HAUNTED
Castles & Houses of
SCOTLAND

Martin Coventry

GOBLINSHEAD
Musselburgh

Haunted Castles and Houses of Scotland

First Published 2004
Reprinted 2005, 2006 with minor updating, 2007
© Martin Coventry 2004

Published by GOBLINSHEAD
130B Inveresk Road
Musselburgh EH21 7AY
Scotland

British Library Cataloguing in Publication Data
A catalogue record for this book is available from the British Library.

ISBN 10: 1 899874 47 X
ISBN 13: 978 1 899874 47 7

Typeset by GOBLINSHEAD using DTP
Printed by Bell & Bain, Glasgow

If you would like a full colour leaflet of our books on Scottish history, travel, castles and the supernatural, please contact us at:
Goblinshead, 130B Inveresk Road
Musselburgh EH21 7AY, Scotland
Tel: **0131 665 2894**
Fax: **0131 653 6566**
Email: **goblinshead@sol.co.uk**

Written, printed and published in Scotland

CONTENTS

PREFACE

This book is about all the different kinds of ghost stories associated with Scotland's castles, and the houses and mansions which superseded them. There are some 450 or so tales of manifestations at 300 strongholds and mansions, meaning many have several different stories. As will be seen, there are a great many of these tales, and I have arranged them thematically (where possible), rather than geographically or alphabetically; and have also tried to offer some explanation as to why they might have been remembered. A separate section, at the beginning of the book, lists the sites alphabetically, and indicates which sites can be visited or stayed at (many are open to the public or are hotels). There is also an index by haunting, as well as a general index.

I have not usually used 'alleged' or 'reputed' or 'said to be' in the stories (the stories became very clumsy and repetitive as everything is 'said to be'), but it should be assumed that in regard to the ghost and ghostly activity this is the case, there being no way to verify supernatural phenomena. The history and factual details are (I hope) just that, and I have given as much background as possible (for which there was room: this book grew in the telling – the extent is three times longer than planned). The stories are stories, however, and no doubt have been embellished down the years, including unwittingly by me.

The existence or truth of some of these ghost stories are refuted or details are not agreed or not known by those who own or manage the castles or houses. Where I know there has been some disagreement, I have noted this. The most obvious castle is Glamis, which rightly, or (more) probably wrongly, has ended up with a fearsome reputation. The Grey Lady and the bogle of Earl Beardie are acknowledged (although not confirmed), while others are not. You will not find any story here about a monster or beast of Glamis – which, though a stock favourite in many books, is hardly a ghost story. Alternatively, an owner or custodian who is especially enthusiastic about ghost stories can unduly influence the popularity and appearance of a bogle.

I, myself, am no nearer one explanation (or even several) as to why belief in ghosts and the supernatural remains so widespread and popular, or why so many sane, rational and sometimes formerly sceptical people still have uncanny and unexplainable experiences. All I can say for sure is that there is phenomena which has been interpreted as haunted activity.

Whether the activity came first, and a traditional or folkloric explanation was placed on the activity; or the story of a murder or tragic event came first, and the activity (or its interpretation, anyway) followed, cannot be determined.

Indeed, the interpretation and identification of apparitions is interesting. I was involved in a television show for an American cable network. One of the segments was about Greyfriars Kirkyard in Edinburgh. The producers were particularly interested in the so-called Covenanters' Prison, and they told me that a medium reported seeing many figures clad in grey clerical robes here, evidence, it was said, of the many Covenanters who had died.

This appears to be wrong. Covenanters would never have worn clerical robes as they were fanatically opposed to even the concept of friaries, let along wearing their garb. There is also considerable doubt as to the circumstances under which people were held here: for how long, how many people, and indeed even how many died. This could have been a mistaken identification, of course, and what the medium claimed to have seen were actually phantom friars; alternatively, the producers misinterpreted the vision. There is no known reason, however, why friars would haunt here. The show, however, was aired with the phantom Covenanters wearing clerical robes.

The reader can draw their own conclusion: a ghostly encounter; a mistaken identification; an incorrect interpretation; or (unwittingly, of course) a false sighting. Like all things in life, the believer will continue to believe, and the doubter continue to doubt. So much in these stories depends on the point of view of the witness. The Drummer of Cortachy is an interesting example. Portents of death were widely believed in Victorian times. Several times in the 19th century phantom music was reputedly heard before a death of the Earls of Airlie or in their family. The drummer was heard, sometimes months before a death, sometimes not even at Cortachy. Was this fitting the facts to the legend? The drummer has not apparently been heard in the 20th century. But if somebody now heard unexplained music at Cortachy would they interpret it as a portent of death or just ignore it?

What is incontestably true is that there are hundreds of these fascinating, grim, gruesome, enigmatic or simply sad stories of ghosts, phantoms, spectres, spirits, wraiths and bogles; portents of death and doom; pipers, drummers and trumpeters; Green, White, Grey, Pink, Blue and Black Ladies; evil and bloody men who were sold to the Devil; headless horsemen, handless wraiths and a cut-in-half woman; dogs, monkeys and even possibly a lion; moans, groans, footsteps and banging at doors: all of which are retold here.

And finally, after nine months of intensive work on this book, it will be nice to get back to the lands of the living. I am starting to feel a little fey myself. It is interesting that ghost stories lose much of their power at fearless noon; while sitting alone at in the small hours of the morning, nobody about, black and moonless, every little noise amplifies, every creak magnifies, you start seeing things out of the corner of your eye ...

Martin Coventry
Musselburgh
May 2004

We have taken the opportunity of the second reprint to update the alphabetical section which lists castles and houses which can be visited or offer accommodation. As ever, this has been checked but things do change and errors are made so check before setting out on any journey.

I would also like take this opportunity to thank everyone who has made this book so successful, and wish readers happy, if a little chilling, reading ...

Martin Coventry
Musselburgh
February 2006

How to Use the Book

The main part of this book is arranged thematically (see the contents pages iii-iv).

Maps on pages x-xiii locate all the sites mentioned.

An alphabetical list of all the castles and mansions in the book follows on pages xiv-xxv. This includes the map number and map reference using the grids of the maps. Indication whether the castle is open to the public as a visitor attraction or hotel then follows, along with contact information where available. This information is believed to be correct at time of going to press, but it is for guidance only and should be checked if any visit is planned. Many places have several stories associated with them, and the page numbers of the main entries in the text are given, along with the page number of any illustration. Please note that the stories in this book are not always confirmed by the castles and mansions. Many mangers and owners are happy to discuss hauntings; while others are not and some may even be hostile.

Selected further reading appears on pages 217-218.

An index of hauntings is located on pages 219-223.

The main index follows on page 224-229. Please note that this lists castles and mansions, but only such individuals and events that are mentioned in the text in relation to the ghost stories.

The National Trust for Scotland
Wemyss House, 28 Charlotte Square, Edinburgh EH2 4ET
Tel: 0131 243 9300   Fax: 0131 243 9301
Email: information@nts.org.uk   Web: www.nts.org.uk

Historic Scotland
Longmore House, Salisbury Place, Edinburgh EH9 1SH
Tel: 0131 668 8800   Fax: 0131 668 8888
Email: hs.explorer@scotland.gsi.gov.uk
Web: www.historic-scotland.gov.uk

viii

Maps and List of Castles and Houses

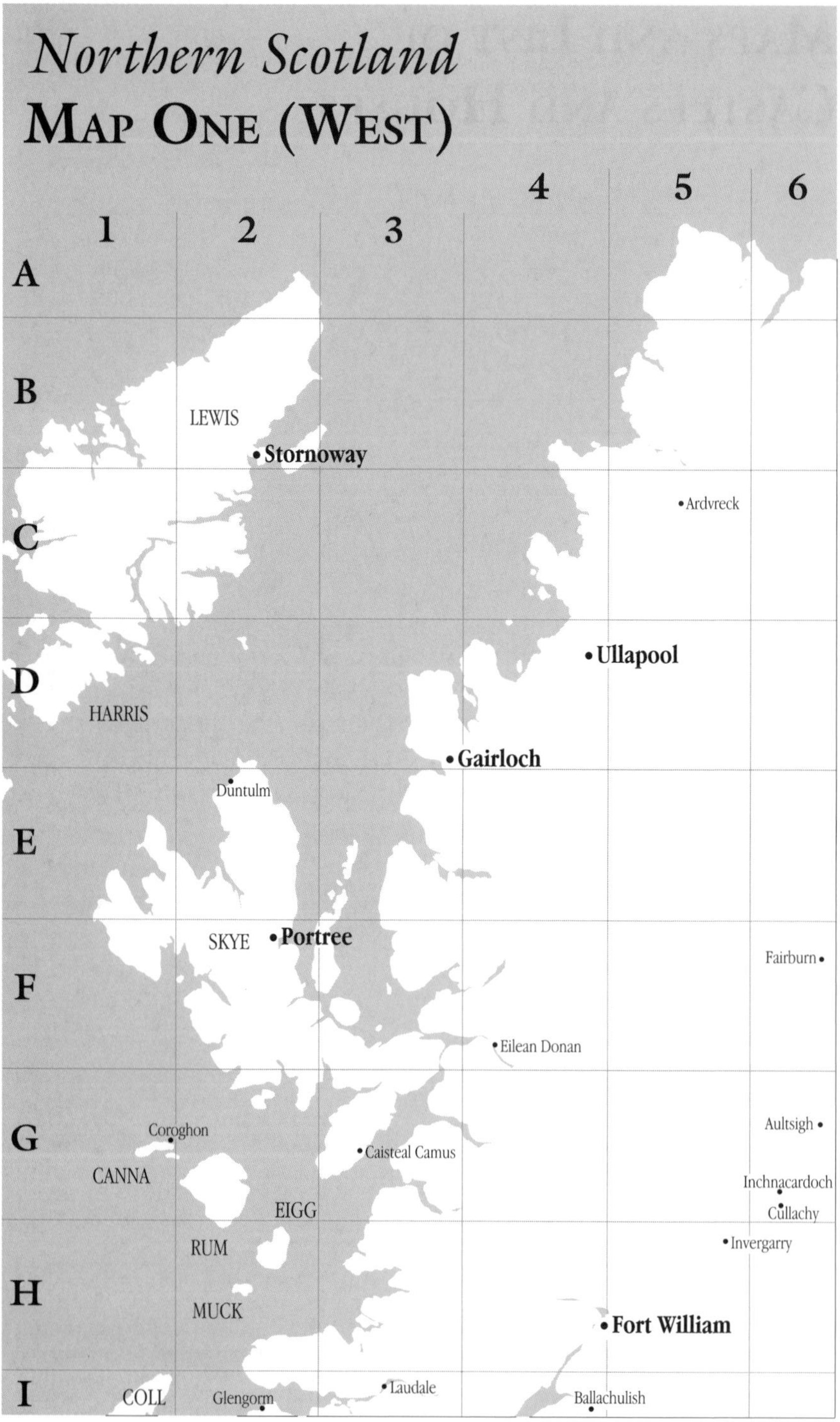

Northern Scotland
MAP ONE (WEST)

	1	2	3	4	5	6

A

B

LEWIS

• **Stornoway**

C

• Ardvreck

D

• **Ullapool**

HARRIS

• **Gairloch**

Duntulm

E

SKYE • **Portree**

Fairburn •

F

• Eilean Donan

Coroghon

Aultsigh •

G

CANNA

• Caisteal Camus

Inchnacardoch

Cullachy

EIGG

RUM

• Invergarry

H

MUCK

• **Fort William**

I COLL   Glengorm   • Laudale   Ballachulish

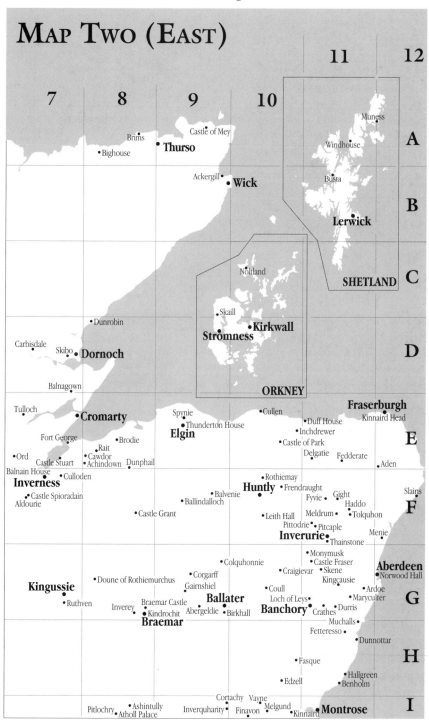

MAP TWO (EAST)

7 8 9 10 11 12

A B C D E F G H I

Muness

Brims
Bighouse
Castle of Mey
Thurso
Windhouse
Busta

Ackergill
Wick
Lerwick

Noltland
SHETLAND

Skaill
Stromness **Kirkwall**

Dunrobin

Carbisdale
Skibo **Dornoch**

Balnagown
ORKNEY

Tulloch
Fraserburgh
Cromarty
Spynie
Cullen
Kinnaird Head
Thunderton House
Duff House
Fort George
Brodie
Elgin
Inchdrewer
Ord
Rait
Castle of Park
Delgatie
Fedderate
Castle Stuart
Cawdor
Achindown
Dunphail
Aden
Balnain House
Culloden
Rothiemay
Inverness
Huntly
Frendraught
Castle Spioradain
Balvenie
Fyvie
Gight
Slains
Aldourie
Ballindalloch
Haddo
Castle Grant
Leith Hall
Meldrum
Tolquhon
Pittodrie
Pitcaple
Menie
Inverurie
Thainstone

Monymusk
Colquhonnie
Castle Fraser
Corgarff
Craigievar
Skene
Aberdeen
Kingussie
Doune of Rothiemurchus
Gairnshiel
Kingcausie
Norwood Hall
Coull
Ardoe
Ruthven
Braemar Castle
Ballater
Loch of Leys
Maryculter
Inverey
Kindrochit
Abergeldie
Birkhall
Banchory
Durris
Braemar
Crathes
Muchalls
Fetteresso
Dunnottar

Fasque
Hallgreen
Edzell
Benholm

Cortachy Vayne
Pitlochry
Ashintully
Inverquharity
Finavon
Melgund
Montrose
Atholl Palace
Kinnaird

J TIREE • Castle Loch Heylipol
• Auchindarroch
Castle Coeffin • Lochnell • Barcaldine
MULL Dunstaffnage • Ardchattan
Dunollie • **Oban** • Inverawe
Moy • Knipoch

K IONA

Inveraray
Cobbler Hotel
• Arrochar

• Barbreck
• Duntrune
Castle Lachlan Rossdhu
Auchendennan
L Dunans Knockderry Cameron Bonhill
Ardincaple
JURA Castle Levan

• Duchal
ISLAY • Rothesay

M GIGHA Skipness
Cara • Largie
• Ardrossan · Dean
• Brodick **Kilmarnock**
N Saddell • ARRAN
Ayr • Sundrum
Campbeltown Dunure • Cassillis
Culzean Cloncaird

O • **Girvan**
• Carleton

P Galdenoch • **Stranraer**
• Dunskey

Q 1 2 3 4 5 6

Southern Scotland
MAP THREE (WEST)

LIST OF CASTLES AND HOUSES

The following is an alphabetical list of all the castles and mansions mentioned in the main text. The map number and reference refer to the maps on the previous pages. Opening and contact information are included and, although these are believed to be correct at the time of going to press, these are for general guidance only and should be checked with the sites before setting out on a visit or stay. Historic Scotland's website is www.historic-scotland.gov.uk and The National Trust for Scotland www.nts.org.uk or www.scotlandforyou.co.uk

Abbotsford   **Map: 4, N10**
Open late Mar-Oct; also by appt. Tel: 01896 752043
Web: www.scottsabbotsford.co.uk
Page(s): 175

Abergeldie Castle   **Map: 2, G9**
Page(s): 40-41, 120   Illus page: 120

Achindown   **Map: 2, E8**
Page(s): 58, 210-211

Ackergill Tower   **Map: 2, B9**
Conference and hospitality centre.
Tel: 01955 603556   Web: www.ackergill-tower.co.uk
Page(s): 16-17   Illus page: 17

Aden House   **Map: 2, E12**
Stands in country park: park open all year.
Tel: 01771 622857 Web: www.aberdeenshire.gov.uk/heritage
Page(s): 57-58

Airlie Castle   **Map: 4, J9**
Page(s): 118

Airth Castle Hotel   **Map: 4, L8**
Tel: 01324 831411   Web: www.airthcastlehotel.com
Page(s): 96

Aldourie Castle   **Map: 2, F7**
Page(s): 94

Allanbank House   **Map: 4, M11**
Page(s): 60-61

Arbigland House   **Map: 4, P8**
Page(s): 56, 169

Ardblair Castle   **Map: 4, J9**
Accommodation available: must pre-book.
Tel: 01250 873155
Page(s): 41-42   Illus page: 7

Ardchattan (HS)   **Map: 3, J4**
Ruins of priory (HS) open all year; garden (private), open Apr-Oct. Tel: 01631 750274 (garden)
Page(s): 22-23

Ardincaple Castle   **Map: 3, L5**
Page(s): 132

Ardoe House Hotel   **Map: 2, G11**
Tel: 01224 860600   Web: www.ardoehouse.com
Page(s): 67

Ardrossan Castle   **Map: 3, M5**
View from exterior.
Page(s): 174-175

Ardvreck Castle   **Map: 1, C5**
View from exterior.
Page(s): 43, 191

Ashintully Castle   **Map: 2, I8**
Accommodation available.
Tel: 01250 881237   Web: www.ashintully.com
Page(s): 33, 166

Atholl Palace Hotel   **Map: 2, I8**
Tel: 01796 472400   Web: www.athollpalace.com
Page(s): 86

Auchen Castle Hotel   **Map: 4, O8**
Tel: 01683 300407   Web: www.auchencastle.com
Page(s): 203

Auchendennan (Loch Lomond Youth Hostel)   **Map: 3, L6**
Tel: 0870 0041136   Web: www.syha.org.uk
Page(s): 108

Auchindarroch   **Map: 3, J5**
Page(s): 102

List of Castles and Houses

List of Castles and Houses

Crathes Castle (NTS) Map: 2, G11
Open Apr-Oct; garden and grounds open all year.
Tel: 01330 844525
Page(s): 12-14 Illus page: 13

Crichton Castle (HS) Map: 4, M10
Open Apr-Sep. Tel: 01875 320017
Page(s): 144-145, 190 Illus page: 145

Cromarty Castle Map: 2, E7
Page(s): 207-208

Cromlix Castle Map: 4, K8
Page(s): 19

Culcreuch Castle Map: 4, L7
Hotel and country park.
Tel: 01360 860555 Web: www.culcreuch.com
Page(s): 57

Cullachy House Map: 1, G6
Page(s): 134

Cullen House Map: 2, E10
Page(s): 158-159

Culloden House Map: 2, F7
Hotel.
Tel: 01463 790461 Web: www.cullodenhouse.co.uk
Page(s): 173

Culross (NTS) Map: 4, L8
Ruins of abbey accessible all reasonable times; parish
church open all year; Palace, Study and Town House
(NTS) open Easter-Sep. Tel: 01383 880359 (NTS)
Page(s): 185-186

Culzean Castle (NTS) Map: 3, O5
Open Apr-Oct, daily; country park open
all year; accommodation available in Eisenhower Suite.
Tel: 01655 884455 Web: www.culzeancastle.net
Page(s): 109, 114

Dalhousie Castle Map: 4, M9
Hotel.
Tel: 01875 820153 Web: www.dalhousiecastle.co.uk
Page(s): 23, 201, 205

Dalkeith House Map: 4, M9
Country park open Apr-Sep. House not open.
Tel: 0131 654 1666/663 5684
Web: www.dalkeithcountrypark.com
Page(s): 108

Dalmahoy Map: 4, L9
Hotel.
Tel: 0131 333 1845 Web: www.marriott.com
Page(s): 91

Dalpeddar Map: 4, O8
Page(s): 33-34

Dalry House, Edinburgh Map: 4, L9
Page(s): 144

Dalzell House Map: 4, M7
Page(s): 68-69

Dean Castle Map: 3, N6
Open all year, Wed-Sun, closed Mon & Tue.
Tel: 01563 522702 Web: www.deancastle.com
Page(s): 123

Delgatie Castle Map: 2, E11
Open early Apr-late Oct; accommodation available.
Tel: 01888 563479 Web: www.delgatiecastle.com
Page(s): 101

Dolphinston Tower Map: 4, N11
Page(s): 131

Donibristle House Map: 4, L9
Page(s): 163-164

Dornoch Castle Map: 2, D7
Hotel.
Tel: 01862 810216 Web: www.dornochcastlehotel.com
Page(s): 178-179

Douglas Castle Map: 4, N8
Page(s): 204-205 Illus page: 204

Doune Castle (HS) Map: 4, L7
Open all year: Oct-Mar closed Thu & Fri.
Tel: 01786 841742
Page(s): 74

Doune of Rothiemurchus Map: 2, G8
House and country park: check opening.
Tel: 01479 812345 Web: www.rothiemurchus.net
Page(s): 131, 159

Dreadnought Hotel, Callander
Map: 4, K7
Tel: 01877 330184 Web: www.swallow-hotels.com
Page(s): 18, 145, 202

List of Castles and Houses

Fernie Castle Map: 4, K9
Hotel. Tel: 01337 810381
Web: www.ferniecastle.demon.co.uk
Page(s): 63

Ferniehirst Castle Map: 4, N11
Open Jul, Tue-Sun. Tel: 01835 862201
Page(s): 83 Illus page: 84

Fetteresso Castle Map: 2, H11
Page(s): 79 Illus page: 79

Finavon Castle Map: 2, I10
Page(s): 166

Floors Castle Map: 4, N11
Open Apr-late Oct.
Tel: 01573 223333 Web: www.floorscastle.com
Page(s): 192

Fort George (HS) Map: 2, E7
Open all year. Tel: 01667 460232
Page(s): 187

Frendraught Castle Map: 2, F10
Page(s): 87-88

Fyvie Castle (HS) Map: 2, F11
Open Apr-Sep, Sat-Wed; Jul-Aug, daily; grounds open
all year. Tel: 01651 891266
Page(s): 46-48, 115 Illus page: 47

Gairnshiel Lodge Map: 2, G9
Available to hire for exclusive use.
Tel: 01339 755582 Web: www.gairnshiellodge.co.uk
Page(s): 98-99, 215

Galdenoch Castle Map: 3, P5
Page(s): 159

Garleton Castle Map: 4, L10
Page(s): 192

Garth Castle Map: 4, J8
Page(s): 20

Gight Castle Map: 2, F11
Page(s): 185, 211

Glamis Castle Map: 4, J10
Open mid Mar-Dec. Tel: 01307 840393
Web: www.glamis-castle.co.uk
Page(s): 38-40, 140-141, 199 Illus page: 39

Glengorm Castle Map: 1, I2
Self-catering apartments/B&B available; coffee shop &
gallery.
Tel: 01688 302321 Web: www.glengormcastle.co.uk
Page(s): 86

Glenlee Map: 4, P7
Page(s): 93-94

Gorrenberry Tower Map: 4, O10
Page(s): 133

Grandtully Castle Map: 4, J8
Page(s): 200

Grange House, Edinburgh Map: 4, L9
Page(s): 192-193

Grangemuir Map: 4, K10
Page(s): 26

Greenlaw House Map: 4, M9
Page(s): 71

Guthrie Castle Map: 4, J10
Accommodation available.
Tel: 01241 828691 Web: www.guthriecastle.com
Page(s): 102-103

Haddo House (NTS) Map: 2, F11
Open Easter, then May-Aug daily; Sep, open wknds
only; garden and country park open all year.
Tel: 01651 851440
Page(s): 181

Hailes Castle (HS) Map: 4, L10
Access at all reasonable times.
Page(s): 169

Hallgreen Castle Map: 2, H11
Page(s): 66, 193

Hermitage Castle (HS) Map: 4, O10
Open Apr-Sep. Tel: 01387 376222
Page(s): 72-73, 137-139, 161-162 Illus page: 138

Holyroodhouse, Edinburgh Map: 4, L9
Open all year: closed during State visits, tel to confirm.
Tel: 0131 556 5100 Web: www.royalcollection.org.uk
Page(s): 77 Illus page: 77

Hopetoun House Map: 4, L9
Open mid Apr-late Sep.
Tel: 0131 331 2451 Web: www.hopetounhouse.com
Page(s): 117

Houndwood House　Map: 4, M11
Page(s): 74, 169

Houston House　Map: 4, M8
Hotel. Tel: 01506 853831
Web: www.macdonaldhotels.co.uk/houstounhouse/
Page(s): 213

Howlet's House　Map: 4, M9
Page(s): 19

Huntingtower (HS)　Map: 4, K9
Open Apr-Sep, daily; Oct-Mar, closed Thu & Fri.
Tel: 01738 627231
Page(s): 126-127　Illus page: 127

Huntly Castle Hotel　Map: 2, F10
Tel: 01466 792696　Web: www.castlehotel.uk.com
Page(s): 66

Inchdrewer Castle　Map: 2, E10
Page(s): 109, 205

Inchnacardoch　Map: 1, G6
Page(s): 134

Inveraray Castle　Map: 3, K5
Open Apr-Oct; closed some Fri.
Tel: 01499 302203　Web: www.inveraray-castle.com
Page(s): 120, 164-165, 213　Illus page: 164

Inverawe House　Map: 3, K5
Smoke houses, shop and nature trail.
Tel: 01866 822446/822777　Web: www.inverawe.co.uk
Page(s): 51, 179

Inverey Castle　Map: 2, G8
Page(s): 171-172

Invergarry Castle　Map: 1, H5
View from exterior. In grounds of Glengarry Castle
Hotel (01809 501254; www.glengarry.net).
Page(s): 133　Illus page: 133

Inverquharity Castle　Map: 2, I9
Page(s): 140

Jedburgh Castle (Jail)　Map: 4, N11
Jedburgh Castle Jail and Museum stand on the site:
open Easter-Oct.　Tel: 01835 863254
Page(s): 116-117

Johnstone Ldge, Anstruther　Map: 4, K10
Page(s): 29

Johnstounburn House　Map: 4, M10
Page(s): 106

Kellie Castle (NTS)　Map: 4, K10
Open Easter, then May-Sep; garden and grounds open
all year.　Tel: 01333 720721
Page(s): 106-107, 176

Kemback House　Map: 4, K10
Page(s): 30

Kilbryde Castle　Map: 4, L7
Garden open by appt only; castle not open.
Tel: 01786 824505　Web: www.gardensofscotland.org
Page(s): 31

Kindrochit Castle　Map: 2, G8
Open all year.
Page(s): 198-199

Kingcausie　Map: 2, G11
Page(s): 97, 201, 213

Kinghorn Castle　Map: 4, L9
Page(s): 94

Kinnaird Castle　Map: 2, I10
Accommodation available; garden occasionally open
under Scotland's Garden Scheme
(www.gardensofscotland.org).
Page(s): 152　Illus page: 152

**Kinnaird Head Castle (HS) (Scotland's
Lighthouse Museum)**　Map: 2, E12
Open all year: tel to confirm details.
Tel: 01346 511022/01975 571331
Web: www.lighthousemuseum.org.uk
Page(s): 65

Kinneil House (HS)　Map: 4, L8
View from exterior; public park open all year.
Page(s): 67

Kirk o' Field, Edinburgh　Map: 4, L9
Page(s): 77, 173

Knipoch Hotel　Map: 3, K4
Tel: 01852 316251　Web: www.knipochhotel.co.uk
Page(s): 170

Knockderry Castle　Map: 3, L5
Page(s): 213

Lagg Tower　Map: 4, O7
Page(s): 150-151

List of Castles and Houses

List of Castles and Houses

Rothiemay Castle   Map: 2, F10
Page(s): 99, 181-182, 202   Illus page: 99

Roxburgh Castle   Map: 4, N11
Page(s): 190

Roxburghe House Hotel (Sunlaws)
Map: 4, N11
Tel: 01573 450331   Web: www.roxburghe.net
Page(s): 56-57, 194

Ruthven Barracks (HS)   Map: 2, G7
Access at all reasonable times.   Tel: 01667 460232
Page(s): 141-142

Saddell Castle   Map: 3, N4
Accommodation available through the Landmark Trust.
Tel: 01628 825925   Web: www.landmarktrust.org
Page(s): 92, 193

Saltoun Hall   Map: 4, M10
Page(s): 94

Sanquhar Castle   Map: 4, O8
Access at all reasonable times.
Page(s): 25, 166-167   Illus page: 167

Scone Palace   Map: 4, K9
Open late Mar-Oct.
Tel: 01738 552300   Web: www.scone-palace.co.uk
Page(s): 214-215

Shieldhill   Map: 4, N8
Hotel.   Tel: 01899 220035   Web: www.shieldhill.co.uk
Page(s): 54-55

Skaill House   Map: 2, C9
Open Apr-Sep; accommodation available.
Tel: 01856 841501   Web: www.skaillhouse.com
Page(s): 98

Skene House   Map: 2, G11
Page(s): 153

Skibo Castle   Map: 2, D7
Exclusive country (Carnegie) club.
Tel: 01862 894600   Web: www.carnegieclubs.com
Page(s): 24-25   Illus page: 25

Skipness Castle (HS)   Map: 3, M4
Access at all reasonable times; chapel, near the sea,
also access at all reasonable times.
Page(s): 128

Slains Castle   Map: 2, F12
View from exterior.
Page(s): 182-183   Illus page: 182

Spedlins Tower   Map: 4, P9
Page(s): 160-161

Spynie Palace (HS)   Map: 2, E9
Open Apr-Sep, daily; Oct-Mar closed Thu & Fri.
Tel: 01343 546358
Page(s): 187, 206

St Andrews Castle (HS)   Map: 4, K10
Open all year; ruins of cathedral, open all year.
Tel: 01334 477196
Page(s): 92, 155, 156-157   Illus page: 156

Stirling Castle (HS)   Map: 4, L8
Open all year.   Tel: 01786 450000
Page(s): 73-74, 193-194, 210

Sundrum Castle   Map: 3, N6
Available to let.
Tel: 01530 244436   Web: www.sundrumcastle.com
Page(s): 85

Taymouth Castle   Map: 4, J8
Page(s): 117-118   Illus page: 117

Thainstone House   Map: 2, F11
Hotel.
Tel: 01467 621643   Web: www.swallow-hotels.com
Page(s): 80

The Binns (NTS)   Map: 4, L8
Open Jun-Sep, Sat-Thu, closed Fri; park land open all year.
Tel: 01506 834255
Page(s): 150, 194

Thirlestane Castle   Map: 4, M10
Open Easter-late Sep: check days.
Tel: 01578 722430   Web: www.thirlestanecastle.co.uk
Page(s): 172

Threave Castle (NTS)   Map: 4, P7
Open Apr-Oct (ferry to castle).   Tel: 07711 223101
Page(s): 208-209   Illus page: 208

Thunderton House   Map: 2, E9
Public house.   Tel: 01343 554921
Web: www.thundertonhouse.co.uk
Page(s): 173

HAUNTED
Castles & Houses of
SCOTLAND

INTRODUCTION

This book concerns the many tales of ghosts which are associated with Scotland's castles. There are hundreds of these tales recorded here, some fragmentary, some detailed. No doubt there are many more tapping at windows and gliding along empty passageways, still waiting to manifest themselves on paper.

Ghost stories have survived far better than many other ancient supernatural or mystical beliefs in this (supposedly) secular age, even outlasting mainstream religion for many Britons. The Reformation and Protestantism in the 16th and 17th centuries and the growth of science and rationality in the 17th, 18th and 19th centuries were major factors in limiting the supernatural universe, killing off kelpies, mermaids and other fearsome beasts (although the Loch Ness Monster still refuses to die, despite the best efforts of scientists), reducing once fearsome fairies to diminutive twee little beings – and brownies to girl guides. Powerful witches were sought and persecuted for a while, but by the middle of the 18th century even this panic of maleficium was seen as superstitious, and had been ridiculed and abandoned.

Belief in ghosts and related phenomena continued, however, and became even more widespread, along with spiritualism, in the 19th century. The Victorians, who are thought to have lived through a very Christian age, became more and more obsessed with dying and necromancy as the century progressed, and built themselves grander and grander tombs and mausoleums (very many people are now buried without even a modest monument). The slaughter of the World War I reinforced this, and prompted an increased belief in spiritualism. It should be noted that all of the most famous spiritualists, barring one who was not tested, were shown to have used fraudulent practices.

As the 20th century progressed, ghosts became more frightening again, along with the growth in cinematic offerings such as the *Evil Dead*, *Amityville Horror* and *Poltergeist*. In fact, even as belief in mainstream religion has decreased, or perhaps because of it, other belief systems, such as parking angels, crystals, wicca, shamanism and white magic have increased. Ghost stories, however, remain as popular as ever. Mortal sentient creatures will always wonder and worry what happens when they die. Ghost stories go some way to meet this morbid curiosity, even if in the end they just confuse things further.

It should be emphasised, however, that this book is about ghost stories, not about ghosts. In recording and repeating these tales, no judgement is made as to their truth, nor indeed even to the existence of ghosts. Many sensible and honest people have experienced uncanny things in Scotland's castles and mansions. Whether these are manifestations of uneasy spirits of the dead; or simply the stirrings of an uneasy imagination is impossible to say. There is also a rich folkloric tradition in ghost stories, and certain assumed beliefs about ghosts, such as all female ghosts are beautiful, they float along, or only appear at night.

Versions of stories vary greatly, and it is not possible to supply a 'correct' tale or account any more than it is possible to substantiate the phantoms themselves. Where possible and applicable, details have been checked, and many places have an 'official' story (or stories). But this process can prove problematic in itself. One castle, now a hotel, has over the years supplied two different versions of their own ghost story, while giving a third account on their website. I have not usually named the witness or witnesses, except where this makes an account clearer, as I have no way to test the veracity or otherwise of a story.

What has been done is to provide as much background information about the story, where this information is available. Where there is doubt about a tale, where there is more than one version, or where I know it is refuted, this has been noted in the text.

Castles and stately mansions are, of course, not the only places to have a resident bogle or two. Most theatres and hospitals, and many hotels, inns and pubs, have eerie tales, and activity can take place almost anywhere, including in the open or in council houses.

Although an apparition is often described as the main feature of a haunting, at least in stories, other activity is more common: especially unexplained footsteps, banging and rapping, electrical equipment being interfered with, and a change in temperature (be really worried if it gets hotter, rather than colder). Reported apparitions are often a patch of fuzzy light or balls or iridescence. Other motifs also appear repeatedly: blood stains; secret chambers and tunnels; stairs; people being walled up in the castle; skeletons being found (literally, sometimes, a skeleton in the closet); ghosts walking through blocked-up doorways.

It has been suggested that the placing of human remains under the hearth or beneath the floor was some kind of offering. There are certainly many stories which involve the discovery of skeletal remains. Whether this is a device in the story, of course, is certainly also possible: it does seem a very difficult and elaborate manner in which to dispose of a corpse. There are also several tales which feature the finding of a secret room. While many may have indeed been secret, it may be that during alterations (often radical changes undertaken over hundreds of years of use) the rooms or closets were innocently sealed to regularise the shape of a room or because they were no longer needed.

In many accounts of ghostly activity, a person wakes from sleep to see an apparition or to find it feels as if a heavy weight is on top of them, forcing them into the mattress. The phantom soon fades or the weight lifts. They find that they cannot move or even scream. This is one phenomenon which may be explained: the sleeper believes they have woken but are still in a dream-like state, known as sleep paralysis. Their ability to move while asleep is naturally curtailed (so that people do not act out their dreams). It takes a moment for the ability to move to be restored, and during this period it can feel as if something is pinning the person, or preventing them even from screaming.

Ghost stories may be frightening and knowing about a haunting can add interest and excitement to a visit to, or stay at, many of the great castles, stately homes and country house hotels of Scotland. But it is the all too real human, mostly male, failings of violence, lust and greed which are much more concerning. Be afraid of those who in the stories murdered, killed and tortured, not the poor dead victims or their restless ghosts.

SECTION ONE
Ladies of Different Colours

T he majority of ghost stories concerning castles involve female ghosts: around 60% of stories where gender is mentioned. Most of these are believed to be young women who died before their time: cruelly murdered, committing suicide, killed by misadventure, or perishing from a broken heart. There are more than 150 of these tales; and many share common elements, not least the victim being imprisoned, usually in an upstairs chamber (rather than a dark and dank dungeon), or being starved to, or falling to, her death. Stairs also feature in many of the tales.

Some have seen these merely as folk traditions, with echoes of the Rapunzel fairy tale. Yet perhaps they are the only means of giving the victim a voice when otherwise the wrongs and injustices that had been done to them would have been long forgotten. These stories are likely to commemorate the exceptional rather than commonplace. If every father or lover treated their womenfolk as badly as in ghost stories, their cruelty would have been everyday and the events would hardly have been worthy of note. Female apparitions tend to be the weak and the victims of violence, cruelty or neglect, while (as will be seen) many male ghosts are powerful, and even the perpetrators of violence.

Apparitions of these dead souls are mostly recorded as Green Ladies (many Green Jeans), although White and Grey Ladies are also common. From the accounts, it is not clear whether the colour refers to the dress that the apparition wears; or, such as in the case of Green Ladies, that they emit a green glow; or that they are a 'stereotypical' phantom. Green was often seen as an unlucky colour in medieval and early modern times, being associated with magic and the fairies (not the diminutive figures of modern fancy but powerful and chaotic supernatural beings). Green is also associated with gruagach or glaistig, a guardian spirit ghost or fairy woman found in Gaelic-speaking areas.

It is similarly not clear whether White and Grey Ladies are apparitions with an absence of colour or whether they are simply clad in white or grey. It has been suggested that ghosts lose their colour over time, fading from their original hue to grey and then insubstantial white as they lose 'energy', eventually becoming no more than a presence. This, as will be

*Ardblair Castle: home to a Green Lady, the spirit of
Lady Jean Drummond, who also haunts nearby Newton.*

seen, is not borne out by the stories, where Green Ladies (often the oldest spirits recorded in a building) are the most commonly recorded apparition and usually, although not always, retain their colour throughout the centuries. Pink, Brown and Blue Ladies are also reported, as well as Black Ladies. These latter ghosts' descriptions come mostly from their Asian or Polynesian appearance.

Green Ladies are common in Scotland (more than one quarter of all tales where a colour is mentioned), more so than White (one fifth) or Grey Ladies (one tenth), which might not have been expected. This may be due to the concept of a 'guardian spirit' or gruagach for a castle or house, which is discussed, along with brownies, in more detail in Section Two. Gruagach are part of the rich Gaelic tradition of supernatural entities, and may have become combined with the more prosaic concepts of ghosts in Lowland areas. Gruagach also overlap with the idea of a harbinger spirit, akin to a banshee from Irish belief. Gruagach would be witnessed as a herald when something bad was going to happen (or, indeed, something good). This coincides with the belief that the appearance of some ghosts, or specific events such as the behaviour of a particular animal or the tolling of bell, heralds disaster or death in the resident family.

CHAPTER ONE
Lust, Cruelty & Jealousy

P erhaps not surprisingly, ghost stories of these type can, almost without exception, be seen as a catalogue of cruelty by men towards women – the exception is Christian Nimmo, who slew her lover, described under Corstorphine Castle, and Agnes at Loch of Leys. The following stories reflect the male's propensity to aggression and violence all the too clearly, as does the next section on property. As mentioned above, however, these are the exception rather than the rule. Medieval and early modern times are seen as being particularly brutal, but if our society was to been seen in terms of current tabloid headlines of child murders, rapes, shootings and terrorist attacks, what would those looking back make of the 21st century?

There are many of these tales and consequently this is a large chapter.

FOUL AND BLOODY MURDER
T ales where the ghost story is thought to have originated from a murder, perhaps to hide a pregnancy, perhaps because of unrivalled cruelty, or perhaps because of uncontrollable jealousy.

M EGGERNIE CASTLE, north of Killin in Perthshire, is an imposing 16th-century tower house in a fine mountainous location. It was built by Colin Campbell of Glen Lyon, but later passed to the Menzies of Culdares family. Meggernie has one of the most intriguing ghost stories, and certainly one of the most gory.

When the castle was held by the Menzies family, one of the lairds had an especially attractive and good-looking wife. Although there was no evidence of infidelity, Menzies could simply not trust her, and his jealousy began to prey on him. Innocent actions were misinterpreted and one day, in a fit of boiling rage, he attacked and murdered his unfortunate wife. When he came to and realised what he had done, Menzies was in a panic. To conceal the poor woman's body, he cut it in two, and hid her remains, either under the floor of (or in a chest in a closet off) what became known as the haunted room. Menzies then left Meggernie for the continent, presumably shutting up the castle for the duration of the trip. When he returned, the murder had not been discovered and he told everyone that his wife had drowned while they were abroad.

Menzies then tried to bury the two halves of his wife, which cannot have been a pleasant task. He managed to retrieve her bottom half and buried it in the family burial ground, but died himself before he could dispose of the rest of her. Indeed, he may have been murdered by one of his wife's family, or one of her own friends, who suspected what he had done. Or he might have been frightened to death by her bogle.

But from then on very strange manifestations began to plague Meggernie, and disturbances became so common that the room on which they were centred was abandoned as a bedroom at one time. The tower was haunted by an apparition of the top half of a woman, consisting of the head and upper torso. Her lower half, from the waist down in a gore-spattered dress, was seen on the ground floor, in an avenue of trees near the castle, and at the burial ground, which local people soon would not frequent after dark.

The ghost was observed on several occasions in Victorian times: once in 1862 by two friends who visited Meggernie. Although they were sleeping in adjacent chambers, the door, through a closet, between the rooms was locked. One of the men woke up, having received what he thought was a very hot kiss. He saw the top half of the phantom, a despairing expression on its features, moving towards the locked door. The visitor was concerned that the kiss might have scorched him, but

Meggernie Castle: haunted by the phantom of a lady murdered and cut-in-two by her husband.

on examination in a mirror could find no trace of the fiery lips. It then transpired that his friend had a similar experience, and both the men reported the manifestation at about 2.30 am. The ghost was bathed in an eerie pink light. They both had similar descriptions of the ghost's appearance and behaviour.

Another account, which happened about a week later, has the upper half passing along a passageway on the first floor: the face again had an expression of dreadful sorrow. The phantom then faded away. A servant then reported seeing the lower half going towards the north tower. And in 1928 a doctor, staying in one of the chambers below the rooms believed to be haunted, described how he had seen the upper part of the ghost, but floating near the ceiling, also emitting a kind of pink glow. This had been preceded by footsteps approaching his room.

There have apparently been many other sightings by local people of the lower part in the area around the burial ground and along an avenue of trees. Other manifestations include unexplained knocking and banging in the castle, which have been witnessed in recent times.

During renovation (probably in the first quarter of the 20th century), the upper bones of skeleton were said to have been discovered beneath floor boards in one of the upper chambers (or in a closet), but the haunting is believed to have continued even after the remains were buried.

Incidentally, some doubt has been cast on the witnessing of the phantom by the two friends in 1862, and it has been suggested that they concocted the story between them.

A story of doomed love between warring clans is centred on Rait Castle, a ruinous stronghold a few miles south of Nairn near Inverness. The castle, a hall-house extended by a round tower, dates from the 13th century, but some 300 years later, in 1524, was held by the Cummings. This was a branch of the once mighty Comyn family, fierce enemies of Robert the Bruce and much reduced from their former power after defeat during the Wars of Independence.

The Cumming laird of the time was harbouring a fatal hatred for the Mackintoshes, a neighbouring clan. The reason for the feud is not recorded. He invited them to Rait for a feast, feigning reconciliation, but intending to have them slaughtered. Indeed, the feast may have been a betrothal or wedding celebration, having pledged his own daughter to the son of the Mackintoshes. But the Mackintoshes came forewarned and heavily armed, and escaped from the feast by cutting their way out, leaving many of Cumming's men dead or wounded.

Cumming suspected that his plotting had been betrayed, and immediately turned on his daughter, fearing that she had actually fallen in love with the son of a Mackintosh. In a red rage, Cumming pursued the poor girl through the castle. In desperation, she climbed out of a window, hoping to make good her escape. But her father drew his sword, and hacked off both her hands so that she tumbled from the ledge, mortally wounded, to die soon afterwards.

Cumming was not long to survive his daughter. While visiting nearby Balblair Castle, he and his followers were set upon by the Mackintoshes and slain.

The spirit of his daughter was not to rest, however. An apparition of a handless girl in a blood-soaked dress began to be seen in the castle. Her ghost, recorded as the Wraith of Rait, is said to have been so frightening that the building was eventually abandoned.

This story had also been recorded in association with Cawdor Castle.

Equally grim, and even more cruel, is the story of the ghost of Ann Grant, which is said to have been active in Borthwick Castle, even in recent times. The imposing tower stands in a picturesque spot some two miles south-east of Gorebridge, in Midlothian in central Scotland.

Borthwick Castle is one of the most impressive of all Scotland's many castles. It stands more than 100 feet tall, and has walls 14-feet thick in places, rising to eight storeys in the wings. It was built in 1430 by Sir William Borthwick, whose fantastic, carved stone effigy, alongside that of his wife, can be seen in the nearby parish church.

Mary, Queen of Scots, had to escape from the castle disguised as a pageboy in 1567, and in 1650 the castle quickly surrendered when besieged by Cromwell's forces. It remains a spectacular building, and is now used as a hotel.

Ann Grant is said to have been a serving girl, who worked in the castle and fell in love with one of the Borthwick lairds. In time their affair became all too evident: she became heavy with child. But this was a man who was not to shirk from extreme action. Borthwick had Ann murdered by slashing her across the belly and leaving her to die in her own blood. A former owner of the castle (believed previously to have been sceptical of ghosts) and a visitor are both said to have witnessed the ghostly re-enactment of Ann's death on two separate occasions.

The murder apparently happened in the Red Room of Borthwick. A pregnant girl, dressed in medieval garb, was pinned between two women (described as midwifes or witches, although how this would be apparent

11

from their apparel is not clear). Ann was then cut across the belly by a soldier with a sword, and left to die on the floor of the room. It has been suggested that this terrible act was to hide Borthwick's indiscretion, although a serving girl being made pregnant by a laird would hardly have been cause for even much gossip in medieval or early modern times. The particularly horrific and messy nature of her death suggests some other motive, but none is recorded. It also seems a strange place to commit such a terrible and gruesome murder, rather than outside where her body might have been disposed of more discreetly.

Other manifestations, apart from these bloody 're-enactments', in the room include a sudden drop in temperature; and scratching noises have been reported coming from the chamber when it was empty. Scratch marks are said to have appeared on the door, and reappeared even after it had been painted. Footsteps have repeatedly been heard at 1.30 in the dead of night on the turnpike stair to the chamber, although again on investigation there was nobody there. On one occasion two guests saw a heavy fire door open by itself, which remained open until they closed it and, during a conference in the Great Hall, crying and sobbing were heard apparently emanating from the haunted room despite it being empty at the time.

One story about the ghost is that it dislikes men (which would certainly be understandable), and on several occasions doors have been inexplicably slammed on toes or fingers. Another detail is that the former owner had the haunted room exorcised – apparently not successfully.

C RATHES CASTLE is a wonderful pile in rolling Deeside countryside some miles east of Banchory. Among many other things, it is famous for the spectacular gardens, laid out over four acres, including a Fountain Garden, Rose Garden and Wild Garden. It is also famous for its own ghost, the Green Lady, an apparition so popular that the chamber on the third floor, where it appears, is called the Green Lady's Room.

Crathes was held by the Burnett of Leys family. Alexander Burnett started construction of the present castle in about 1552 and the family held it until 1952 when it passed to The National Trust of Scotland. The Burnetts had come to prominence during the Wars of Independence, and were given the Horn of Leys by Robert the Bruce, a bejewelled horn of ivory encrusted with jewels, which can be seen in the High Hall of the castle.

The ghost story probably dates first from the 18th century, when the apparition was first recorded crossing the room to an old fireplace: a girl

Crathes Castle: haunted by a Green Lady, the ghost of a girl seen walking to a fireplace with a baby in her arms.

in a green dress with a baby in her arms. The phantom was seen often, and has been witnessed in modern times. One account describes the ghost as being a luminous block of ice, not human shaped, but it moved like someone walking. There was also a small apparition with the large luminous shape. The appearance was accompanied by a sharp drop in temperature.

The chamber the ghost haunts is described as being especially cold, and was formerly a bed chamber: many sleepers reported a feeling of tension or a strange presence which prevented them from getting a proper night's rest. It is also reported that some visitors to the castle will not enter the Green Lady's Room despite being ignorant of the story. A guide felt an invisible person brush past her. Indeed, Queen Victoria is said to have seen the ghost, and in some accounts an appearance was believed to herald a death or misfortune in the family.

There is more than one version recorded of the tale behind the haunting. The spirit seems in life to have been the daughter of the then laird or a lass in his protection. She either found herself pregnant after dallying

13

with a servant or was harshly used against her will by one of the laird's companions with the same result. She lost the baby, the small skeleton being found by workmen in a small recess under the hearthstone of the fireplace some time in the 19th century. It is presumed the baby, at least, was murdered.

The Burnetts' earlier stronghold was at LOCH OF LEYS, about which another ghost story is recorded. This was their original castle, occupied from the early 14th century but abandoned when Crathes was built. It stood on an island in the now drained loch, but there are no upstanding remains. Medieval artefacts from the castle are on display at Crathes.

Bertha was an attractive young woman, a relative of the Burnetts, who was staying at Loch of Leys. The son of the house, Alexander, and Bertha fell in love some time before 1543, but Alexander's mother, Agnes, did not want them to marry. The old laird had died, and Agnes wanted an advantageous match for her son. Alexander was called away on business, but as soon as he left Bertha began to ail and soon was very ill. Alexander returned home some time later to find that Bertha had died that very day. There was to be no imprisonment in an attic room for Bertha: Agnes had had her poisoned to free her son.

But Bertha's ghost sought revenge and appeared to Agnes. So terrified was Agnes by the apparition that her heart stopped and she died in terror. The apparition is still said to appear on the anniversary of Bertha's death.

Alexander Burnett went on to marry Janet Hamilton in 1543, and this was the advantageous match for which Agnes might have wished. Janet came with a large dowry, and it was with this new wealth that Alexander was able to build Crathes.

The COBBLER HOTEL, at Arrochar at the northern end of Loch Long, stands on the site of a castle or old house of the MacFarlanes, who held lands here from the 12th century. There was a clan seat here in 1697, known as Arrochar House, and the present building incorporates the foundations. The MacFarlanes were a reputedly wild lot, but in 1767 had to sell the property to the Colquhouns of Luss, their former enemies.

There is a ghost story associated with Arrochar House, although the spirit now haunts the present building, which is used as a hotel. There are at least two versions of the tale.

The less-grim version is that the young daughter of one of the

MacFarlane lairds fell in love with one of the Colquhouns. The two clans were constantly fighting, and such a relationship was doomed. Inevitably, her father discovered her dallying, and forbade them to meet. She ignored his warnings and kept seeing her love. Becoming furious at this lack of loyalty and respect, MacFarlane had her locked in one of the chambers of the house. She was allowed no food or water, and within a short time she was dead. Her phantom, a Green Lady, was then witnessed in the building.

Another version is that the MacFarlane (or Colquhoun) chief came home one day unexpectedly and discovered his wife in a Biblical clinch with one of his neighbours. MacFarlane, taken by a red rage, first slew his neighbour, then mortally wounded his wife. Bleeding copiously, she dragged herself along a corridor and died in one of the chambers. Despite the provocation and when he came to himself, MacFarlane was horrified by what he had done, and hanged himself. The ghost of his wife returned as a Green Lady, and appeared when one of the family was about to die or misfortune strike.

Lying three miles north and east of Maybole in Ayrshire, CASSILLIS HOUSE is a large mansion, developed out of a strong tower dating from the 14th century. The building was altered and extended in later centuries, but still has a vaulted basement with a prison built into the very thick walls. Cassillis was held by the Kennedy family from 1373, and they were made Earls of Cassillis in 1509. The first Earl was slain at the Battle of Flodden four years later, while the second was assassinated by Sir Hugh Campbell of Loudoun, and the third was probably poisoned when he was a Commissioner for the marriage of Mary, Queen of Scots.

As mentioned under Dunure, the fourth Earl roasted the Commendator of Crossraguel Abbey until he signed over the lands to the Earl. This is not quite as unreasonable as it sounds: the Kennedys had bequeathed much land to the abbey down the centuries, and did not want it given to whomsoever Stewart chose.

Cassillis House is still occupied by the Kennedys, and became their main seat after Culzean Castle was passed to The National Trust for Scotland.

One tale is that Cassillis is haunted by Lady Jean Hamilton, wife of John Kennedy, sixth Earl of Cassillis. She has been witnessed in the Countess Room, and it is here her apparition has often been seen, looking out of a window. It is thought that she hopes for the sight of her lover, Sir John Faa of Dunbar.

Cassillis House: *haunted by Lady Jean, who was imprisoned by her husband and made to watch the execution of her lover Johnie Faa 'the gypsy laddie'.*

This is linked to the old ballad *Johnie Faa*, the gypsy laddie, when a spell was placed on the lady of the house so that she ran off with Faa. The Earl was having none of it, however, and pursued them. When he caught them, he summarily hanged Faa, making Lady Jean watch, and imprisoned her in Cassillis (or Maybole) Castle.

There does not appear to be any historical evidence for the details of the ballad: indeed surviving letters suggest the sixth Earl and Lady Jean were on good terms.

A CKERGILL TOWER, two or so miles north of Wick in Caithness, is a strong tower house with later extensions, after being remodelled in Victorian times. It originally had a 12-foot-wide ditch and rises to six storeys including the attic.

Ackergill was long a property of the Keith family, who were major landowners in Caithness. They feuded with another northern family, the Gunns, and there were repeated outbreaks of violence between the two clans in the 15th century.

Helen Gunn was a lovely creature, and is known as the Beauty of Braemore. Her father held lands at Braemore, which is in a remote part of Caithness, some miles west of Dunbeath on the Berriedale Water. Helen had fallen in love and was betrothed to be married. Dugald Keith of Ackergill, however, desired her for himself. Keith sought her out at her father's house in Braemore on the night before her wedding, killed several of her family and their retainers, and kidnapped Helen, despite her protests that she was already promised to another. Dugald carried her off to Ackergill, where he had her imprisoned in one of the attic rooms. Helen would have nothing to do with Dugald and, rather than submit to him, the poor woman threw herself from the battlements and was dashed on the ground below. From that day on the castle was haunted by a Green Lady, Helen's apparition, clad in green. There is said to be an ancient rowan tree, known as Fair Ellen's Tree, at Braemore.

Ackergill Tower: Helen Gunn 'the beauty of Braemore' was kidnapped and imprisoned here; rather than submit to her abductor, she threw herself to her death from the parapet.

The abduction is thought to have taken place before 1426, possibly before the present castle was built, although there may have been an older stronghold on the site.

One version of the ghost story of Dunrobin Castle is similar to many details of this tale.

CALLY CASTLE stood about half a mile south of Gatehouse of Fleet in south-west Scotland, but little now survives except one wall. It was a property of the Stewarts, but later passed to the Murrays. They abandoned the castle, and built themselves a new mansion in 1763-5. This was altered and extended down the years, is now used as the Cally Palace Hotel, and lies in 150 acres of grounds.

One tale is that a young woman, perhaps a servant or nanny, was murdered in the building by being thrown from one of the upper chambers. In 1975 a guest reported seeing the phantom of the girl, who was clad in green, fleeing from a man. His arms were outstretched and covered in blood.

The DREADNOUGHT HOTEL in the middle of Callander in Stirlingshire was built in 1802 by Francis MacNab, the chief of his clan. It is a large imposing building, modified down the years, and used as a hotel. 'Dread nought' is the motto of the MacNabs. There has apparently been a hostelry here since the 17th century.

It is haunted by the ghost of a girl. There are at least two versions of the story behind the haunting. One is that she was a servant girl who was made pregnant by MacNab, and he tossed her out of one of the windows on the upper floors to rid himself of her. A second that he walled up his wife somewhere in the building.

The hotel is also said to be haunted by MacNab himself, as well as the sobbing of a child.

The Loch Ness Youth Hostel, at AULTSIGH on the banks of Loch Ness, is housed in what was the Aultsigh Hotel. The apparition of a young woman, with jet-black hair and flashing eyes, has been seen, both in the youth hostel and in the surrounding countryside. Other manifestations include ghostly footsteps crossing and recrossing the floor of one of the rooms.

Annie Fraser was an attractive lass, and was desired by two brothers, Alasdair and Malcolm McDonnell. Annie became a bone of contention between them, and appears to have favoured Alasdair. She was spending some time with him on the hill behind the house, presumably in a romantic liaison, when they were surprised by Malcolm. Filled with ire, Malcolm attacked and slew his brother, and then strangled or stabbed the unfortunate Annie. Dragging her body back to the house, he hid it under floor boards in an abandoned chamber. Aware his terrible deeds would not go undiscovered for long, he fled the house by boat, but the vessel capsized and he drowned crossing the loch.

The unexplained footsteps are said to come from the room where Annie's body was concealed.

Lying in Auchinlea Park, PROVAN HALL, some three miles west and north of Coatbridge, is a fine courtyard house, dating from the 15th century: it has been described as 'probably the most perfect pre-

Reformation mansion house in Scotland'. The lands were originally held by the Bishops of Glasgow, but passed to the Baillies after the Reformation, then the Hamiltons, and finally to a Reston Mathers (who is said to haunt the house). The building is owned by The National Trust for Scotland, but managed by Glasgow City Council.

Provan Hall has a White Lady, an apparition of which has been witnessed at the garden gate, calling for her son. The tale is that the woman and her child were murdered in one of the first-floor bedrooms by one of the lairds.

The scant ruins of HOWLET'S HOUSE stand in a remote but scenic spot some miles north-west of Penicuik in Midlothian. For many years, travellers and visitors to the area reported seeing the phantoms of a young couple, increasing speculation about murderous deeds at the house. Eventually the bodies of a young man and woman were found in a shallow grave and, when they were given a proper burial, the apparitions were not seen again.

The story goes that the owner of Howlet's House, although in advancing years, had married a young and lovely wife. For some time the girl seems to have been content, but her eyes started to wander towards a handsome servant, and before too long they had started a passionate affair. Soon afterwards the couple disappeared. Her old husband told all who would listen that they had run off together, taking his money. He then left the area himself.

It is assumed that her husband had discovered his wife and the servant in a compromising position, then murdered them and hidden their remains.

CROMLIX CASTLE, located some miles north of Callander in Stirlingshire, was once a strong fortress, but nothing remains today except a scatter of stones. There was an ancient barony of Cromlix, which was a property of the Chisholms.

One story is that Ann Chisholm of Cromlix was romantically entwined with Sir Malaise Graham of nearby Kilbryde, a neighbouring tower house (which has its own ghost story that may be confused with, or based on, Ann). Graham appears to have tired of his love, and murdered her and hid her body in Kilbryde Glen. Her ghost, an apparition in a white blood-stained dress, was seen there repeatedly and did not rest until her remains were found and given a Christian burial.

GARTH CASTLE lies some six mile of Aberfeldy, and is a somewhat dour tower, dating from the 14th century and said to have been built by Alexander Stewart, the Wolf of Badenoch (who is reputed to haunt what is now Ruthven Barracks). The castle was restored after falling ruinous, and is still occupied.

Garth was held by the Stewarts, and Neil (or Nigel) Stewart of Garth was reputedly a particularly unpleasant fellow. He cannot have been very old when in 1502 he seized one of his neighbours, Sir Robert Menzies, and imprisoned him at Garth after burning Weem Castle, then threatened to torture and kill him in an attempt to make him sign over lands. This nearly got Stewart executed, and he was only saved by the intervention of the Earl of Atholl.

By 1545 it seems he had become tired with his wife Mariota. She was found dead below the castle walls, and it was suspected that a stone had hit her on the head after being flung from the walls of Garth. Suspicion fell on Menzies, but nothing could be proved. Things were to catch up with him, however, and he was eventually imprisoned in his own dungeon until his death in 1554.

An apparition, believed to be that of Mariota, has been seen several times in the vicinity of Garth.

NEAR Wigtown in Galloway are the scant remains of BALDOON CASTLE, a stronghold of the Dunbars, who owned the property until about 1800. The ruins are haunted by the apparition of a woman in a blood-splashed wedding dress.

In 1669 Janet Dalrymple of Carscreugh was in love with Archibald Rutherford, a younger son of Lord Rutherford, but he was poor and her parents were against their marriage. They chose Sir David Dunbar of Baldoon, who was the heir to Baldoon, and persuaded Janet to marry him. At first she had refused, but over time they wore her down. The couple were married at the church in Old Luce, and then went to Baldoon Castle for their wedding-night celebrations. Eventually they retired for the night.

A large commotion was heard coming from their bedchamber. When the door was finally forced open, all was far from well. But, as Dunbar would not speak of what happened that evening, there can only be speculation about the events. Janet was either killed on her wedding night after having tried to slay her new husband, or died insane soon afterwards, or she possibly committed suicide. One version suggests it was the Devil who tried to slay Dunbar, and so frightened Janet that she could not bear to go on living. In any event, Janet died within a short time of her unhappy marriage celebrations.

Her apparition is said to be seen at Baldoon most often on the anniversary of her death, 12 September, although at other times she is also said to search through the ruins. Dunbar recovered sufficiently to marry a daughter of the Montgomery Earl of Eglinton, while Janet's lover, Archibald, never married and died in 1685.

Sir Walter Scott's *Bride of Lammermuir* (and then Donizetti's opera) were inspired by this story.

BALNAGOWN CASTLE, which was held by branches of the Ross family until 1958, is a substantial but much-altered tower house, dating from the 14th century. It stands in Easter Ross, about six miles south of Tain. The Ross family were a wild lot in the 16th century, and the lairds were constantly in trouble with the authorities. Katherine Ross (known as Lady Foulis), sister of the then laird of Balnagown and wife of Robert Munro of Foulis, was charged with witchcraft, incantation, sorcery and poisoning. Although some of her acquaintances were burned, she managed to escape execution herself by ensuring the jury at a retrial was made up of her own people – the charges were found not proven.

Balnagown is haunted by the spirit of what is described as a Scottish princess who was murdered in the castle. Her apparition is a Grey Lady, dressed in a grey frock, and it has green eyes and auburn hair. The ghost once appeared in the dining room, then walked to the drawing room,

Balnagown Castle: *haunted by the ghost of a 'Scottish princess', murdered and walled-up in the building.*

and there vanished. It is said that she was not frightening, and even seemed friendly. Manifestations were witnessed in the 20th century when her apparition was again seen. The remains of the woman are believed to be walled up somewhere within the castle, but whether this was to kill the poor woman or only to hide her body is not recorded.

Balnagown has a second ghost, 'Black Andrew' Munro, a cruel and unpleasant character, whose story is related later in the book.

CASTLE FRASER is a large and grand building, consisting of a massive Z-plan tower house from the 16th century. It is located six miles or so south-west of Inverurie in Aberdeenshire, was held for many centuries by the Fraser family, and is now in the care of The National Trust for Scotland.

One tale is that a young girl or princess was violently murdered near the fireplace in the Green Room of the Round Tower of the stronghold. The date is given either in the far past or in the 19th century. Her body was dragged downstairs, leaving a smear of blood on the steps, before being buried. The hearth and floor were also liberally bedaubed with gore. After disposing of her corpse, the floor and stair were repeatedly washed, but no matter how much effort was put into the cleaning, the blood could not be removed. It is said that the stair was eventually boarded over to hide the evidence of the murder. Of course, there could be many more prosaic reasons why this would be done, not least if the stone treads were uneven after many years of use, or so that the treads would not be so cold.

An apparition clad in a long black gown, believed to be of Lady Blanche Drummond, who died in 1874, has also been seen here, and was reported in 1995. It is said to have had no face, and was seen in the library and passageways. Blanche was married to Colonel Frederick Mackenzie Fraser, and her portrait hangs in the Green Room.

Set in a peaceful location on the north bank of Loch Etive, some miles north-east of Oban, stands ARDCHATTAN PRIORY. It was founded in 1231, but was dissolved during the Reformation, and the property went to the Campbells. They built a house, incorporating part of the buildings (which had been torched in 1644 and 1654), while the church was used by the parish until 1731. The Campbells still occupy Ardchattan, and there is a fine four-acre garden.

A ghost story dates from when the priory was still in use. A young nun fell in love with one of the monks, and she would visit him in the priory.

They arranged a bolt hole should they be discovered, but it was an airless pit in the floor. The prior had found out about their assignations, however, and burst in on them. The girl had time to make flight to her refuge, but the prior had the bolt hole barricaded, burying her alive, so that she either suffocated or died from thirst. The nun's ghost then went on to haunt the buildings.

The remaining ruins of the priory are in the care of Historic Scotland and open to the public, as is the garden of Ardchattan House.

DALHOUSIE CASTLE, which stands south of Dalkeith in Midlothian, is an imposing castle and mansion, now used as a hotel, but long the seat of the Ramsays, who were made Earls of Dalhousie. They still hold the title, but the castle was sold and the family now live at Brechin Castle in Angus.

In the middle of the 16th century, a Lady Catherine was mistress to one of the Ramsays. Ramsay's wife, however, found out about her husband's affair, and had Catherine seized and imprisoned in one of the upstairs chambers. Catherine was starved to death.

Her ghost, a Grey Lady, has been seen several times on the stairs, in the dungeons, and along the Black Corridor (the original battlements which have been incorporated into the present building). Other manifestations include the swishing of her dress, and tapping or scratching at doors. The ghost was witnessed in one of the bedrooms during renovation work in 2000. Other disturbances include a waitress having her hair pulled, and a guest being tapped repeatedly on each shoulder, both apparently when nobody was present. It is not clear if this was by Lady Catherine or another spirit.

Located to the south and west of Edinburgh, CRAIGHOUSE, a much-altered tower house, dates from the 16th century and was built by the Symsons. It later passed to the Dick family, who were ruined supporting Charles I, then the Elphinstones. It was subsequently part of a psychiatric institution, but is now in the campus of Napier University.

In 1712 Craighouse was occupied by Sir Thomas Elphinstone, who had a grown-up son, John, by his first wife. Sir Thomas decided to remarry, and choose Elizabeth Pittendale, a pretty young girl many years his junior, as his new wife. The couple were married, and came to live at Craighouse.

Sir Thomas grew jealous, and began to feel that Elizabeth was showing undue interest in his son John (Elizabeth may have met John before she was married, although she did not know that he was Thomas's son). It would appear that her husband's fears were groundless and, although Elizabeth was attracted to John, nothing happened between them. Nevertheless, one day Sir Thomas surprised the couple together after bursting in on them. Fearing the worst, rage took the older man, and he attacked his wife and brutally stabbed her to death. John escaped and fled, but the next morning Sir Thomas was also found dead, having taken his own life.

Despite the circumstances surrounding their deaths, Elizabeth and Sir Thomas were interred in the Elphinstone burial vault.

John inherited Craighouse, but chose not to live there, and the castle was let to tenants. But an apparition of Elizabeth, a Green Lady, began to plague the occupants. Her ghost, dressed in a green frock, was repeatedly seen, and there were other manifestations and disturbances. The tenants became very anxious and frightened, but eventually it became clear that the spirit of Elizabeth was unhappy that she had been buried beside Sir Thomas. When her remains were removed from the Elphinstone vault, the manifestations ceased.

It is believed that when John Elphinstone died, he was interred beside Elizabeth.

S tanding in Sutherland, some miles west of Dornoch, SKIBO CASTLE is a magnificent mansion, which was rebuilt by the famous industrialist and philanthropist Andrew Carnegie in 1898. Carnegie was born in Dunfermline in 1835, and was one of the richest men in the world after making a fortune from railways and iron and steel in America. The mansion is now home to an exclusive country club, and Madonna and Guy Ritchie were married here.

This was, however, the site of an ancient castle, held by the Bishops of Caithness from the 13th century, and then the Gray family following the Reformation.

The old castle was long haunted by the phantom of a girl, fleeing through the chambers, her clothing dishevelled and torn. Other manifestations included unexplained cries and screams of terror coming from unoccupied areas. It is said that during renovations (there were several during the building's history) the remains of a girl were found walled up in one of the castle chambers. The bones were given a proper burial, and it is said the haunting ceased after this had been done.

The story is that a girl went to the castle at a time when it was not

Skibo Castle: *at one time the apparition of a dishevelled and terrified young woman was seen in the building.*

being used by the owners. The only occupant was the keeper of the castle. He attacked and assaulted the poor young woman, and then murdered her and hid her body. As there was nobody else in the building, there was no-one to hear her terrified cries.

S ANQUHAR CASTLE, just south of the burgh of Sanquhar itself, was once a strong and important stronghold of the powerful Crichton family. The property was sold to the Douglases of Drumlanrig in 1639, and they abandoned Sanquhar for their magnificent new mansion of Drumlanrig. Sanquhar fell into a crumbling ruin, although some consolidation was undertaken until 1900.

The castle is haunted by a White Lady, believed to be a phantom of the young and golden-haired Marion of Dalpeddar (Dalpeddar was a small estate, with its own tower house, some three miles south-east of Sanquhar – it has its own ghost story, which seems more than just a coincidence). The accounts state that she disappeared in 1590, and she was seduced and cruelly murdered, probably by Robert Crichton of Sanquhar. Certainly a female skeleton was found, stuffed face-down in a pit or hole, with some golden hair still stuck to the skull, when the castle was excavated in 1875-6. The White Lady is believed to have appeared before a death in, or misfortune was about to strike, the resident family.

Grangemuir, about a mile north of Pittenweem in Fife, dates from about 1807, but stands on the site of a much older building, which was occupied by the Bruce family. The later house is still occupied.

Grangemuir (or Grangemyre) was haunted by the ghost of a pretty girl called Buff Barefoot, called so because she would wear no shoes or socks. She had been found abandoned, although with a bag of gold, when she was an infant. Buff had two admirers (one a son of the family who owned Grangemuir) being an attractive lass, but her affections appear to have become a bone of contention. The poor girl ended up murdered, although the exact circumstances are not recorded. Her killer was captured, while her other suitor committed suicide.

There were then many manifestations at Grangemuir, not least the sound of heavy footfalls in the building, made by unseen bare feet. Her apparition was also observed. The disturbances were apparently so frightening that the old house was abandoned, and the new building put in its place. The builders were careful enough not to reuse any of the materials from the previous dwelling.

Old Woodhouselee is now a very ruinous castle, consisting of little more than cellars, and stands on a crag, just over one north-east of the Midlothian town of Penicuik. The castle may have been built by the Sinclairs, but passed to the Hamiltons. The building was demolished towards the end of the 17th century, and replaced by Woodhouselee, a new house near Fulford, itself now gone.

In January of 1570 at Linlithgow, James Hamilton of Bothwellhaugh shot and killed James Stewart, the infamous Regent Moray. Moray, the illegitimate brother of Mary Queen of Scots, was instrumental in getting Mary to abdicate; and he was made Regent in the name of the infant James VI. He also had a long-running feud with the loyal Hamiltons, and had imprisoned the head of their family. This may have been grounds enough for Hamilton of Bothwellhaugh to assassinate Moray, but he may have had a far more personal reason.

Some time before the killing in 1570, the Regent Moray (or one of his supporters) had appeared at (Old) Woodhouselee on a freezing night in January, presumably looking to imprison or kill Hamilton. Hamilton was not at home, but Hamilton's wife and her young baby were seized and thrown out of the castle into the grounds in only their night clothes, or even naked. The infant died from the cold, and Lady Hamilton went mad from grief. When she died, perhaps as late as 1609, an apparition of her was then often reported at Woodhouselee, especially on freezing moon-lit nights, either searching through the castle and grounds for her baby or with the infant in her arms. At least one account also has her at the 'new' Woodhouselee, perhaps translated here with many of the building materials, although this may simply be a confusion with 'Old' Woodhouselee. She has been described both as a White Lady, but also as a Green Jean.

Hamilton, himself, escaped and fled to France, where he continued to work on behalf of Mary, Queen of Scots (she was then imprisoned in England). He died in 1580.

M AINS CASTLE is a plain but striking tower house, dating from the 15th century, located near East Kilbride. It was long held by the Lindsays of Dunrod, one of whom, with Robert the Bruce, had infamously stabbed the Red John Comyn at Dumfries in 1306. Indeed, Mains had originally been a property of the Comyns. Once while out curling on a local pond, a later Lindsay was so angered by one of his servants that he had him drowned by pushing him under the ice. The

Mains Castle: haunted by the phantom of a woman strangled to death by her husband.

castle was ruinous at one time, but has been restored.

Mains is haunted by the phantom of a woman. The story goes that her husband returned home unexpectedly. She was dallying with another man, and just had time to hide her lover in the castle. That night, she knotted bed sheets together so that her lover might climb from a window and escape: it is not recorded whether she also meant to flee. But she was caught during the act, and her furious husband murdered her by strangling her. Her apparition and those of the bed sheets are both said to have been witnessed.

She is said to have been a sister of William the Lyon, King of Scots in the 12th century. The present castle, of course, would not have been in existence then, although there was an earlier castle on a nearby motte.

On Canna, one of the Small Isles (which also include Muck, Eigg and Rum), are the scant remains of COROGHON CASTLE atop a steep rock. The ruins are said to be haunted by the ghost of a woman who was imprisoned here by one of the MacDonalds.

BROOMHILL CASTLE, just south of Larkhall in Lanarkshire, was for hundreds of years held by a branch of the Hamiltons, but was demolished after a fire gutted the building in 1943, and little remains. The Hamiltons supported Mary, Queen of Scots, and the castle was torched in 1572. It was rebuilt, then remodelled and extended in later centuries.

Broomhill's ghost story is unusually late, and dates from about 1900, when the house was occupied by the McNeil Hamiltons of Raploch. The site of the house and grounds, and even a nearby inn, are haunted by a Black Lady. She is said to be the phantom of a beautiful Indian girl – perhaps a servant, perhaps a princess – who was reputedly mistress to Captain Henry McNeil Hamilton, owner of Broomhill (he died in 1924). The girl disappeared about 1900, and it is believed by some that she was murdered.

Strange manifestations then plagued the house, and her apparition was seen, looking out from the windows in the house, in the grounds, and in Morgan Glen. Broomhill was reported on *Tonight*, a television programme in the 1960s, when an exorcism was performed. At that time it was still possible to enter part of the cellars, although these have since been sealed.

The ghost has also been witnessed at the nearby Applebank Inn. A lintel from Broomhill House was used in an extension to the establishment, perhaps bringing the ghost along with it. Objects are said to have mysteriously disappeared at the inn, while others are moved about without explanation.

Another Black Lady haunted LOGIE HOUSE in Dundee, although the building was completely demolished in the 20th century. It is said that in life that she was an Indian princess, captured by one of the owners when they worked for the East India Company, around the turn of the 19th century. The poor woman was imprisoned at Logie, and died there. Her ghost returned to plague the house, and there are also reports of her haunting the area around the site.

AUCHLOCHAN HOUSE, south of Lesmahagow in Lanarkshire, also has a Black Lady who haunts the grounds, the lovely black wife of one of the owners, the Browns of Auchlochan. The woman, in this case, appears to have died of natural causes. The building is now used as a nursing home.

JOHNSTONE LODGE in Anstruther, a town house of 1829, is believed to be haunted by Tetuane Marama, a Tahitian princess, the wife of George Dairsie. Her ghost is also a Black Lady, and she was buried in the burgh's burial ground: there is a memorial on the south wall of the church.

Wellwood House, which stood near Muirkirk in Ayrshire, has been demolished. It incorporated a stronghold or old house of the Campbells, which dated from about 1600, into a 19th-century mansion. It was removed in 1926.

The house had a ghost, the phantom of a young lass, known as Beanie (also spelt in one account as Beenie). Her apparition would be seen, going from a room in the old part of the building, through the house, to the grounds. There she would weep. If anyone approached the phantom, it would slowly disappear. The poor girl is said to have been deeply in love but she was murdered, possibly by a jealous rival and possibly on the stairs of the house: it is recorded that a blood stain could not be removed from the steps.

Located on a cliff-top above the River Ericht two miles north of Blairgowrie, CRAIGHALL, or Craighall-Rattray, is a grand baronial mansion, which incorporates some of an old tower. It stands in a fine wooded estate. The property had passed to the Rattray family by the 16th century, and they still live at Craighall.

One of the chambers in the old part of the building is haunted. The Rattray family supported Charles I, and as a result the castle was besieged by Cromwell's forces sometime in the first years of the 1650s. Eventually it was taken, but the family had hidden themselves and could not be found. A young servant girl was seized, but would not reveal their whereabouts. She was taken to what is now known as the North Room, and the soldiers dragged her to the window. She would still not betray the family, although repeatedly threatened, and was finally thrown from the window to be dashed on the ground below.

The chamber from which she was thrown then became haunted by her ghost. Tapping sounds were reported coming from the window, and the room is described as often having a frightening feeling. Other manifestations are reported throughout the mansion, including unexplained footsteps when nobody is present, and knocking and banging. People staying at Craighall are said to have been woken from sleep feeling as if there is a great weight on their chests.

Craighall also has Grey Lady, who may be responsible for many of the manifestations, or may be the phantom of the servant girl.

KEMBACK HOUSE, some miles east of Cupar in Fife, probably dates from the beginning of the 18th century, but was altered in 1907. It replaced an earlier building, possibly a castle or fortified house, which was a property of the Schivas family.

Nearby Dura Den, the 16th-century Dairsie Bridge, and the house are haunted by a White Lady. She is believed to be the wife of the Schivas laird in the troubled times of the 17th century. Her husband, a Covenanter, had taken refuge in a cave in Dura Den, and was being hunted by the government. She brought him food, but was eventually arrested, although she would not betray the whereabouts of her husband. The poor woman was taken to Dairsie Bridge, and there hanged. An alternative version is that she was the wife of a Miles Graham, and after being tortured did reveal his hiding place: he was, of course, executed. A chamber in Kemback House is known as the White Lady's Room.

Located some five miles or so west and north of Thurso in the north of Scotland, BRIMS CASTLE is a 16th-century L-plan tower house with a walled courtyard. It was built by the Sinclairs, but is now an impressive ruin, although apparently not in the most savoury of situations.

The building is said to have a White Lady, which has been seen on many occasions. James Sinclair of Uttersquoy, a nearby property, had a very attractive daughter, who became involved with Patrick Sinclair of Brims. Patrick appears to have tired of his love, and the poor lass was

30

murdered, her body hidden in the castle. There is also a story that a coffin was ordered from Thurso, but for whom was never discovered.

K ILBRYDE CASTLE, near Dunblane in Stirlingshire, is an L-plan tower house, dating from the 15th century, but extended in around 1877. It was originally a property of the Graham Earls of Menteith, but was sold to the Campbells of Aberuchill in 1669. The house is still occupied by the Campbells, and the gardens, which have been restored and developed, are open to the public.

One story is that the castle and the grounds near the old chapel were haunted by a White Lady, the ghost of a woman murdered here. The apparition was seen on several occasions, but when approached would fade away. It seems too much of a coincidence that a White Lady, the spirit of Anne Chisholm (of Cromlix Castle), haunted Kilbryde Glen, and this may be a confusion of tales.

C ASTLE LEVAN, near Gourock in Renfrewshire, stands on a strong site overlooking the Clyde, and dates from the 14th century. It was built by the Morton family, but later passed to the Semples, and then the Stewarts of Inverkip in 1649. The building became ruinous, but has been restored and reoccupied, although there is a now a housing estate in its grounds.

The castle has accounts of a White Lady, the ghost of Lady Marion Montgomery, her apparition having been seen in the building. Marion appears to have been a cruel lady, and mistreated the locals and her tenants, so much so that she got into trouble with the authorities, being sentenced to death by Mary of Guise. This would place the tale around 1550, although the sentence was not carried out. When her husband discovered what she had been up to, he had her locked up in one of the chambers, and Marion was starved to death.

A s mentioned above, most of these stories concern the violent deeds of men. There are always exceptions, however, as the White Lady of Corstorphine, the phantom of Christian Hamilton, wife of Andrew Nimmo, demonstrates.

Nothing remains of CORSTORPHINE CASTLE, which was once a large and princely stronghold, long held by the Forresters: the castle was burned out and then mostly demolished at the end of the 18th century. The Dower House, the old church, and a large doocot in Dovecot Road (off Saughton Road North to the west of Edinburgh) survive from this time. Incidentally, the doocot is said to have supernatural protection: anyone demolishing it would be doomed to a quick death.

The Forresters were an important family, and there are carved tombs for Sir Adam Forrester, Provost of Edinburgh (who died in 1405), and Sir John Forrester, Lord Chamberlain during the reign of James I, (and their wives) in the nearby Corstorphine Old Parish Church.

Christian was deeply in love with James Forrester, second Lord Forrester, although she was his niece; and they met under a sycamore tree (supposedly planted in 1429: an old sycamore tree survives at one end of Dovecot Road). It was at the tree that they had a violent argument, possibly about the fact he drank and philandered rather too much. During the course of the fight, Christian stabbed and killed Forrester with his own sword. The argument may have also been because she wished to marry him: he had apparently got a dispensation so that he could wed her (they also had a daughter).

Christian was speedily arrested, taken to the tolbooth in Edinburgh, tried and sentenced to death, although she claimed that she only acted in self defence. Christian, disguised as a man, managed to escape from her imprisonment, but she was pursued south and recaptured at Fala. Being brought back to Edinburgh, she was executed by beheading on 12 November 1679 at the Mercat Cross in the city. She is said to have conducted herself well and bravely, and was wearing a white frock.

Her phantom, a White Lady, has been repeatedly seen by the old sycamore tree and around the former grounds of the castle. One account has her sometimes seen with the fatal sword.

PROPERTY

Property has always been a motive for misdeeds and murder, and medieval and early modern times were no different. There were several high-profile cases, such as those involving Lady Foulis and the Erskines of Dun, when relatives would resort to witchcraft and murder to ensure or enhance an inheritance. There are, however, fewer ghost stories of this kind than might be expected, although the cruelty involved in these few is exceptional.

ASHINTULLY CASTLE, 12 miles or so north of Blairgowrie, in Perthshire, is a fine L-plan tower house, dating from the 16th century, and was restored in later centuries after falling ruinous. For many years it was owned by the Spalding family, before coming to the Rutherfords, and it is still occupied. It does have, however, a particularly unpleasant ghost story.

At some time in the past, during the period it was held by the Spaldings, the castle was owned by a young woman, Jean (or Jane), in her own right. Her uncle, however, wanted the lands for himself, and did not see her as a barrier to inheritance. Jean was in one of the castle chambers, having her hair combed by a serving girl. This day she was wearing a green frock. As mentioned above, green was seen as an unlucky colour and associated with the fairies. Perhaps she was tempting fate, although it is difficult to see how another choice of dress would have saved her.

Her uncle sought her out in her chamber. It is not recorded whether they argued or even passed any words, but the outcome was he slit poor Jean's throat, and then also slaughtered the young maid, concealing her body by stuffing it up the chimney of the chamber (for years afterwards it was noted that the chimney did not draw well). Jean's corpse was dragged to the burial ground, and there interred, a headstone marking her grave.

Jean's ghost, a Green Lady (Green Jean), returned to manifest itself in the castle, and has also been seen in the small walled burial ground. Phantom footsteps have also been heard around the building.

DALPEDDAR was formerly a small estate with its own tower house, some three miles south-east of Sanquhar. Reports over many years were made of an apparition of a tall woman, sometimes with a boy, clad in white, being seen repeatedly on the roadside by a large hawthorn bush. The wee lad would be seen to be weeping. On closer investigation, however, nobody was found. These accounts were made over many years, one describing how a tall woman, dressed in white, walked down the middle of the road. Her face could not be seen as it was obscured by a large bonnet, which was also white.

The remains of a woman and child were finally found buried by the roadside near the hawthorn tree: the young woman had had her skull split.

The story goes that, during the first quarter of the 16th century, the woman, Lady Hebron, was heir to the lands and small fortalice of Dalpeddar. She married and had a son, but her husband died, leaving her a widow. The boy's uncle wanted the estate for himself, and Lady Hebron and her young son disappeared, leaving the uncle to inherit.

It does also seem too much of a coincidence that a Marion of Dalpeddar was reputedly murdered in 1590 as Sanquhar Castle and the stories may be linked or confused.

WRIGHTSHOUSES stood on the site of what was later James Gillespie's School, then the Blind Asylum, off what is now Gillespie Crescent in Edinburgh. A castle or fortified house stood here, which may have dated from the 14th century, but it was demolished in 1802. It was held by the Napiers, but passed to the Clerk family in 1664.

At the end of the 18th century, Wrightshouses was the residence of Lieutenant General Robertson of Lawers. One of his servants was sleeping in a bedroom when he was greatly disturbed during the night when he witnessed the apparition of a headless woman with a baby in its arms. The servant saw the ghost on several occasions, and it always emerged from the hearth stone of the fireplace. The servant must have been glad when Robertson returned to his own home.

The building was demolished only a few years later, and it is believed that the bones of a woman and child were found beneath the hearth. The woman had had her head severed, perhaps to fit in the cavity beneath the stone, perhaps as part of her brutal murder.

The story behind the haunting is that, after 1664, Wrightshouses was occupied by a James Clerk, his wife and child. James was slain in battle, leaving his infant son his only heir. Clerk's younger brother, however, wanted the property for himself, and he murdered the lad and his mother, then concealed the crime by hiding their remains under the fireplace. In another version the woman and son were dumped in a chest, and the lady's head was severed to fit it into the space. It was then walled up into a cupboard. When the house was being demolished, the remains were found.

A similar story to this has also been told about nearby Bruntsfield House, after Gillespie's School moved here.

S tanding some miles south-east of Dumfries, COMLONGON CASTLE has a very tragic ghost story, concerning Marion Carruthers of Mouswald. Comlongon consists of a strong-walled keep to which was added a mansion in the 19th century. It was held by the Murray family from 1331 until 1984, and the building is now used as a hotel.

Marion Carruthers was heir, along with her sister Janet, to the lands and tower house (only one wall of which is now left) of Mouswald, a property nine miles west of Annan. Her father, Sir Simon Carruthers, had had no sons, and Marion's husband would acquire her portion of Mouswald as her dowry. Whether Marion had a lover is not recorded, but she was betrothed to a man she did not want or love, Sir James Douglas of Drumlanrig (or to John MacMath, his nephew, according to one account). He was far more interested in her estate than her physical assets. Maxwell of Caerlaverock also had designs on the property, and seized Mouswald Tower in the meantime.

Marion could not be persuaded to marry and, according to one account, was held in Hermitage Castle. She managed to escape, and fled to Comlongon and the protection of her uncle, Sir William Murray, to whom she offered half her dowry. Even the Privy Council ruled against her, and in 1563 poor Marion was commanded to place herself into the guardianship of Borthwick Castle, in Midlothian, until the matter was resolved. In the end, it was found against her and in favour of Douglas,

Comlongon Castle: *Marion Carruthers fell to her death from the old keep: did she commit suicide or was she murdered?*

and she was ordered to marry him.

It ended, however, seven years later when Marion was found dead at the foot of the keep at Comlongon, below the watch-tower – it was reported that no grass will grow at the spot where she hit the ground. It was now 25 September 1570. It was said that she did 'wilfully take her own life by leaping from the lookout tower' and that she 'did break her head and bones'.

What exactly happened, however, is not known. Marion may have jumped from the keep, the many years of conflict or the prospect of marrying a man she did not want finally having got to her. There is also a more sinister explanation. The Douglases found a way into the castle and sought out Marion. When she still refused to wed, they took her to the watch-tower and threw her to her death. Marion was said to have committed suicide, and she was not buried in consecrated ground.

Her weeping apparition, a Green Lady, was then repeatedly seen in the castle and grounds, and the sounds of her crying have also been heard. A ghostly presence, which forces itself past people, has been recorded on at least two occasions. One reason given for the restlessness of her spirit is that she was not given a proper burial and still seeks restitution.

The Douglases, of course, acquired Marion's half of Mouswald.

CARLETON CASTLE is a ruinous tower, standing in a picturesque location six or so miles south of Girvan in south Ayrshire. Ghostly cries and screams have often been heard from the vicinity of the old fortress.

Carleton was held by the Cathcart family, and Sir John Cathcart was renowned for having been married seven times, although each of his wives had suddenly died or mysteriously disappeared. He did, of course, get to keep their dowries: money or property given to him each time he was wed (quite a Bluebeard), although he may simply have tired of them. When his seventh wife met her demise, he decided to take another: May Kennedy of Culzean – although she may have had her doubts about Cathcart from the beginning. May's home, the Culzean Castle of the day, many miles up the coast, was then a relatively modest tower house, although it was incorporated into a massive and splendid new mansion for the Earls of Cassillis by Robert Adam in the 18th century. No doubt, however, May's dowry would have been generous: the Kennedys were a wealthy and prominent family.

One day May and Cathcart were walking along cliffs at Games Loup, a couple of miles south-west of the tower (and near Sawny Bean's Cave).

Cathcart suddenly seized May and tried to fling her off the path to her death. Or he told her to strip naked, before intending to throw her to her death – this was so he could keep her clothes and jewellery rather than for any sexual motive. This she agreed to, but only if he would turn his back, as she felt bashful in front of her new husband. Cathcart then turned his back on her, somewhat unwisely as it turned out.

May was more than ready for him and, in the ensuing melee, it was Cathcart who ended up dead at the foot of the cliffs.

It is not recorded whether the cries from Carleton are his or those of his victims.

Witchcraft and Magic

W itchcraft and magic was seen as a widespread problem in the 16th and 17th centuries, one which frightened and even obsessed sections of both the church and state, and a large proportion of ordinary people. Around 4,000 individuals, most of them women of ordinary status, were accused of witchcraft in Scotland. It is perhaps surprising, then, to find so few ghost stories associated with those women, either in castles or elsewhere, despite the fact many were executed. Perhaps ordinary women were too impoverished even to return as phantoms.

While the vast majority of witchcraft prosecutions and accusations about dallying with the Devil were made against women, the majority of ghost stories involving witchcraft or the Devil are about men. These are covered in Section Three.

Janet Horne from Dornoch is believed to be the last case of a supposed witch being executed, and she is thought to have been burnt in 1722 or 1727 (along with another woman). Janet is said to have been up to all sorts of wickedness, not least turning her lame daughter into a pony and riding her to meetings with the Devil. A large stone marks the spot of Janet's death, and the story goes that at times the apparition of an old woman can be seen, being consumed by the flames. She is described as struggling and cursing as the fire rages beneath her (one story is that she was burned in a barrel of tar after being dragged through the streets of Dornoch). It was, of course, usual to throttle witches before they were burnt, which cannot have been much conciliation except for a less-appalling death.

This story also illustrates how difficult it can be to reconcile stories with written records, many of which are (of course) fragmentary. There is confused evidence for the Dornoch case, which is also true in the cases of other famous 'witches', such as Maggie Walls, Kate MacNiven and Kitty Rankie, the latter being described below under Abergeldie.

The tragic death of Janet Douglas, Lady Glamis, is, however, all-too-well documented.

G LAMIS CASTLE, some miles north of Dundee in Angus, is said to be one of the most haunted buildings in the world, although a visit will confirm there is no unearthly or malevolent atmosphere – or even anything particularly spooky about the place. What is undoubtedly true is that it is one of the most-fabulous buildings and -magnificent castles in the whole of Scotland.

Glamis is associated with Macbeth and Duncan, but this is because of Shakespeare's Scottish play rather than any historical connection. Glamis is not mentioned until 1264, some 200 years after the events (it is also recorded that Duncan was slain after a battle with Macbeth, but this was near Elgin in Moray). It also seems unlikely, therefore, that Malcolm II was murdered here in 1034.

Glamis was built by the Lyon family, who have held the lands since the 14th century. They were an important lot: Sir John Lyon was Chancellor of Scotland, and the family were made Earls of Strathmore and Kinghorne. The Queen Mother, Elizabeth Bowes Lyon, who died in 2002, was a member of the family.

Janet Douglas was the beautiful sister of the Douglas Earl of Angus, and was a popular woman of good character. She married John Lyon, sixth Lord Glamis, although he died in 1528 and she was left a widow. They had a young son, another John. Janet apparently remarried, wedding Walter Campbell of Skipness.

James V was on the throne at the time. He had been a child when his father, James IV, was slain at Flodden in 1513. James IV's widow, Margaret Tudor, married Archibald Douglas, sixth Earl of Angus, two years later. Douglas was an ambitious man, and manipulated and even imprisoned the young James V. The king escaped in 1528, assumed control of the kingdom, and then went on to pursue a vendetta against the Douglases.

Although Janet appears to have been completely innocent, she was accused of witchcraft and trying to poison James V. Although she had made an able and eloquent speech in her defence, the poor woman was imprisoned, along with her young son and new husband, in a dark pit at

Glamis Castle: home to a Grey Lady, the sad spirit of Lady Janet Douglas, who was burned alive for witchcraft.

39

Edinburgh Castle for so long that she almost went blind. Campbell tried to escape from the castle, but was killed when he fell from the castle rock.

Janet was found guilty, of course, and was executed by being burnt alive on Castle Hill at Edinburgh on 3 December 1537. She has been described as 'in the prime of her years, of a singular beauty, and suffering through all, though a woman, with a man-like courage'.

Glamis was forfeited to the Crown, and Janet's infant son was also sentenced to death, although the sentence was not to be carried out until he came of age. James V seized Glamis Castle and the family's lands, and it was not until he died in 1542 that John Lyon was released (after the deathbed confession of one of the accusers) to become seventh Lord Glamis. John recovered the property, although his castle and lands had been plundered by the king's retainers in the meantime.

The spirit of Janet Douglas returned to Glamis. A Grey Lady was witnessed repeatedly, especially sitting sorrowing or kneeling praying in the family chapel, as well as being witnessed in the clock tower. Unexplained hammering and banging noises, sometimes heard at Glamis, have also been linked to Janet's death.

One account has the Grey Lady sitting in the chapel in 1716 when James VIII and III (although never crowned) touched local people in an attempt to cure them of scrofula (also known as the King's Evil). It was described on another occasion as being a small figure, when it was seen praying at one of the pews. The witness could observe the figure closely, but the sun shone through the phantom, making a pattern on the floor. There have been numerous other sightings down the years.

There are also stories of the ghost of a tongueless woman, and a White Lady, who haunts an avenue up to the castle, but these apparently have no foundation. As does the tale of a servant girl who was a vampire, and was walled up when she was caught draining one of her victims.

Glamis also has the famous story of Earl Beardie in a walled-up room, but that is told later.

Located in the rolling countryside of Royal Deeside, west of Ballater, ABERGELDIE CASTLE is a 16th-century tower house of the Gordon family. The castle was attacked and torched in 1592, and was used in the Jacobite Rising of 1689-90. Abergeldie is near Balmoral, and Queen Victoria leased the castle in 1848 to house guests. It is still home to the Gordons.

The tale goes that Catherine Frankie, also known as Kitty Rankie or

French Kate, was a French serving girl in the castle at the end of the 16th century. She became well known for having second-sight, and gained a reputation for being a witch. Margaret, the lady of the house, became concerned that her husband had not returned home from a journey abroad as expected, and consulted Kitty as to his whereabouts. Kitty told her mistress that he was delayed during the passage because he was fooling about with other women. The lady then told Kitty to sink his ship and drown her husband, and this Kitty did by raising a great storm.

Margaret was not very grateful, and Kitty might have been wiser to have given some other explanation as to Margaret's husband's delay. The lady of the castle had the girl imprisoned in the dungeon of Abergeldie, and accused her of witchcraft. Kitty was found guilty and then burned at the stake. The Brahan Seer would have done well to have heeded this story.

Kitty's apparition was then seen on many occasions at Abergeldie, most often in the clock tower. Mysterious and unexplained noises were also recorded. The bell is reputed to ring by itself as a harbinger of death or misfortune in the family.

Incidentally, there is no contemporary written record or evidence of a Catherine Frankie or Kitty Rankie being accused and executed for witchcraft.

Two castles are thought to share the same ghost. NEWTON CASTLE, near Blairgowrie in Perthshire, is a strong 16th-century tower house, and was a property of the Drummonds. Nearby ARDBLAIR CASTLE, also a 16th-century tower house, was held by the Blairs, and is about half a mile away. As with many neighbouring families and clans in medieval times, the two families shared in a long-term bitter feud which led to a cycle of murder and revenge.

Both castles are said to be haunted by a Green Lady, dressed in a frock of green silk, and the story dates back to the middle of the 16th century. The ghost is reputed to be the spirit of Lady Jean Drummond of Newton, who had fallen in love with one of the Blairs of Ardblair. Such a match was simply out of the question under the circumstances, and neither family wanted a wedding.

According to one tale, Lady Jean is said to have died of a broken heart when she was promised to another suitor, drowning herself in a local marsh. An alternative version is that she had been told her suitor was dead, and killed herself in despair in the river Ericht.

***Newton Castle:** haunted by the ghost of Lady Jean Drummond, whose phantom has also been seen at Ardblair.*

Another tale, related in an old ballad, is that she, advised by a local witch, enlisted the help of the fairies when the ardour of her lover had lessened. These fairies were dangerous beings, however, and by taking a wedding dress which they had woven, a shifting green in colour, she was inviting disaster. She had hoped that the magical dress, the 'witchin claith o' green', would ensure marriage to her lover.

In the ballad, she does indeed get married, but then is struck dead just after her vows. Perhaps an illustration that you should be careful for what you wish. Another version states that she got her green dress from water kelpies.

Accounts record that her apparition has been seen in the late afternoon and early evening on sunny afternoons, sitting in the gallery of Ardblair Castle, staring out of the window, or searching through castle chambers of Newton, and perhaps sadly singing in the North Tower. The apparition has also been reported in the grounds of the two strongholds. It is usually said to be sorrowful rather than frightening, although it was apparently disconcerting enough to persuade evacuees to flee and return to Glasgow during the World War II. A report does have her 'dripping and rather sinister' in the policies of Newton.

In one account, she is said to be buried on Knockie Hill. On Halloween at midnight, her head stone is reputed to revolve three times before she rises from her grave.

In a lonely and picturesque situation in the north-west of Scotland, ARDVRECK CASTLE is a ruinous castle dating from the 15th century. The lands were a property of the MacLeods of Assynt, and the castle was sacked in 1672.

The story goes that the chief of MacLeod wanted a grander castle than he could afford. Knowing that he was wicked fellow, the Devil tempted him with a splendid stronghold, but on condition that MacLeod would sign over his soul. MacLeod would not do this, but instead promised the hand of his beautiful young daughter in marriage. The Devil, in the guise of a handsome young man, successfully courted the daughter: the poor young woman had no idea she was betrothed to Satan. The wedding took place, and it was only on her wedding night the new bride realised what her father had done. In terror and shame, she climbed to the top of the castle and threw herself off. It is said that her weeping apparition has been witnessed often in the castle ruins.

Ardvreck is particularly noteworthy for its grandeur in a remote setting. The tale, however, would seem aimed at the MacLeods, perhaps because a MacLeod had the famous Marquis of Montrose imprisoned in 1650 after he took refuge here following his defeat at the Battle of Carbisdale.

Standing on the banks of the Dee, MARYCULTER HOUSE dates from the 17th century, but has a much longer history. The present building stands on the site of preceptory (similar to a priory) of the Knights Templar, an order of holy knights dedicated to serving God and protecting pilgrims to the Holy Land. The preceptory was founded by Walter Bisset in 1230 (the main preceptory was at Temple in Midlothian) but the Templars were suppressed by the Pope in 1312. Following the Reformation, the lands came into the possession of the Menzies family, and they built a house here. The building is now used as a hotel.

The ghost story goes back before the dissolution of the Templars, and concerns a beautiful Saracen woman and one of the Knights, Godfrey Wedderburn of Wedderhill. Wedderburn fought bravely and honourably in the Holy Land and, when badly wounded, he was tended to by a Saracen woman, who recognised his piety and goodness despite being of a different faith. They became friends, but the regard the couple had for each other was strictly pure and innocent. When Godfrey had fully recovered, he sadly bade the woman farewell and returned to the preceptory.

Much later, Godfrey was still at Maryculter when he was visited by the

Saracen woman, who had travelled all the way to Scotland to see him again. The couple were delighted when they were reunited. The Preceptor, the head of the establishment, however, was less than enamoured. He simply would not believe that they had never been anything except friends; neither could he, nor his Knights, have any dealings with a Saracen, their sworn enemies. The Preceptor would not believe Godfrey, no matter how much he protested, and claimed that he had broken his vows to God. The Preceptor forced Godfrey to slay himself with his own sword. The Saracen woman was appalled and also killed herself, but not before cursing the Preceptor for forcing Godfrey into an early grave.

As she breathed her last, lightning struck the Preceptor, leaving a charred hollow in the ground where it had struck: nothing was ever found of the man. The hollow became known as the Thunder Hole, and can still be seen, although it was formerly much deeper.

Godfrey and the Saracen woman are said to have been buried side by side, presumably not on sanctified ground. His apparition, on a horse, was then seen riding over the hill of Kingcausie, while the story goes that the phantom of the Saracen has been observed in the woods near the house.

CHAPTER TWO
Love & Death

To fall in love and to be in love is as popular today as it ever was. In the age of the castle, however, the affection of the daughter of an Earl or laird was not hers to give. Marriages were arranged to form alliances, heal feuds or secure lands, and, of course, to provide a nobleman with a male heir to carry on his line. A beautiful young woman could be betrothed to an ugly old man, who had already survived many wives and fathered many children, provided only he was of sufficient rank. Inevitably, many of these young women fell in love with men of too low a status for the approval of their father, or sometimes they loved a member of a rival family or clan. These matches were most likely doomed.

No doubt these relationships often became physical, and more than one unwed lusty noble woman or serving girl was to find herself carrying her lover's child. A potential husband would want to be certain that any offspring were his, and so many families would want to conceal a pregnancy, or even take more extreme measures.

It should also be said that these ghosts, when their appearance is described, are always young and beautiful. It seems from the tales that plain or unattractive women do not haunt Scotland's castles.

Perhaps one of the clearest illustrations of the difference in status between women and men in the medieval and early modern period is that there are no stories of the son of a nobleman being imprisoned for falling in love with a servant or ordinary lass.

This is quite a large section, so it has been divided into The Breaking of a Heart; Death by Misadventure; and Suicide.

THE BREAKING OF A HEART

These include stories where the girl was jilted, spurned, abandoned or prevented from seeing or meeting her lover. The poor lass would often go into a decline and eventually die or, in the case of Lillias Drummond, could not apparently provide her husband with a male heir.

Located in the north-east of Scotland, some miles from Turriff, Fyvie Castle is a huge, grand and imposing building, remodelled and enlarged down the centuries by a succession of owners. It was originally held by the Crown, but passed to the Lindsays, then the Prestons, Meldrums, the Seton Earls of Dunfermline, the Gordons, and finally the Leith family, before passing to The National Trust for Scotland. The castle has 48 acres of grounds and parkland, and there is an 18th-century walled garden and fine loch-side walks.

Fyvie has a fascinating ghost story, dating from the turn of the 17th century.

Lillias Drummond was the wife of the powerful Alexander Seton, who was made Earl of Dunfermline in 1606 by James VI and was Chancellor of Scotland. Lillias appears to have been a good wife, but unfortunately, although they had four daughters who survived into adulthood, she did not produce a son, albeit hardly an occurrence for which she was responsible. On 8 May 1601 she died, at the age of about 30, young even for the times. Within six months (in fact he was betrothed in just a few short weeks), Seton had remarried, wed to Grizel Leslie.

Lillias had died at Seton's house in Fife, presumably at Dalgety which was his favourite residence (and where he was buried at St Bridget's Kirk in 1622 after dying at Pinkie House). Although it has been suggested that Lillias was starved to death, there is no evidence for this, and she more likely died of a broken heart or just from natural causes, such as giving birth at least five times (another daughter died in infancy) before she was 30.

Whatever the truth of it, and there must have been doubts as to the cause of her death at the time, Alexander Seton went on to wed Grizel Leslie, his step-niece, on 27 October 1601. They spent their wedding night in what is now the Drummond Room at Fyvie Castle.

All night they were disturbed by sighing and moaning coming from the window. When they got up in the morning, they found an inscription, facing outwards, distinctly carved with fine lettering into the outside of the window sill (which is some fifty feet above the ground): D[ame] LILLIES DRUMMOND. The inscription is still there, and can be seen during a visit to the castle. Whether or not this was carved by a ghost is open to question, of course, but what is true is that this is a very strange place for Lillias to have had her name inscribed – or for a stone to be reused. It could be that this part of the story arose from this inscription, and not the other way around. A 'Green Ladye' is, however, mentioned in documents dating from the 17th century.

*Fyvie Castle: there are stories from the 17th century of a
Green Lady – the ghost is said to have carved her name on a
window sill D[ame] LILLIES DRUMMOND.*

How ever the inscription got there, the castle was plagued by Lillias's
ghost, described as a Green Lady, most often seen on the main stair but
also in the passage to the Douglas Room (or Murder Room), where
there are blood stains which cannot be removed. Her phantom is said
to herald a death or misfortune in the resident family, and to have made
her presence felt before the death of Cosmo Gordon in 1879 and
Alexander Gordon a few years later. Indeed, Cosmo is reported to have
been shaken out of his bed by invisible hands, and on a later occasion a
great blast through the building blew the covers off several beds.

One account has the phantom with a candle in its hand and pearls in
its hair, and describes how it wore a green brocade dress, and emitted a
soft illuminance. It is also reported that the phantom has been seen as a
just a patch of light or as a glow, witnessed often at night in one of the
bedchambers. In recent times a visitor told one of the guides, who are
on hand in many of the chambers, that she had seen the phantom of a
lady in the Gordon Bedroom.

Grizel Leslie, herself, was also not to live into old age, and died only
five years after she was married to Seton. She had three children in this
brief time, and they did have a son, but he died young. Their two
daughters were called Jean and, interestingly, Lillias. Alexander Seton
then married Margaret Hay, by whom he had several children, including
Charles, who became second Earl of Dunfermline. Alexander, himself,
died in 1622, while Margaret Hay was to live nearly another 40 years.

The Seton Earls of Dunfermline did not survive the next generation, and James, the fourth Earl (and Alexander Seton's grandson), was forfeited in 1690 and died without heirs four years later. The title became extinct.

Lillias's four daughters married into the noble families of Scotland: Anne, the Erskine Earls of Kellie; Isobel, the Maitland Earls of Lauderdale; Margaret, the Mackenzie Earls of Seaforth; and Sophia, the Lindsay Lords and later Earls of Balcarres.

Fyvie Castle also has a Grey or White Lady, the story going that a young lass was starved to death (anyone who tried to rescue her was slaughtered) in a secret chamber behind what is now the Gun Room. The small room was discovered when workmen were altering the building, and in it they found her remains. When the bones were buried, activity and disturbances became worse, and the ghost is said to have been particularly active in the 1920s and 1930s. One account describes a woman in a white flowing dress, who sailed across a room and disappeared through a door. Manifestations apparently lessened when the remains were returned to the secret chamber and sealed within.

It is possible that Lillias's manifestations and that of this Grey or White Lady have become confused. Lillias is also believed to haunt Pinkie House, and Fyvie has stories of a ghostly drummer or trumpeter, but that tale, along with the Weeping Stones of Fyvie, is covered later.

PINKIE HOUSE, in Musselburgh, in East Lothian is a fine rambling mansion which still has some original 16th-century ceilings in the long gallery. The property was acquired by Alexander Seton (see above) when he was given the lands of Dunfermline Abbey (this part of East Lothian was a portion of the great wealth held by the abbey) by James VI. Seton died here in 1622. The house was visited by both Charles I and Bonnie Prince Charlie, and is now part of Loretto, a private school.

As at Fyvie, the house is believed to be haunted by Lillias Drummond (although she is also called Green Jean in one account), a Green Lady, and her appearance bodes ill for the resident family. Her apparition, or perhaps another, is sometimes accompanied by a child.

NEIDPATH CASTLE stands near the Border burgh of Peebles, above the River Tweed. It is a strong L-plan keep, dating from the 14th century and survived a siege by Oliver Cromwell in 1650. The castle was owned by several of the great families of Scotland: Frasers, Hays and Douglases. Sir Walter Scott visited the castle, and he was to write

*Neidpath Castle: home to the ghost of a
girl who died from a broken heart.*

about the Maid of Neidpath in verse. The castle can be visited.

Jean Douglas, born in 1705, was the youngest daughter of Sir William Douglas, Earl of March. She fell in love with one of the Scotts of Tushielaw, a landed family but not high enough in the pecking order of the day for the child of an Earl. Her father would not let them marry, and tried to stop them meeting. When this did not work, he had Scott sent away, hoping that Jean would forget him. But the poor girl was in love, would consider no other as suitor, and she became thin and ill. So ill, in fact, that her father feared she would die.

Eventually Scott returned and her father relented. But, either because Scott had found another lover or because Jean herself had so changed because of her poor health, Scott failed to come to her or even to recognise her when she was at a window of Neidpath and he passed by the castle. This was too much for the poor girl, and she soon died of a broken heart.

But her restless spirit, known as the Maid of Neidpath, began to haunt the castle. An apparition of Jean was reported, clad in a full-length brown dress with a large white collar (although she has been described as a White Lady by some). Other manifestations have also been described, even in recent times: doors open and close by themselves, knocks and other unexplained noises are heard, objects move by themselves. Some people feel the castle has an oppressive atmosphere, and one visitor, although unaware of the ghost story, is said to have been so scared she fled the building and would not return.

C ASTLE GRANT, which dates from the 15th century, is an imposing building near the Moray town of Grantown-on-Spey. As the name suggests, it was the seat of the Grant family. One of the bed chambers in the old part of the castle, which is known as Barbie's Tower, is haunted.

In the 16th century Lady Barbara Grant, daughter of the then laird, fell in love with a man well below her station, while her father chose another to be her husband, an ugly character renowned for his cruelty. Barbara would not hear of this new suitor, and was imprisoned in a dark closet off one of the attic rooms until she changed her mind.

The poor girl would not relent, no matter how harsh her confinement, and refused to marry anyone but her love; her father would not relent either, and she remained in the closet for several weeks. Eventually, she died of ill treatment and a broken heart.

Castle Grant: *there is a tale of a small sad spectre, the ghost of Lady Barbara, imprisoned for falling in love with the wrong man.*

Her apparition began to haunt the chamber by the closet where she had been imprisoned, although her small ghost is not believed to be frightening. It reputedly appears from behind tapestries hiding the entrance to the closet, goes across the room and, after washing its hands, then disappears through the entrance to the turnpike stair.

AUCHINVOLE HOUSE, just south of Kilsyth, was an altered 16th-century tower house, built by the Stark family, but has been completely demolished except for a doocot and some walling. One of the chambers was said to be haunted by the apparition of a woman. The phantom would be seen looking out from one of the windows, the story going that the ghost was looking to where the girl's lover was buried by a tree stump on the river bank, after he had been treacherously slain. They had been betrothed to be married, but the girl died of a broken heart, spending the last days of her life staring forlornly from the window.

INVERAWE HOUSE, in a fine location by Taynuilt in Argyll, has long been held by the Campbells and parts may date from as early as the 14th century. The building is harled and whitewashed, and was added to down the centuries. It is said to have a Green Lady, a phantom of Mary Cameron of Callart (called the Maid of Callart, but also recorded as a Green Jean).

She had been married to the laird, Diarmaid Campbell, who had rescued her from Callart when her family caught plague: she alone survived. They had a large family, but Diarmaid died in 1645, along with many other Campbells, from wounds received at the Battle of Inverlochy (he is buried at Ardchattan, along with the Red Fox, Colin Campbell of Glenure, the victim of the Appin Murder, mentioned under Barcaldine Castle).

Mary's apparition has been reported in the Ticonderoga Room of the house, and activity was witnessed in 1912, when loud screams were heard coming from the empty chamber. Her apparition was described in the 1940s as being slim and pretty, with long blonde hair, garbed in a green dress. It was witnessed walking along a gallery to the Ticonderoga Room. On another occasion, a guest in the room was turned over in bed. The ghost is reported to be friendly, though, and to have helped people on several occasions. It also apparently only appears to members of the Campbell family.

Inverawe House is still occupied, and there are fine smoke houses.

B USTA HOUSE (which is pronounced Boosta) is in a fantastic tranquil location, some ten miles north of Lerwick on Shetland. The house dates from 1588, and was held by the Giffords of Busta, who were Scottish incomers and made their money as merchants and fish exporters. Busta has its own harbour and extensive grounds, and is now a popular hotel.

The hotel has a tragic ghost story. Barbara Pitcairn was a pretty maid (or perhaps guest at the house), and she attracted the attention of the eldest son of the house, John. They loved each other but, aware his parents would disapprove, John was secretly married to Barbara by the local minister, and she fell pregnant.

Many years before, in 1714, Thomas Gifford, John's father, had married Elizabeth Mitchell, and they went on to have four sons, including John the eldest. In a terrible tragedy, however, all four sons were drowned in a boating accident on Busta Voe. This left Barbara a widow, and Gifford without an heir.

Barbara produced papers proving that she had wed John, and in time she had a son, who was called Gideon. The son was adopted as Gifford's heir, but Barbara was so ignored and mistreated that she was forced to leave both Busta and her son. She retreated to a house of a poor relation in Lerwick, where she died at the age of only 36 years old.

Barbara's sorrowful apparition searches Busta, looking for the son that was so cruelly wrenched from her, and has been witnessed in the house. In the past few years, a child saw, and tried to offer food to, a 'woman' in the bar, although others there could not see anyone or anything.

Elizabeth Mitchell's ghost may also haunt Busta. There have been several sightings, including in the Linga Room, of the phantom of a grey-haired woman, garbed in a brown dress and lace cap (the apparition is believed to be too old in appearance to be Barbara). One occupant tried to speak to the phantom, but it rose to its feet, walked away and then vanished. The ghost has been reported by different guests on three separate occasions, including twice being seen on consecutive nights. Another guest described how a woman stood at the end of the bed, and then faded away when he showed alarm at her presence. A dog was greatly distressed on entering the room and howled the place down: its behaviour returned to normal when another bedroom was offered.

An apparition (whether this was Barbara or Elizabeth is not known) was also seen by the receptionist and a guest in the bar servery area. The figure walked behind the receptionist into an area reserved for staff, and there vanished through a wall. A pale face was also witnessed at one of the windows, seen at one of the upper floors, which then faded away.

Other manifestations include the sound of heavy footfalls in the Foula Room despite the chamber being unoccupied. Electrical equipment and lights are said to switch themselves on and off. The month of May has been identified as the time when most manifestations occur, round the anniversary of the deaths of the four Gifford brothers.

Another occurrence happened in the Foula Room, where there was a foul smell, described as being like sewers and dead animals. A minister and his wife were staying in the room, and the stench was only apparently there when they were in the chamber. They were given another bedroom, and the smell disappeared. But when they went back to the room, the smell returned. Other guests were given the Foula Room, and the stench did not trouble them. Despite a thorough investigation into the cause of the smell, nothing was found to explain its presence.

CASTLE CARY, which dates from the 15th century but also reuses Roman masonry from the sites along the Antonine Wall, stands about two miles north-east of Cumbernauld in central Scotland. It was held by the Livingstone family, but by the first half of the 17th century had passed to the Baillies. It was torched in 1645 by men under the Marquis of Montrose and by the Jacobites in the 1715 Rising. Fifteen years later it was owned by the Dunbars.

The castle has a White Lady, the phantom of Lizzie Baillie. Elizabeth Baillie was the lovely daughter of the then laird, although she rejected all potential husbands selected by her father. In time he found that she had fallen in love with a poor Highlander who had only a few acres of land to his name. Her father forbade them from meeting, but she ignored his warning. Finally he had her imprisoned in an attic chamber until she would renounce her lover. But one night Lizzie slipped out of her chamber onto the battlements and jumped from the top of the tower. Her lover, along with some strong friends, had spread a blanket and caught her as she fell. The couple then eloped, and lived happily until Lizzie discovered that her escape had killed her father. She could no longer be happy herself, and died before her time.

It is said that Lizzie's apparition searches through the chambers of the castle for her father. The phantom has been seen in many parts of the old castle, but most often on the main stair.

Castle Cary has a second ghost, but that story is covered later.

Located near Moffat in the turbulent Border area formerly frequented by independent but feuding reivers, Lochhouse Tower is a strong 16th-century tower house, which was built by the Johnstones. The tower has been restored and is still occupied.

The tower is haunted by the ghost of Lillias Johnstone, who lived here around the turn of the 17th century. Lillias was the lovely sister of the chief of the Johnstones. She fell for Walter French, another local laird, who lived at nearby Frenchland Tower, but her brother did not like French and they quarrelled. This dispute led to the killing of Lillias's brother, a death in which Walter French was implicated. French fled abroad, believing that Lillias could not marry someone who had a hand in her brother's death and, when he returned, he married the daughter of Maxwell of Breckonside.

Although young and beautiful, Lillias would take no other lovers nor suitors as she still only loved Walter French. When she finally died, her ghost returned to haunt the tower.

Shieldhill, which is said to date from as early as 1199, incorporates an ancient castle into the large mansion, and stands in wooded parkland some miles north-west of Biggar in Lanarkshire. The lands were held by the Chancellor family, but since 1959 the house has been used as a country house hotel. The building is haunted by the young and beautiful daughter of one of the Chancellor lairds.

The ghost is a Grey Lady, and has been described as being clad in a grey cloak. It has been witnessed in recent times, walking towards the burial place in the grounds, as well as in one particular room (which is available to guests). The apparition is mostly seen in the old part of the building, and uses the original stone stair to move from floor to floor. Other reported manifestations include television channels changing by themselves, chairs and other objects moving, and unexplained noises and footsteps when there is apparently nobody about.

There are several versions of the story behind the haunting, and these only agree that a young woman died before her time.

One is that she fell pregnant to a gamekeeper's son, and her baby was still born and then buried without her knowledge. The poor lass wept herself to an early grave. Another is that she planned to elope with her lover but she fell to her death from the upper floors; another that her father ordered that she was to stop seeing her lover and in despair she committed suicide. The least pleasant is that she was raped by soldiers returning from a battle in the middle of the 17th century and was made pregnant. The new-born child was taken from her and left to die, and in terrible grief she took her own life.

Whatever the truth of it, this is believed to be a very sad spectre.

D UNTULM CASTLE has several ghost stories: indeed, it is claimed by some that the building was so disturbed by all the different spirits that the MacDonalds abandoned it for a new house some miles south at Monkstadt (itself now a ruin). Duntulm is located on the north coast of Trotternish on Skye, some miles north of Uig, and little now remains, although it is a wonderful location on cliffs, looking out to the Outer Hebrides.

Margaret was the sister of MacLeod of Dunvegan, and was unfortunate enough to have lost an eye in an accident. The poor woman was married to one of the MacDonalds, when their main seat was at Duntulm. MacDonald grew tired of his wife, and eventually sent her back to Dunvegan, on a one-eyed horse with a one-eyed servant and accompanied by a one-eyed dog. Safe to say, MacLeod was furious. Margaret's weeping ghost returned to the castle.

Interestingly, there is a similar story of the Earl of Ross sending his one-eyed wife, the sister of the MacDonald Lord of the Isles, back to him on a one-eyed horse with a one-eyed dog and servant. Why exactly anyone would want to anger the Lord of the Isles, one of the most powerful men in Scotland, in such a manner is certainly open to debate.

Duntulm has several other stories which are described below.

L ying some three miles or so west of Dunbar in East Lothian stands the fine mansion of BIEL. It has an ancient castle at its core, and was a property of the Hamiltons. They were made Lords Belhaven in 1647, and Biel was held by the family until 1958. John Hamilton, second Lord Belhaven, strongly opposed the Union of Parliaments. There is a plaque on the outside of the house with the inscription in Latin: 'The first year of the betrayal of Scotland'. The house is still occupied.

John Hamilton, third Lord Belhaven, was married to Anne Bruce. She was the granddaughter of Sir Andrew Bruce of Earlshall, a notorious persecutor of Covenanters (and said to haunt Earlshall). Anne was very beautiful, but found out that her husband was having an affair. John was made Governor of Barbados but was drowned after his ship sank in 1721 before he could take up his post. Even after his death, Anne showed no interest in other men. She was renowned for her pallid complexion, and spent much of her time walking through the grounds of Biel, a pale lonely figure. When she died, she began to haunt the vicinity of the building, especially a path known as The Lady's Walk. Her ghost became known as the White Lady of Biel.

Perched on a steep rock on the island of Lismore, CASTLE COEFFIN is a ruinous and overgrown castle of the MacDougalls of Lorn. It is said to be named after one of its ancient owners, Caifen, the war-like son of a Norse king. An old story tells that Beothail, his gentle sister, died heartbroken after the man she loved was slain fighting in Scandinavia. Beothail was buried on Lismore, but her ghost returned to haunt the castle: her voice was heard, 'crying in the wind'. She did not rest until her remains were taken to Norway and buried beside her love.

When she was dug up, however, a bone from her foot was missed. Her ghost again gave those at the castle no peace until it was found and buried with the rest of her.

Two miles east of Kirkbean in Dumfries and Galloway stands ARBIGLAND HOUSE, a fine classical mansion, built by William Craik in 1755 to replace an older house. The property was held by several families before coming to the Craiks in 1679. John Paul Jones, founder of the American Navy, was born at nearby Kirkbean and worked on the estate as a gardener.

The grounds around the house are haunted by the daughter of one of the Craik lairds, known as the Ghost of the Three Crossroads. She is believed to have fallen in love with a groom called Dunn, but her parents thought the lad was beneath her station and forbade them to marry. Dunn then disappeared: he may have been murdered by the girl's brothers, and she reportedly fled the house, and was not seen again: perhaps she was also killed. Whatever end she came to, whether slaughter or misadventure, her apparition has been seen in the grounds, and occasionally in the house. Dunn's ghost, on a phantom horse, has also been reported near the main gates.

Situated near Kelso in the Borders, is ROXBURGHE HOUSE HOTEL. The building was formally known as Sunlaws, and dates mostly from 1853 after the previous house was destroyed by fire. It stands in a quiet location in 200 acres of gardens and wooded park land. It was a property of the Kerrs of Chatto, and Bonnie Prince Charlie was entertained here in November 1745. The house was used to hold German prisoners of war during World War II, acquired by the Duke of Roxburghe in 1969, and is now a hotel.

The hotel is haunted by the apparition of a Grey Lady, described as being clad in grey. She walks along an area on the ground floor, covering the corridor from the kitchen, through to the inner hall, and then along the path leading out from the conservatory up to the Japanese bridge. The story goes that she is searching for her baby, but there is no clue to her identity. The ghost has been seen several times in living memory.

CULCREUCH CASTLE, set in acres of its own parkland in the Fintry Hills in Stirlingshire, is a fine building which dates from the 15th century. The stronghold was long a seat of the Galbraith family, although they had to sell it in 1630 because of debt. The building has possibly one of the largest bat colonies in the UK residing in the roof space above the dining room. It is now used as a hotel.

At certain times, usually in the wee hours of the morning, soft music from a clarsach (an iron-strung harp) can be heard, most usually in the Chinese Bird Room (so called because it has early hand-painted Chinese wallpaper, dating from 1732, and a rare survivor in Scotland), as well as in the adjoining chamber and the Laird's Hall.

The story goes one of the Buchanan family, along with his mistress, visited Culcreuch in 1582. This Buchanan got into an argument with Robert Galbraith, son of the 16th chief, and was mortally wounded by Galbraith. The bleeding man was carried to what is now the Chinese Bird Room, accompanied by his mistress, and here he died. His mistress was distraught, but to comfort herself began to play her clarsach, and the plaintive music has been heard often, even in recent times. Some, however, have suggested this may be the sounds coming from the bat colony.

STANDING in a country park some miles west of Peterhead near Mintlaw, ADEN HOUSE is now a roofless ruin but stands on the site of a castle. The lands were a property of the Keiths, before coming to the Russells of Montcoffer in 1758.

The apparition of a young woman was reported here in the first part of the 19th century. The daughter of the then laird fell in love with one of her father's servants. Her father forbade the couple to meet, and took to locking the door of her chamber. The servant lad is said to have got a ladder, climbed up to the girl's room, and the two ran off together, at least this is what was believed. What then happened is not certain, whether the lass died or not, but a phantom of the girl was then witnessed. A later occupant of the bed chamber had it partitioned, walling off the 'haunted' portion.

O n the Cawdor Estate, about one mile south of Cawdor itself, ACHINDOWN is a small mansion, dating from about 1700. It was held by the Munroe family. The Battle of Culloden was fought nearby, and Hamish Munroe sheltered fleeing Jacobites in the basement. Government troops searched the building, found the Jacobites, and shot them, as well as Munroe himself, against the garden wall: the marks of the musket balls can be seen marking the wall.

There are reports of several sightings of the apparition of a girl in the garden, seen picking flowers. The phantom is described as having brown hair, wearing a blue-print dress, and being barefooted. The ghost is believed to be the phantom of Elspeth Munroe, daughter of the Hamish mentioned above. The girl is said to have run off with a poor shepherd from the estate, although to what fate she then came is not recorded.

There is also a story about another haunting, but that is covered later.

L ocated in Cults in Aberdeen, NORWOOD HALL is a fine mansion, which was rebuilt in 1881 for the Ogston family. It is now used as a hotel. Nearby are the scant remains of Pitfodels Castle, which was held by the Reids, but later passed to the Menzies family.

The building is haunted by the phantom of woman, believed to be the mistress of Colonel James Ogston. It is thought that the poor woman hoped that Ogston would leave his wife for her, but he never did. Alternatively, it is his wife who has been seen here: she despaired because he would not give up his mistress. Ogston's own apparition has also been witnessed at Norwood.

DEATH BY MISADVENTURE
Stories where the heroine is killed by accident.

Lying about one mile north-east of Golspie in Sutherland, DUNROBIN CASTLE is a magnificent fairy-tale fortress, more akin to a whimsical Continental chateau than a dour Scottish stronghold. Although the building dates from the 1300s, it was remodelled in later centuries, and has fine formal gardens. The castle has been the seat of the Earls and Dukes of Sutherland since the 13th century, and has many magnificent rooms. The castle still owned by the same family, and the building is open to the public.

There are at least two versions of the ghost story, which only agree on the manner of the victim's death: falling from an upstairs window.

Margaret Gordon was the daughter of the 14th Earl of Sutherland (who was Earl from 1609 until 1679). She fell in love with Jamie Gunn, a son of one of the Earl's retainers. Such a mismatched union would never have been approved of by Margaret's father, and he had Margaret imprisoned in one of the attic rooms, next to what is now known as the night nursery. Gunn decided to rescue his love as Margaret's health suffered during her incarceration. A rope was smuggled into the chamber, and Margaret tried to escape out of the window. Her father, getting suspicious, flung open the door of the chamber. Margaret was so surprised by his sudden entry that she let go of the rope and fell to her death.

An alternative version, which appears in the guidebook for the castle, is that in the 15th century the then Earl of Sutherland attacked the

Dunrobin Castle: *haunted by the ghost of a lady: daughter of one of the Earls or a beautiful prisoner?*

Mackay clan, and during the fighting captured a beautiful young Mackay lass. The Earl was determined to marry his attractive prisoner, presumably a noble woman, but she refused him, and he had her locked up in what became known as the haunted room. She had no hope of escape until she fashioned her sheets and other linen into a make-shift rope, then used this to climb out of the window. The Earl burst in during her attempt, and was so consumed with fury that he cut the knotted sheets with his sword. The poor girl fell to her death beneath the tower. This version bears many similar details to that of Helen Gunn of Braemore, who died by falling from the battlements of Ackergill Tower after being seized by Keith of Ackergill.

From that time on, sobbing and wailing was often heard coming from the haunted room, so much so that at one time the chamber was abandoned. The guidebook reports, however, that the ghost has neither been seen nor heard in living memory. The apparition is described as a White Lady in one account.

The only activity reported at Dunrobin is in Duchess Clare's Bedroom, where footsteps are heard when nobody is present. One time the apparition of a man was seen on the landing and then vanished through a closed door. There does not appear to be any connection between this manifestation and the ghost story related to the haunted room.

ALLANBANK HOUSE was a small 19th-century mansion, which replaced an earlier house dating from the 17th century, although this newer house was itself demolished in 1969. It was a property of the Stewarts, and Robert Stewart of Allanbank was made a baronet of Nova Scotia in 1687. The house stood some four or so miles east of Duns in Berwickshire in the Borders.

In the 1670s Robert went to Paris, and there he met and became romantically linked to a lovely Italian or French or Flemish-Jewish girl called Jean (or Jeanne: it may be a coincidence, of course, but many Scottish ghosts are called Jean ...). Jean was besotted and wanted to marry (she may have originally been a nun, most likely a Sister of Charity), but Stewart seems to have tired of the girl; and no doubt his parents would also have disapproved. Robert planned to leave Paris and abandon Jean in the city, no matter how much she begged to be allowed to go with him. Jean was desperate and, as his carriage left, she threw herself in front of the horses. Either by accident or design, she was thrown under the hooves and carriage, and trampled to death: one of the wheels is said to have rolled over her head. If Robert thought he was then free of the jilted girl, he was wrong. An alternative version of the tale is that she pursued Robert to Scotland, and was killed under his carriage at the gates of Allanbank when he was with his new betrothed.

Jean's ghost certainly followed Robert back to Scotland, and began to haunt the house and the gardens of Allanbank. On arriving home, John was greeted by her apparition at the gates. The phantom had her arms open, and was described as being clad in a dress of white lace, her shoulders and bodice soaked in blood from her mangled head.

Her apparition became well known, and was called Pearlin Jean because of the lace frock the apparition wore: it apparently also sported high heels. Other manifestations included doors opening and closing by themselves, and ghostly feet and the rustling of a gown were frequently heard round the passages of the house. The room in which the ghost was most often witnessed was closed up and abandoned.

Jean was certainly making her presence felt, and the disturbances were to continue after Robert's death. Indeed, her appearance became so common that servants learned to live with manifestations as if nothing out of the ordinary was happening. The building is also said to have been exorcised on several occasions, but to no effect.

The old Allanbank House was demolished in 1849, and a new mansion built, but the manifestations are said to have continued, being reported at the turn of the 20th century and later: although by then they were less vigorous in nature. This 'new' house was itself demolished in 1969.

Standing near Longforgan west of Dundee, CASTLE HUNTLY is a large and impressive building, constructed by the Grays in the 15th century. They held the property until 1614, when it was sold to the Lyon Lord Glamis: indeed, there was said to be a tunnel from here to Glamis Castle – which, if true, would be no mean feat as the two strongholds are more than ten miles apart. Castle Huntly is still occupied, although now by a Young Offenders' Institution.

The castle is haunted by a White Lady, the ghost of a daughter of one of the Lyon lairds. The story goes that the poor girl became pregnant by one of the castle servants, and was imprisoned in an upstairs chamber (which was later known as the Waterloo Room) to hide her condition. The girl tried to escape out of the window of the chamber but fell some 100 feet to her death; another version is that she was pushed out of the window to hide her pregnancy. Either way, her ghost then haunted the Waterloo Room, as well as the grounds, especially around the Bogle Bridge. It is recorded that the apparition was seen often at one time.

TULLOCH CASTLE, which may date from the 12th or 13th century, stands about one mile north of Dingwall in the far north-east of Scotland. It was owned by several families in turn, until coming to the Davidsons in 1762, who held it until 1945. After being used as a hospital during World War II, and then a school, the castle now houses a fine hotel.

Along with many other fortresses, Tulloch is said to have had a tunnel, which connected it to Dingwall Castle about a mile away. These stories are not usually given much credence but, interestingly, part of a collapsed subterranean passageway can be seen in the middle of the front lawn.

Tulloch is haunted by a Green Lady, which was seen often during its use as a hospital. The phantom was apparently identified as a figure in a

Tulloch Castle: *A Green Lady haunts the building, the ghost of a girl who died by falling down the main stairs.*

portrait hanging in the Great Hall. A chamber in the castle is called the Green Lady's Lounge.

The story is that a young girl disturbed her father when he was in a compromising position with a female who was not the daughter's mother. The girl was so startled that she stumbled from the room and then fell down the main staircase of the castle, dying from her injuries.

MUCHALLS CASTLE, near Stonehaven some miles south of Aberdeen, dates substantially from early in the 17th century, and was long a property of the Burnetts (also see Crathes Castle). It is an impressive courtyard castle, although there was a stronghold here for hundreds of year before the present building. James 'VIII', the Old Pretender, visited

Muchalls in 1716 during the Jacobite Rising, although by then the rebellion was faltering, and he soon sailed back to the Continent.

The castle is haunted by a Green Lady. The story is that a young woman, a servant at the castle, was drowned in a cave which opened onto the sea at the Gin Shore in a cove about a mile from Muchalls. At that time, the cave was reached by a subterranean stair and tunnel from the wine cellar or from the present dining room. The cave was used for smuggling, gin being a major commodity, and her lover was away on ship.

The girl had seen his vessel, and had been waiting for him in the cave when she fell into the sea and was drowned. Her apparition was reported in 1906, and in the 1970s. On this latter occasion it was dressed in a lime-coloured frock, and was seen sitting in front of a mirror in one of the chambers, arranging her hair. The phantom vanished when the room was entered. This room was also sometimes found to be exceptionally cold.

On another occasion, the then owner saw the apparition of a woman cross the former dining room, and disappear through the entrance to a cupboard. This was later shown to be the opening into a secret passage.

A nother stronghold with a female apparition is FERNIE CASTLE, the West Tower of which is haunted. The building dates from the 16th century, and was held by several families, including the Fernie family, the MacDuffs, Balfours and Arnots. The castle is now used as a hotel, and is located four miles west of Cupar in Fife.

The apparition is said to be garbed in a green gown with a high neck, and has been observed in one of the castle's chambers. Unexplained knocking at doors has also been heard, and electrical equipment is reputed to switch itself on and off, apparently at random. The ghost is believed to be searching through the rooms for her lover.

The tale behind the haunting is that a young woman fell in love with a man of whom her father disapproved. She tried to elope with her lover, but before they could escape they were pursued to Fernie by her father's men. They couple tried to hide in a small chamber in the West Tower, but the girl was found and was to be returned to her father. In the resulting struggle, she fell from a window to her death.

DEATH BY SUICIDE

The ladies in the following stories are said to have committed suicide. If this was the case, they would not have been buried in consecrated ground and would have been thought to have spent eternity in purgatory. This would explain why their spirit was restless as they search for a proper burial, and the peace it was believed that would bring.

CASTLE OF MEY was the much-loved Caithness home of Elizabeth Bowes Lyon, the Queen Mother, who died in 2002. The building dates from the 16th century, when it was owned by the Sinclair Earls of Caithness, and stands about seven miles north-west of Castletown in the far north of Scotland.

Lady Fanny fell in love with the son of a ploughman. Her father was the fifth Earl of Caithness (who put down a rebellion in Orkney in 1615),

Castle of Mey: *Lady Fanny, daughter of the Earl of Caithness, fell to her death from the castle parapet: her grieving spirit, a Green Lady, has been witnessed here.*

and Sinclair had her imprisoned in an upstairs chamber, now known as Lady Fanny's Room, in the attic of the castle to prevent her meeting her lover. She derived some comfort, however, from seeing the man working below in the fields. The Earl wanted her to forget him and had the window on that side blocked up. Having no hope, Fanny flung herself from another window, and was dashed on the ground below; alternatively, she fell as she leaned out too far. Her sad spirit, a Green Lady, was then said to haunt the castle. The ghost was apparently witnessed in 1953 when the castle was being renovated.

In Fraserburgh, in the far north-east of Scotland, is Kinnaird Head Castle. It was built by the Frasers, but in the 18th century was converted to carry a lighthouse and is now part of Scotland's Lighthouse Museum. Near the castle is a smaller tower known as the Wine Tower, which was apparently once used as a chapel. Below it is a sea cave.

Sir Alexander Fraser of Philorth built the harbour at Fraserburgh (the town was formerly called Faithlie), although he ran out of money and had to sell much of his lands. His daughter, Isobel, fell for a man of whom her father disapproved. Despite warning them, they would not stop seeing each other. Sir Alexander seized the man and had him chained in a cave below the Wine Tower, although it appears that Fraser only wanted to frighten his daughter's lover. Unknown to Sir Alexander, a storm blew up, however, and lashing waves and the incoming tide drowned Isobel's lover. When she found his lifeless body, the girl was stricken and threw herself into the sea and she too was drowned or, alternatively, she threw herself from the Wine Tower onto the rocks below.

Whenever a gale blows, an apparition can be seen by the Wine Tower, a desperate girl searching for her lover.

Located in a remote spot, all traces of Myredykes Tower, once a strong castle, are gone, but it stood about 10 miles north-east of Newcastleton in the Borders. The lands were held at one time by the Elliots.

The tower had a Green Lady, the ghost of Jean Elliot. She was a lovely lass, but would take no husband, no matter how handsome or rich. Her brothers suspected that she was dallying (she may even have fallen visibly pregnant), and took to following her. They discovered that she often met a handsome young man at nearby Hob Knowe. One time, after she had returned to the castle, they fell upon and slew her lover. One version records that he was the son of the Queen of the Elves. With his last breath, he cursed the family, saying that the last foundations of the castle would be washed away by Jean's tears. The brothers were fearful, and fled the Knowe.

Jean discovered her lover's lifeless body the next day, and in great despair threw herself in the Liddel Water and was drowned. Her weeping ghost, clad in a sodden green dress, was then repeatedly seen and heard, both in the castle, by the Liddel Water, and at Hob Knowe.

None of the sons were to have an heir, and the property passed within a generation to the Croziers. The manifestations continued, however, and the tower was soon abandoned and became ruinous.

The last vestige is said to have been swept away when the river was in spate.

C ASTLE OF PARK stands some miles north-west of Aberchirder, in Banff and Buchan, in the north-east of Scotland. It was a property of the Gordons, and was developed down the years into a large mansion, surrounded by fine parkland.

Park has several ghost stories, and one is that it is haunted by the ghost of a young servant girl who became pregnant and was dismissed from service. The poor lass despaired and, feeling she had no future, committed suicide. Her apparition, a Green Lady, has been seen in the grounds and in the castle, sometimes looking out from one of the second-floor windows. A guest saw the apparition of a cloaked and hooded woman.

H ALLGREEN CASTLE is a much altered L-plan tower house, incorporating work from the 14th century, standing just east of Inverbervie in Kincardineshire. It was a property of the Dunnet family, and then the Raits, and a newer mansion has been added.

The building has stories of a ghost of a young woman who committed suicide after the death of her child.

Apparitions of two serving girls have also been witnessed in one of the basement chambers, which still retains its original stone vault. Their appearance is heralded by a dramatic drop in temperature.

S tanding in seven acres of parkland just north of Huntly in Aberdeenshire, HUNTLY CASTLE HOTEL, formerly known as Sandiestone and Huntly Lodge, was originally built around 1750 as a hunting lodge for the Gordon Dukes of Gordon.

A former seat of the Gordons was at Huntly Castle, which is in the care of Historic Scotland and open to the public, about a quarter of a mile to the south, and materials were used from this magnificent ruin to build this new house. The lodge was extended in 1832 and became the seat of the Duke's eldest son. The building is now used as a hotel.

The hotel has a Green Lady. The story is that she found herself with a child but without a husband: the baby may have been fathered by a 'gentleman' of the house.

The poor girl felt abandoned and committed suicide.

Ardoe House, to the south-west of Aberdeen, is a fine baronial mansion, dating from 1879, and built for the soap magnate Alexander Ogston. It has been a hotel since 1947, and sits in 30 acres of Aberdeenshire countryside.

The building is haunted by a White Lady. One version of the story is that a daughter of a previous owner (at an earlier house on the site as the estate was purchased by the Ogstons in 1839) was raped and fell pregnant. The poor lass despaired, and killed herself and her baby. The apparition has also been identified as Katherine Ogston, wife of Alexander Milne Ogston. The phantom was witnessed in 1990 at the main stair before vanishing at the entrance to the hotel: her portrait hangs there.

The fine old mansion of Kinneil House, which is set in a public park near the West Lothian town of Bo'ness, dates from the 16th century and has original painted ceilings. It was long held by the Hamiltons, who had a strong tower house here. The family were made Dukes of Hamilton in 1643, after which they remodelled Kinneil. The building was occupied by Cromwell's forces in the 1650s, from when the ghost story is believed to originate.

The ghost is thought to be that of Ailie or Alice, Lady Lilburne. She was said to be the young wife of a Cromwellian colonel, billeted here in the 1650s, or the mistress of the Duke of Hamilton, depending on the version of the story. The first Duke of Hamilton was executed in 1649 by Cromwell, while the second died in 1651 at the Battle of Worcester so, if she was a mistress, it is likely she was held here against her will. Whatever the reason, she detested Kinneil and wanted to flee from the house. After having tried to escape on more than one occasion, she was imprisoned in one of the upper chambers. Getting more and more desperate, she finally threw herself to her death from a window of the house into the glen of the Gil Burn, some 200 feet below. Her screams and wails are sometimes heard on dark winter nights, and her spirit haunts the glen through which the Gil Burn flows. She has been described as a White Lady.

Braemar Castle stands in a picturesque and mountainous part of Scotland, and dates from the 17th century. It was built by the Erskine Earls of Mar to protect against neighbouring clans, but was burned by John Farquharson of Inverey in 1689. Later it was altered by the military when it was used against the Jacobites and illegal whisky distillers. The

Braemar Castle: *the ghost of a young lady, who believed she had been spurned, haunts the castle.*

castle has a claustrophobic pit prison, unventilated and measuring just six feet by twelve.

Braemar is haunted by the apparition of a blonde-haired young woman, who reputedly appears to men who have been recently married. The light tread of a woman has been heard in the building when there is nobody about. Her spirit is thought to search the building for her husband, and a sighting of the spectre was recorded in 1987.

The story goes that a newly married couple were staying in the castle in the second half of the 19th century. The couple were inexperienced in the ways of love, and the young wife was very worried about pleasing her husband. When she woke early the next morning, she found he had gone. Believing she had been abandoned, that he could not stay with her as she had failed to meet his needs, she was devastated. She fled the nuptial bed, climbed to the top of the tower, and threw herself off to her death. Her husband had, apparently, only left early to go hunting.

D ALZELL HOUSE, which is near Motherwell in Lanarkshire, incorporates a castle into the fine old mansion. It belonged to the Dalziel Earls of Carnforth, but was sold to the Hamiltons of Boggs in 1649. The north wing was used as a hospital during World War I, but the building has since been divided into separate houses.

The house apparently has four female ghosts: White, Green, Brown and Grey Ladies.

The White Lady is thought to be the ghost of a young servant lass, who fell pregnant although unmarried. Perhaps because she was abandoned, perhaps because of the shame, in despair threw herself from the parapet to her death. She is said to be observed near the point where she fell.

Sightings of a Green Lady have been reported in the Piper's Gallery and in one of the bedrooms, and other manifestations include unexplained flashing lights, footsteps and other noises. The smell of strong exotic perfume has also been recorded, and is said to herald a fleeting appearance. A Brown Lady is recorded as having appeared in the former nursery. A Grey Lady, wearing a grey nurse's uniform, haunts the north wing, and comes from when the house was used as a hospital. No stories are recorded as to why these last three ghosts should appear at Dalziel.

Located on the picturesque island of Arran, BRODICK CASTLE, an ancient stronghold but much extended and remodelled in later centuries, has a long association with the Hamiltons, who were both Earls of Arran and Dukes of Hamilton. In 1958 Brodick was taken over by The National Trust for Scotland, and there are extensive gardens and parkland.

One ghost story concerns a servant girl who fell pregnant by one of the garrison during the time Brodick Castle was held by Cromwell's forces. The young woman committed suicide at the Old Quay below the castle. Her apparition was apparently seen on many occasions in the old part of the building, and is described as wearing a grey dress with a large white collar. Another version is that the spirit is one of three women starved to death in the dungeons around 1700 because they had plague.

One account states that the phantom is most often seen on the back stairs, and goes from there to the servants' area.

Rothesay Castle, on the island of Bute in the Firth of Clyde, is an impressive walled castle with a later tower, surrounded by a water-filled moat. The castle was a favourite residence of both Robert II and Robert III, and in 1401 Robert III made his son David, Duke of Rothesay, a title that the Prince of Wales, as the heir to the throne, now holds. As is mentioned below, though, David did not do well from the title, being starved to death at Falkland by his uncle. Rothesay Castle is now in the care of Historic Scotland.

A ghost story goes back to the 13th century, when the castle was besieged by Vikings. A Lady Isobel was sheltering in the stronghold, but the Norsemen took the castle, and slaughtered many of the people

Rothesay Castle: *an old ballad tells how Lady Isobel's family were slaughtered by Vikings and, rather submit to them, she killed herself on the Bloody Stair.*

they found, including Isobel's family. A Viking wanted Isobel as a mistress, and might have spared her life, but she would have none of it and slew herself. Her apparition is said to have been witnessed on the Bloody Stair.

Set on the banks of the Tweed in the Scottish Borders, and close to the fine ruins of the ancient abbey, is DRYBURGH ABBEY HOTEL. The hotel is housed in a castellated mansion, dating from the middle of the 19th century, and stands on the site of a much older building, which was known as Mantle House. The hotel has undergone a major renovation in the last few years, and stands in ten acres of grounds and gardens.

Dryburgh Abbey was founded by David I in the 12th century, and became a rich establishment, although it is now a shattered but very picturesque and interesting ruin. This is the burial place of Sir Walter Scott (see Abbotsford). It is said, incidentally, that the cloister and ruins are haunted by ghostly monks, who were fraudulently involved in trying to acquire land from a dying laird. Many churchmen, it seems, substituted the love of women for a love of property.

Not all did, though. The ghost story dates from before the abbey was dissolved. A girl from Mantle House fell in love with one of the monks of the abbey, and the two became lovers. When the abbot found out about the couple, he had the monk slain – this must have been one instance of strict observance of monastic vows than was usual for the times. When the girl discovered what had been done to her lover, she was inconsolable, and cast herself into the River Tweed, where she was drowned. Her apparition, a Grey Lady, has been seen on the chain bridge over the Tweed and in outbuildings of the hotel. Disturbances apparently increased during renovation work. Indeed, the Grey Lady is only thought to be witnessed when something happens in the building which concerns it directly, such as building work.

Although it has been demolished, GREENLAW HOUSE was a large 17th-century house. It stood just north of Penicuik in Midlothian at Glencorse, and was incorporated into a large barracks and prison in 1804. The prison was built to house Napoleonic prisoners, and by 1813 could hold some 6000 men. It was used as the military prison for Scotland until 1888 and the army depot for south-east Scotland from 1875. The site is now occupied by other buildings.

A young woman from the neighbourhood fell in love with one of the French prisoners at Greenlaw in the early part of the 19th century. The prisoners were allowed out to exercise, and here it was that she met her lover. Her father disapproved and had the girl imprisoned so she could not meet her lover. At the same time, her lover is said to have been murdered, possibly by her father and his choice of suitor, or to have been moved elsewhere. When the young woman was set free, she was distraught and threw herself into a gorge, above the River North Esk, now known as Lover's Leap and where they had used to meet. Her apparition has been seen here on many occasions, running through the woods, or standing alone and forlorn.

CHAPTER THREE
Some Other Ghostly Ladies

The following collection of stories are more diverse or fragmentary or the story behind the haunting has not been firmly established. In most cases, no reasons are given as to why the ghost should haunt the way it does. As explored above, many stories have a tragic origin. There are, however, many tales where in life the person has been happy and even loves the place they haunt.

MARY, QUEEN OF SCOTS

It is perhaps not surprising that Mary is said to haunt several of Scotland's castles: her ghost is also believed to have been seen at several sites in England, not the least accounts of her headless phantom, head in its hands, being driven in a spectral coach. Mary spent a very short part of her life in Scotland, although the few years were momentous, both for her and her kingdom's history. During her several progresses, she visited many castles, although it is not clear why she should necessarily haunt so many of them. Also included are other stories regarding her ladies, as well as Darnley and even John Knox.

Mary was born in 1542, and her father James V died soon afterwards following the disastrous battle of Solway Moss. Regents ruled for her, and she was soon sent to France, where in time she married the Dauphin, the heir to the French throne. He died young, and in 1561 she returned to Scotland. The Reformation was gathering pace in Scotland, complicating things for Mary as she was a Catholic. She married Henry Stewart, Lord Darnley, from the powerful Lennox-Stewart family, but the two were not to remain wed for long.

HERMITAGE CASTLE is one of the strongholds said to be haunted by Mary, and at the time was held by James Hepburn, fourth Earl of Bothwell. On 8 October 1566 Bothwell got into a fight with one of the local families, the Elliots, and was stabbed by Little Jock Elliot of Park (Elliot was shot during the fray and died from his injuries). Bothwell returned to Hermitage to recover.

Mary Queen of Scots was at Jedburgh, and hurried to Hermitage on 16 October to tend Bothwell, a meeting which only lasted a couple of hours. Mary could not stay at Hermitage, being a married woman, and left the same day to return to Jedburgh and what is now known as Mary Queen of Scots House. The Queen had fallen in a bog en route during the long and difficult 25-mile journey. She subsequently contracted a fever, which nearly killed her, and was bedridden for a week.

Bothwell and Mary were later married (it was claimed that Bothwell had kidnapped and forced her to wed) after the murder of Henry Stewart, Lord Darnley, her then husband, at Kirk o' Field, a deed in which Bothwell was implicated. Bothwell fled after the debacle at Carberry in 1567, going to Orkney, then Norway, but was imprisoned in the Danish castle of Dragsholm (he had abandoned his first wife, Jane Gordon, to marry Mary; and Jane had him incarcerated for spurning her). Bothwell's mummified body is said to survive at Dragsholm castle. Mary herself was imprisoned at Lochleven Castle (see below).

An apparition of Mary is reported to have been seen at Hermitage, clad in a white dress, although how it was identified so certainly is not recorded.

Hermitage has two other ghost stories: the evil Lord Soulis, and the unfortunate Sir Alexander Ramsay of Dalhousie.

S TIRLING CASTLE is, along with Edinburgh, simply the most fantastic castle Scotland has to offer. It stands on a high rock overlooking the burgh in the centre of Scotland, and is a fascinating complex of historic buildings. Alexander I died at the castle in 1124, as did William the Lyon in 1214. Edward I of England captured the castle in 1304, but it was recovered by the Scots after the Battle of Bannockburn ten years later. James II was born here in 1430, as was James III in 1451. Mary, Queen of Scots, was crowned in the old chapel in 1543, and the future James VI was baptised here in 1566. The Jacobites besieged the castle, albeit rather ineptly, in 1746, but soon had to withdraw.

One apparition seen at the castle is a Pink Lady, a phantom of a beautiful girl in a pink silk gown. The ghost has been witnessed as far away as the Church of the Holy Rude on the way up to the castle, but mostly frequents Ladies' Rock between the castle and the burial ground of the church. It has been identified as the spirit of Mary, Queen of Scots, although another story is that it is the spectre of a woman who lost her husband during the siege of 1304 and is still searching for him. There is an account of an appearance from 1976.

Stories of a Green Lady are also told, a herald of trouble, most often associated with fire. One tale is that she was a lady in waiting to Mary, and that she saved her queen when the bedclothes caught fire. Another version is that she was the daughter of a governor of the castle, who fell in love with one of his men. Her lover was accidentally slain by her father, and in despair the girl threw herself from the walls at the highest point of the rock.

This ghost has been seen in recent times, once so terrifying a cook in the kitchens, when the stronghold was still occupied by the army, that the man fainted. He had discovered her at his elbow, apparently engrossed in what he was doing. The figure was described as misty-green. The man apparently knew nothing of the story before the sighting.

B y the attractive village of Doune, some miles north-west of Stirling, DOUNE CASTLE is a magnificent pile in a spectacular location. Two strong towers are linked by a lower range, which form two sides of a courtyard. The building dates from the 14th century, and was built by Robert Stewart, Duke of Albany. He virtually ruled Scotland during the reign of Robert III, and died in 1420. When James I was released from captivity in England, he had Albany's son executed and seized the castle. Mary, Queen of Scots, stayed at Doune on several occasions. The building was restored in the 19th century, may be visited, and is now in the care of Historic Scotland.

An apparition of Mary, Queen of Scots, is believed to have been seen here. Several photos taken in the castle are said to have revealed 'spirit balls', patches of light. In some cases, of course, these can be caused by specks of dust reflecting light from a flash.

A t HOUNDWOOD HOUSE in the Borders, sounds of ghostly horses have also been reported, linked to a visit here by Mary, Queen of Scots, in 1565. A ring of hers was found near the house.

Houndwood House also has a ghost called Chappie.

T HE COVENANTER HOTEL in Falkland in Fife (which stands near the old palace at which Mary certainly stayed) is haunted by an apparition, which has been identified as Mary. A female figure has been seen on several occasions, and items have been thrown across rooms without explanation. The present building dates from 1771, although it may be on the site of an older dwelling.

M entioned above in relation to a brutal ghost story, BORTHWICK CASTLE is also connected with Mary. She had to flee from here in

1567, along with her third husband Bothwell. Mary was disguised as a pageboy, after being besieged by her enemies – her apparition has been observed. Although, of course, if she was that well disguised, how could anyone be sure that this was not the phantom of a 'real' pageboy? From here, she went on to Carberry Hill, and was held and then imprisoned at Lochleven.

S tanding just east of Kinross, LOCHLEVEN CASTLE, in a wonderful location on an island in the loch, is another stronghold that Mary is believed to haunt. The castle consists of a small keep with a courtyard, and it was captured from the English by William Wallace during the Wars of Independence. The castle is in the care of Historic Scotland, and a ferry takes visitors out to the island in the summer.

Mary was imprisoned here after giving herself up in 1567 at Carberry Hill. During her stay, she was forced to abdicate the throne in favour of her infant son James VI, who had been taken from her. It is likely she also had a miscarriage. She managed to escape the following year.

Her apparition has been seen at the castle.

C RAIGNETHAN CASTLE is also said to be haunted by Mary (although it is not even certain that she visited here). The castle is a fantastic ruin in a picturesque situation, with a strong, squat tower, defended by a ditch with a unique caponier (a low structure built in a ditch to defend it), and is now in the care of Historic Scotland.

Craignethan Castle: *one of several castles believed to be haunted by the ghost of Mary, Queen of Scots.*

The castle was a property of the loyal Hamiltons, and Mary is said to have spent the night at Criagnethan before the Battle of Langside in 1568. The Hamiltons made up a large part of her force, but they were defeated by the Regent Moray – and Mary fled south to eventual imprisonment in England. After many years in various castles, Mary was accused of plotting against the English queen and was executed by beheading. The phantom of a headless woman, clad in white, has been reported at Craignethan, and this has been identified by some as Mary. Why her ghost would return to Craignethan at all, never mind minus her head, is not obvious. It is also difficult to see how it would be possible to identify a headless apparition with any certainty: unless the apparition carries the head under its arm, of course ...

Other manifestations at Craignethan include the phantom of a woman, dressed in Stewart-period dress, seen in the outer courtyard. Two visitors followed the apparition, thinking it was the custodian in period clothes, before it unexpectedly vanished. At the later house here the voices of women from unoccupied areas, mysterious pipe music, and other sounds have been heard. Other manifestations have been witnessed in the tea room (which is also in this building), including pans falling off the cooker and pictures being moved around the walls. The tea room can have a very chill atmosphere, and a custodian's dog refused to go into the room, even though it was happy in the rest of the castle.

Author's note: this is the only building in which I have had any experience which could find its way into the book. We visited Craignethan, for a second time, one beautiful sunny day in summer. The castle was reasonably busy. It should also be said that I have been in many many ruined castles in many seasons, including the dead of winter, many deserted by all except Joyce and me. I have never seen or heard anything unexpected or uncanny.

I visited the toilets at Craignethan, which are in the outer courtyard and in same building as the tea room and the custodian's house. The bathroom, however, had a very unpleasant and cold feeling to it, unexpectedly so for a warm day, and I felt I should leave as quickly as possible and that I was being watched. I had just bought a new guidebook, which found its way in the toilet pan despite my best efforts to stop it. I had visited Craignethan some years before, used the toilet, and had no such sensation, so I was doubly perturbed. This was also before I knew of any ghost story concerning Craignethan. Anyway, this my only ghost story concerning a castle: and not a very dignified one.

This is not the only toilet which may be haunted: see Balnain House.

S tanding at the end of the Royal Mile in Edinburgh, HOLYROODHOUSE is an impressive royal palace, begun in the 16th century and still the official residence of the monarch in Scotland. The ruins of the abbey church of Holyrood adjoin, founded as an Augustinian establishment, dedicated to the Holy Cross: David I donated the Black Rood of his mother, St Margaret, to the abbey. David Rizzio, the secretary of Mary, Queen of Scots, was murdered at the palace. A plaque marks the spot, and for many years it was said that blood from his violent murder could not be washed off.

Holyroodhouse: *the palace is the residence of the monarch in Scotland, and home to a Grey Lady.*

The Queen's Audience Chamber is reputed to be haunted by a Grey Lady, said to be one of Mary's companions in life. One account describes the apparition as being very faint. Ghostly footsteps have also reportedly been heard in the long gallery.

C ESSNOCK CASTLE, near Galston in Ayrshire, dates from the 15th century, and was a property of the Campbells. Mary, Queen of Scots, stayed here after being defeated at the Battle of Langside in 1568. One of her ladies died here, and haunts the building. Cessnock was visited by John Knox, and his ghost has also been seen here. The two bogles may not be the most companionable of spirits.

T he ghost of Henry Stewart, Lord Darnley, who was of course Mary's second husband, is believed to haunt the site (near Old College of the University of Edinburgh) of KIRK O' FIELD, where he was murdered. The house in which he was staying was blown up with gunpowder, while he himself, and his servant, were strangled.

Some Green Ladies

There are further stories of this 'colour' of ghost elsewhere in the book, as well as under the section on gruagach, this being a very common colour for a female ghost. Some quarter of all stories about ladies are Green Ladies or have them clad in green. As noted earlier, many are called Jean and it is not clear whether the ghost wore a green dress, appeared in a green glow, or this is a 'stereotypical' apparition. Although the reasons behind some of the hauntings may be guessed at, most stories are fragmentary or are mostly concerned with manifestations of apparitions.

Standing by the sea, Wemyss Castle, near Kirkcaldy in Fife, is a grand pile with a 15th-century castle at its core, remodelled into a large mansion. This was the main stronghold of the Wemyss family, made Earls of Wemyss in 1633, and the family still occupy the building. Mary, Queen of Scots, first met Henry Stewart, Lord Darnley, here in 1565.

The castle is said to have a Green Lady, known as Green Jean, which is reported to have been seen in all parts of the building, both by the family and by servants.

The apparition was described in the 1890s as 'tall and slim and entirely clad in green, with her visage hidden by the hood of her mantle'. In 1904 it is said that she enlivened Christmas celebrations when sightings were made of her, and one of the family walked alongside the phantom until it disappeared.

There is no story behind her appearance.

Wemyss Castle: *residence of a Green Lady, seen in the 1890s, and in 1904 during Christmas celebrations.*

Fetteresso Castle, a mile or so west of Stonehaven, stands on the site of a castle and dates from the 17th century. It was held by the Keith Earls Marischal, who had their main stronghold at nearby Dunnottar. The castle was burned by the Marquis of Montrose in 1645. The Keiths sold the property to the Duffs, who had the castle remodelled into a mansion.

Fetteresso has a Green Lady. An apparition has been seen, once a hooded figure with a baby in its arms. The sounds of unexplained footsteps and the swish of a dress have also been heard, going repeatedly up and down the stairs. On another occasion footsteps were heard, along with the noise of something heavy being dragged. The phantom once disappeared into a wall, which was later shown to be a blocked-up doorway.

Fetteresso Castle: *the apparition of a girl, clad in green, has been seen here, sometimes with a baby in its arms.*

The ghost also haunted a house on the High Street in Stonehaven, which has since been demolished, and the Green Lady (or another, of course), an apparition in a flowing dress, has been reported on roads around the area, including the Slug Road. Indeed, one theory is that an underground passageway connected Fetteresso, this house in Stonehaven and Dunnottar Castle. When the house was demolished, a blocked-up tunnel was found, but its destination could not be determined: it is presumed it was used for smuggling.

There is no story recorded behind the haunting.

CAROLINE PARK, in the Granton area of Edinburgh, is a mansion which incorporates an old tower house, and was formerly known as Royston. It was held by the Logans, the Mackenzies, and the Campbells, then passed by marriage to the Scott Dukes of Buccleuch. The building is located in Edinburgh's waterfront project.

The house is haunted by a Green Lady, believed to be the phantom of Lady Royston, wife of Sir James Mackenzie, younger son of Lord Tarbat. Her apparition, dressed in an emerald-coloured robe with mystical devices, is said to appear by the old well on certain days; and, from there, it goes to the main door of the building. The phantom then vanishes, to reappear in the small courtyard, when a bell tolls. The bell was said to have been heard on many occasions, sometimes tolling by itself around midnight.

Caroline Park also has the distinction of the only castle to have a story of a spectral cannon ball.

STANDING in 40 acres of private gardens and park land, THAINSTONE HOUSE, a hotel just south of Inverurie in Aberdeenshire, is a classical mansion which dates from the 18th century, although with later extensions. An older house here was sacked by Jacobites in 1745.

The mansion has a Green Lady, an apparition clad in a green cloak, the daughter of one of the owners of the property. The story goes that the girl was badly injured in a riding accident, and was brought back to the building, where she died in one of the bedrooms – what is now Room 406. An alternative version is that she was burned to death when the older house was torched.

An account describes how pets will not enter one of the rooms, and objects have been mysteriously moved: a glass being smashed, and a woman's make-up bag being deposited and emptied on the floor. Reports have also been made of furniture being moved about without explanation. A man staying in the room reported feeling a great weight on his chest, which slowly released as he fully woke. He turned on the light, but nothing could be seen. Parts of the hotel are also said to be especially cold.

A member of staff, who was working in the small hours of the morning, described how he turned and walked through a misty entity which was in the rough shape of a person. When he turned back, there was nothing to see.

To the south of Dunfermline in Fife is PITREAVIE CASTLE, which was built in the first few years of the 17th century by the Wardlaws. It was acquired by the Beveridge family in 1885 after falling ruinous, and was restored and enlarged. The building was used by the Royal Navy and then the Royal Air Force, but the base has been closed.

It was nearby that the Battle of Inverkeithing was fought in 1651. A Royalist force, mostly made up of Highlanders, was completely routed by Cromwell's troops, with the loss of many lives; many more were taken prisoner. A party of badly mauled MacLeans sought help from those at Pitreavie, but their pleas were ignored, and they were then fired on. The MacLeans cursed the Wardlaw family, the result being that the laird of the time died 18 months later, and within 50 years the Wardlaws had lost ownership of the castle.

The ghost stories date from this event. The building has both a Green and a Grey Lady, while a headless Highlander has been reported in the vicinity of the castle. The apparition of the ladies were most often witnessed in the wee hours of the night.

Manifestations reported when the building was in use by the RAF included a WAAF being pushed down stairs by an invisible force, a cleaner being grabbed by the shoulder although nobody else was present, and phone calls being received from a room which was known to be empty.

NEWARK CASTLE, or Newark of St Monans, is a ruinous stronghold, which stands by the sea west of the village of St Monans in Fife. The building dates from the 15th century, although altered in later years, and was held by the Kinloch family, then the Sandilands, before coming to the Leslies. One of the family was David Leslie, the Covenanter general, who defeated Montrose at Philiphaugh (see Newark Castle, near Selkirk). Leslie went on to lead the Scottish army that was crushed by Cromwell at Dunbar in 1650, then at Worcester a year later. He was captured and imprisoned in the Tower of London for nine years. He died in 1682. The property passed to the Anstruthers, then the Bairds.

The castle has a Green Lady, another Green Jean. She is believed to have been Jean Leslie, daughter of David Leslie mentioned above. The swish of her dress has also been heard on occasion. There is no story behind her appearance, although caves below the castle were used for smuggling, and it has been suggested that the ghost might have been invented to scare off people from the castle at night. It is not, however, unusual for a castle to have a Green Lady.

An apparition of David Leslie is reported to have once been seen in St

Monans Parish Church, a fine old building on a cliff-top location with an interesting burial ground. The church can be visited in the summer.

MELDRUM HOUSE, just north of Oldmeldrum in Aberdeenshire, is now a hotel and golf club, but the building incorporates a 13th-century castle. It was owned by the Meldrum family, then the Setons, Urquharts and Duffs.

Meldrum was said to have a Green Lady, which had been witnessed often, but in recent sightings, including in 1985, the apparition is reported to be clad in white. The ghost is said to have given a customer of the hotel a cold kiss during a thunder storm; another guest reported an unseen weight forcing them into their mattress while lying in bed; while on another occasion the phantom was seen walking along a corridor on one of the upper floors.

Other accounts had her only appearing to, and looking after, unattended children. Youngsters have reported a friendly woman in white who would keep them company while their parents were away.

Some miles east of Banchory stands DURRIS HOUSE, a greatly altered tower house, which was a property of the Frasers until the end of the 17th century. Durris was torched by James Graham, Marquis of Montrose in 1645, but was restored; the house is still occupied, although it has been divided into three residences.

Durris has a story of a Green Lady, believed to be the apparition of the wife of a Fraser laird in the 1640s. The poor woman thought she was responsible for getting the house burned after cursing Montrose and, in an agony of despair, drowned herself in a nearby river. One account states that she is never seen by women.

BALGONIE CASTLE, near Glenrothes in Fife, is a picturesque stronghold, dating from about 1360, and has a fine great hall. It was held by the Sibbalds, the Lundies, and then the Leslie family. James IV visited in 1496, as did Mary, Queen of Scots in 1565.

The fortress has a Green Lady, Green Jeanie, although it has apparently not been witnessed since 1994. The ghost is described as being pea-green in colour with a full-skirted dress, or a flowing skirt and a hood which conceals her face. The ghost is believed to be the spirit of one of the Lundie family. It has been most often observed in the ruinous 18th-century wing, where it stops at a window to look out into the courtyard while walking between two chambers. Indeed, in 1842 it was described as being a well-known ghost. The phantom is also said to have been seen on the road between Coaltown and Milton of Balgonie.

B ALLINDALLOCH CASTLE, set in fine gardens and grounds in Moray countryside, is an impressive sprawling mansion, which incorporates a 16th-century Z-plan tower house. The lands had passed to the Grants by 1499, and is one of the few castles to be occupied by the same family who built it, the Macpherson-Grants.

The castle has a Green Lady, which has been seen in the Dining Room, which would have been the great hall of the original tower. The Pink Tower, one of the original bed chambers, has a fireplace dated 1546. In this room have been reported sightings of the apparition of a beautiful woman, dressed in a pink crinoline gown, with or without a large straw hat, sitting in a chair. According to the guide book, the ghost was a relation of the Macpherson-Grants, who lost a child in 1750, and it now watches over the family.

There is also a tale of a young girl, whose spectre has been witnessed at the nearby Bridge of Avon. She was jilted by her lover, and her apparition reportedly crosses the bridge every evening. When a new bridge was built, workmen reported seeing her phantom on several occasions.

B IGHOUSE (pronounced Begus) LODGE is (as the name suggests) a large mansion, standing in four acres of grounds, some 14 miles west of Thurso in Sutherland. It dates from the 18th century, and was on lands held by the Mackays from 1597, although they had an earlier house at Kirkton. They eventually sold the property to the Duke of Sutherland.

It is believed that a woman hanged herself in one of the chambers at the end of the 19th century, although it is not recorded why. Her ghost, a Green Lady, haunts the building, and especially the room in which she died. Several times she has been observed walking through walls.

F ERNIEHIRST, near Jedburgh in the Borders, dates from the 16th century and was built by the Kerrs, now Marquis of Lothian. For some 25 years, following 1523, it was held by the English, although then recaptured with the beheading of the English commander; and it was attacked again in 1593 by James VI. For some years the castle was used as a youth hostel, but it is now occupied again as a home by the Kerrs. Ferniehirst has stories of a Green Lady, seen mostly in one of the bed chambers, although this story is refuted.

Ferniehirst Castle *(previous page): there are stories here of a Green Lady, which haunts one of the bed chambers.*

Located about one mile north of Newmains in Lanarkshire, MURDOSTOUN CASTLE is a modern mansion but incorporates part of a 15th-century castle. It was held by the Scotts, but passed in the middle of the 15th century to the Inglis family, then was sold to the Hamiltons in 1719. It was the first building in Scotland to have electric lights. The building has a Green Lady, seen in the East Dressing Room, but she has not apparently been witnessed in living memory.

Standing on Huntly Street in Inverness, BALNAIN HOUSE was built in 1726 for the Duff family. In 1746 it was used as a hospital by the Hanoverian army after the Battle of Culloden, then by the Ordnance Survey in the 1880s for compiling maps of the Highlands. It was later divided into flats, became derelict, but was restored; in 1997 it was bought by The National Trust for Scotland. It did house a museum of musical heritage, but this closed in 2001 due to financial difficulties, and the building is now used as offices for the Trust.

The house has what has been described as a Green Lady, although there is no certain story behind her appearance. One recent sighting may have been in 2000, when one of the staff saw a mysterious lady behind her when looking in a mirror in the ladies' toilets for the Cellar Bar. The apparition was described as small, dressed in old-fashioned clothes, and appeared to be in black and white. One tentative explanation for her appearance is that she searches for her lover or husband who was wounded or killed at Culloden.

To the south and east of Prestonpans in East Lothian, PRESTON TOWER is an imposing and foreboding tower, set in its own gardens with an avenue of tree. It dates from the 15th century, although it may include older work, and two extra storeys were added in the 17th century. It was long a property of the Hamiltons, and was torched in 1544, then again in 1650 by Cromwell. The tower is owned by The National Trust for Scotland, but looked after by East Lothian Council. Two other old houses stand nearby: Hamilton House and Northfield House.

Preston Tower is another stronghold which has stories of a Green Lady.

CASTLEMILK, now giving its name to a housing estate south and east of Rutherglen in Glasgow, was a large and altered castle and mansion, but little remains except some of the basement. It was originally a property of the Comyns, then the Douglases, Hamiltons and the Stewarts. It was purchased by Glasgow Corporation in 1938, and was used as a children's home until the 1960s, after which it was demolished.

The grounds and woodland around the site of the castle are haunted, both by a Green Lady and a White Lady, seen near a bridge over the burn: it is not clear whether these are refugees from the castle. There is also the Mad Major, but that is covered later.

BRUNTSFIELD HOUSE, which is now part of Gillespie's School, stands in the Bruntsfield area of Edinburgh. The building is a 16th-century Z-plan tower house, with later modifications, although on an older site. The property was long held by the Lauder family, then the Fairlies and the Warrenders. It was sold in 1935 to the City of Edinburgh.

One story is that the house has a Green Lady. A secret room was found in the 19th century, and the tales goes that a woman and her child were discovered walled up in the building.

It could be that this story, along with the school, was translated from Wrightshouses.

SUNDRUM CASTLE has a Green Lady, that haunted the old part of the building around the vaulted dining room. She is believed to have been the wife of one of the Hamilton lairds, after they acquired the property in 1750, but she has apparently not been witnessed since the castle was renovated and divided into separate residences.

Sundrum is a large mansion, and incorporates a keep built by the Wallace family. It passed to the Cathcarts, before going to the Hamiltons, and stands four or so miles east of Ayr.

Located near Balmedie in Aberdeenshire, Menie House dates from the 18th century, but stands on the site of an ancient castle of the Forbes family. The house has a Green Lady, which has been most often seen at night in the basement of the old part of the building. The ghost is reported as being more friendly than frightening.

The magnificent mansion of Duff House, just south of Banff and now used to display works of art from the National Gallery of Scotland, was built for the Duffs of Braco by the famous architect William Adam (although they fell out over the cost). It is said to be haunted by a Green Lady.

Ethie Castle, reputedly haunted by the spirit of Cardinal David Beaton (covered in more detail later) also has a Green Lady.

On Mull, some miles west of Tobermory, Glengorm Castle has tales of a Green Lady. It is a castellated mansion of 1860, with no older origins.

Although neither a castle nor a mansion, it is interesting that many other buildings have acquired stories of Green Ladies. The Atholl Palace Hotel was built in 1875-8 as a hydropathic establishment, and is an imposing baronial building overlooking Pitlochry. It is still a hotel, and stands in 48 acres of grounds.

One of the towers is said to have a Green Lady, and the phantom has reportedly been seen in one of the bedrooms numerous times by both staff and customers. Indeed, manifestations were so common, and disturbing, that the chamber, which had formerly been for customers, was changed so that only staff slept there. The ghost, however, was then witnessed in neighbouring bedrooms. The story goes that the hotel had the room exorcised.

SOME WHITE LADIES

W*hite Ladies are the next most common colour of ghost, accounting for just under one fifth of all tales.*

S ome miles east of Huntly in Aberdeenshire is FRENDRAUGHT CASTLE, which dates from the 17th century, but may incorporate some of an ancient stronghold. This older castle, then held by the Crichton family, was torched and burned out in an infamous fire of 1630. The castle was rebuilt in 1656, then altered in later years, and is still occupied, although now by the Morison family.

The Crichtons were an important family in Scotland, but Sir James Crichton and his wife Elizabeth Gordon, daughter of the Earl of Sutherland, found themselves in a feud with a branch of the powerful Gordon family, whose head was the Marquis of Huntly, over the boundary between lands they owned.

Crichton had shot and killed Gordon of Rothiemay (also see Rothiemay Castle), for which he was fined, the money to be paid to John Gordon, the new Lord Rothiemay. Sir James then wounded Leslie of Pitcaple (also see Pitcaple Castle) with an arrow but, when this came to court in October 1630, it was found in his favour. Leslie had threatened Crichton, and Sir James was given an escort back to Frendraught by, strangely enough, John Gordon of Rothiemay, and Viscount Aboyne, another John Gordon, who was the son of the Marquis of Huntly. Crichton and the Gordons had apparently made up, and they spent the evening drinking, eating and blethering. The Gordons and their servants stayed the night, and were lodged in the old part of the building.

But that night the castle caught fire and the old part was engulfed in a fierce blaze. There was only a wooden stair to the Gordons' chambers, and they could not escape. Viscount Aboyne could have survived, but was killed trying to rescue his kinsmen. In total about a dozen people were burned to death, but Crichton with his family and people escaped the blaze without injury. Indeed, they are said to have done nothing to help, and Gordon of Rothiemay and his servants may even have been locked in their rooms.

Foul play was suspected. Sir James and Elizabeth were accused and tried at Frendraught in April 1631, but were acquitted, although one of their servants, John Meldrum, was found guilty of arson (although he was tortured into a confession). He was hanged, drawn and quartered at the Mercat Cross in Edinburgh.

Lady Rothiemay was not satisfied with this 'justice', and she employed men to pillage and harry Crichton's property and people. Although warned repeatedly, Lady Rothiemay was finally imprisoned in 1635 as the attacks under her instigation continued. The poor woman was soon released.

Frendraught is haunted by the apparition of Elizabeth Gordon, described as being a dark woman dressed in a white gown edged with gold. She has been seen on the main stair or back stairs of the house, looking out from a window, and in the grounds and woods. Other manifestations are said to be crashing noises, cries for help, arguing, unexplained heavy footsteps descending the stairs (heard in 1948), the sounds of people arguing, and doors being opened and shut, and then locked. Electrical equipment has also been affected, and on several occasions a television, video and fan heater were found to have been switched on in the morning, despite being turned off before going to bed. Disturbances were frequently reported, especially in the 18th and 20th centuries.

One explanation which has been given is that Elizabeth was involved in the torching of the house, that it was even by her instruction, and she is a guilt-ridden spectre. It was claimed that Gordon of Rothiemay had been locked in his room so could not escape, and that she had disposed of the keys in the well. There is some evidence for this tale: in the 1840s, the well was cleared out and the keys apparently found.

E DZELL CASTLE, standing some miles north of Brechin, is believed to have a White Lady. The castle is a fine ruinous building with a magnificent formal walled garden with a dinky summer house. It was long a property of the Lindsays, whose mausoleum is in the nearby burial ground: the castle and mausoleum are in the care of Historic Scotland and both can be visited. One story is that a Lindsay laird hanged a gypsy lad for poaching. The gypsy lad's mother was distraught and cursed Lindsay for his cruel act: Lindsay's pregnant wife died that day, while he himself was soon devoured by wolves. The castle later passed from the Lindsays.

The White Lady is believed to be the spirit of Catherine Campbell, the second wife of David Lindsay, ninth Earl of Crawford. They lived at Edzell, and Catherine died quite suddenly. She was placed in her coffin, buried with her jewellery and raiment, and taken to the nearby kirkyard where she was put in the family vault. But during the night of her interment, a sextant broke into her coffin in an attempt to steal her rings. He could not get the rings off, and was going to cut off her

Edzell Castle: *stories tell of a White Lady, the ghost of a woman who was buried alive and only awoke when a sextant tried to cut a ring from her finger.*

fingers when Catherine suddenly came back to life. The poor woman had been in a coma, and only then regained consciousness. She fled back to Edzell in a terrible state. Here, however, she is said to have died at the gates of the castle from exposure. The story goes that Catherine's spirit, a White Lady, then began to haunt the old stronghold, including the walled garden, as well as the burial ground of Edzell Old Church, which has the Lindsay Burial Aisle.

Her ghost is said to have been witnessed, both in and around the old castle, in recent times. She has been described as being quite small with a white floral dress with billowing sleeves and blur for a face, and is also said to exude a sickly smell or faint odour of scent. On another occasion, the description was of a figure like a piece of white lace, and faded after a couple of seconds. This smell is thought, by some, to be embalming fluid.

One version of the story, however, does not have Catherine dying at the gates, so the identity of the ghost might be questioned.

Tolquhon Castle is a large, now ruinous courtyard castle, dating from the 15th century, but much altered and extended in following years to make it a comfortable residence. It stands about four miles east of Oldmeldrum in Aberdeenshire, and was originally held by the Preston family, but in 1420 passed to the Forbeses, who held it until 1716. The main part was built by William Forbes, seventh Laird, who remodelled the castle: his carved tomb survives at Tarves.

Recent sightings of a White Lady, described as being slim and clad in a long white dress, have been reported by several visitors to the castle. The phantom is said to be seen standing unmoving at the top of a turnpike stair. The ghost is believed to be sorrowful, but there is no story as to its identity. Other manifestations include unexplained footsteps around the buildings, and once the sound of humming.

There are also stories of a Grey Lady, seen wandering through the buildings at midnight. Groaning has also been recorded, although it is not clear who could have (legitimately) been in the ruin at this time to report it.

The Custodian's House, near the castle, is also apparently haunted. Unexplained knocking on the windows has been reported several times at night.

CLAYPOTTS CASTLE, near Dundee, has a White Lady. She has been identified as a phantom of Marion Ogilvie, seen at a castle window on 29 May each year, the anniversary of her husband's death, waving a white handkerchief (the theory goes that she was waving to her husband at St Andrews!). Marion was the mistress (and wife) of Cardinal David Beaton, by whom she had several children. Beaton was murdered and hung (like meat) from a window at St Andrews Castle in 1546. Her apparition has apparently been witnessed often, but there is a small problem with the story, or at least the identification of the ghost: there does not appear to have been a castle here in 1546. Indeed, Melgund or

Claypotts Castle: *the building has both a White Lady and the story of a brownie.*

Ethie Castle would be a better candidate. The present building is a Z-plan tower house, dating from no earlier than 1569, and it does not appear there was an earlier building on the site.

The lands had been owned by abbey of Lindores, but passed to the Strachans and then the Grahams, one of whom was John Graham of Claverhouse, Viscount Dundee, who was killed at Killiecrankie in 1689.

With fine views of the surrounding countryside to the south-west of Edinburgh, DALMAHOY is a grand symmetrical mansion, which was built by the architect William Adam about 1720. It had long been held by the Dalmahoy family, when it was sold to the Dalrymples, before coming to the Douglas Earl of Morton in the middle of the 18th century. The building is now a hotel and leisure complex.

A White Lady, the apparition of Lady Mary Douglas (daughter of the Earl of Morton who purchased the property from the Dalrymples in about 1750) is reputed to have been seen at Dalmahoy, even in recent times. The phantom has been reported in both the corridors and the rooms of the old part of the building. The ghost is said to be friendly, and a portrait of Mary hangs in the hotel.

Set in a peaceful location just north of Dufftown in Moray, BALVENIE CASTLE is a large walled stronghold with a deep ditch, dating from the 13th century, but added to in later centuries. The Comyns had a castle here, but it was captured by Robert the Bruce in 1308, and the fortress passed to the Douglases, then the Stewarts, Innes family, and the Duffs. The phantom of a woman, a White Lady, has been reported here, as well as an apparition of a red-haired groom with two horses, and the mysterious sounds of a flute playing.

FALKLAND PALACE, in the pretty village of Falkland north of Glenrothes in Fife, is a magnificent Renaissance building and was used by many of the Stewart monarchs, including James V, who died here, reputedly in the King's Room in the restored cross house; Mary, Queen of Scots (one story is that she haunts the Covenanter's Hotel in Falkland); James VI; Charles I; and Charles II. David, Duke of Rothesay, son and heir of Robert II, was imprisoned at Falkland in 1402 by his uncle Robert Stewart, Duke of Albany. David died mysteriously, probably by being starved to death. The palace is now in the care of The National Trust for Scotland, and is open to the public. There is a fine garden, as well as the original Royal Tennis Court, which was built in 1539.

The tapestry gallery is reputedly haunted by a White (or Grey) Lady. One account has the ghost moving along the length of the gallery before disappearing through a wall, where there had formerly been a door. She is also described as emitting a 'greyish' (faint?) light. The lady is said to have waited in vain for her lover, who never returned from battle.

C ARBISDALE CASTLE stands some three miles north-west of Bonar Bridge in Sutherland in the far north of Scotland. It dates mostly from 1910-11, and was built on the site of Culrain Lodge for Duchess Blair, second wife of the third Duke of Sutherland (their castle is at Dunrobin). The Duchess and her husband's family did not get on, and she had to build the mansion outwith the Dukes of Sutherland's demesne. The Duchess bought land just in Easter Ross, and had a magnificent home built, with a large tower, so that it could be seen from many parts of the Duke of Sutherland's lands – no doubt intended to annoy her husband's relatives. It is now a youth hostel.

The castle is haunted by a White Lady, which has been witnessed in many parts of the building, although the manifestation is not recorded as being especially frightening. The ghost has been identified as the widowed Duchess.

R OSSLYN CASTLE, along with tales of spectral flames, phantom dogs and black horsemen, also has a White Lady. It is not clear if she is the spectral guardian of a great treasure here, which is hidden in a secret chamber.

S T ANDREWS CASTLE, covered in more detail later, is believed to be haunted by Archbishop John Hamilton, and perhaps David Beaton. There are also stories, however, of a White Lady being seen near the old stronghold, and on the adjacent shore. It seems likely that this is the same spirit believed to have been seen (more often) in the ruins of the cathedral. This ghost is described as being clad in a white dress with a veil which obscures its face.

T he grounds around BIRKHALL HOUSE have a White Lady, a harbinger of doom or death in the resident family.

S ADDELL CASTLE, north of Campbeltown on Kintyre, has a White Lady, who haunts the battlements of the tower. There is also the spectre of a monk.

SOME GREY LADIES
Grey Ladies appear in about one tenth of tales.

The ruins of MACDUFF'S CASTLE, near East Wemyss in Fife, are in a picturesque location, and were long held by the Wemyss family (see Wemyss Castle). The ruins are frequented by a Grey Lady, the apparition of Mary Sibbald. Mary absconded with a gypsy laddie after apparently helping herself to property which belonged to others. She

Macduff's Castle: the ghost of a woman, whipped to death after being found guilty of theft, haunts the ruins.

was captured, and accused of, and tried for, robbery. The poor woman was sentenced to be whipped, but the punishment was so severe that she died. Her phantom has also been reported in the Wemyss Caves: her trial is said to have been held in the Court Cave.

GLENLEE, a mansion which was greatly enlarged in 1822, was a property of the Miller family in the 18th, then the Smiths in the 19th century.

It is visited by a Grey Lady, believed to be a phantom of Lady Ashburton, garbed in a grey silk dress. The apparition has been seen on more than one occasion. The sounds of ghostly footsteps were reported, along with the rustle of a silk dress. It is thought that the lady was either murdered by a thieving butler or was taken by remorse after being involved in a plot to kill her own husband.

One account describes how an apparition moved silently from the door of a chamber, across the floor, to the entrance of a dressing room. The same witness, when ill, heard a knock on her bedroom door. When she answered it, she found a phantom-woman's face looking at her, which then faded out of sight down a gloomy corridor.

B URLEIGH CASTLE is about one and a half miles north of Kinross, east of Milnathort, and is a picturesque ruin consisting of the remains of a keep and an unusual round corner tower which is corbelled out to square. It was a property of the Balfours, and visited several times by James IV. In 1707 the Master of Burleigh fell for a servant girl, but he was sent abroad to forget her. In the meantime, she married Henry Stenhouse, school master of Inverkeithing, but when Balfour returned from exile he shot and killed the poor man. Balfour was seized and sentenced to death, but managed to escape after changing clothes with his sister. He died, unmarried, in 1757.

One tale is that the castle is haunted by Grey Mary.

T here was a royal castle at KINGHORN in Fife, dating from the 12th century, but of which there were no remains by 1790. It was here that Yolande de Dreux, the young and beautiful wife of Alexander III, awaited him one night in 1286. Alexander fell from nearby cliffs and was killed (see Jedburgh Castle), a monument marking the spot.

One story is that Yolande's ghost still searches the area for her husband. Her apparition, a Grey Lady, has been seen in the area and in the Kingswood.

S ome miles south-west Haddington stands SALTOUN HALL, a fine mansion which incorporates work from as early as the 12th century. It was a property of the Abernethy family, but later passed to Sir Andrew Fletcher, who was so prominent in resisting the Union of Parliaments in 1707. The building has a Grey Lady.

A Grey Lady also haunts ALDOURIE CASTLE, and the apparition has been reported walking from a bed chamber in the ancient part of the building to the old hall, where she disappears. The castle stands some miles south-west of Inverness on the banks of Loch Ness, and dates from the 17th century, although it was extended in later years to form a baronial mansion. It was a property of the Frasers, Grants, then the Mackintoshes, and was recently sold again.

Near Galston in Ayrshire are the impressive ruins of LOUDOUN CASTLE, once the grand home of the Campbell Earls of Loudoun, and now the centre of a family theme park. The building had been accidentally burned out and gutted in 1941.

Loudoun has a Grey Lady, seen repeatedly before and after the fire, and even in recent years. Before the castle was abandoned, the Grey Lady was apparently observed so often that her presence was ignored.

There are also accounts of a phantom dog.

Loudoun Castle: *there are tales of an apparition of a Grey Lady and a spectral hound.*

The grounds of BALLECHIN HOUSE are haunted by a Grey Lady, the phantom of a nun. The apparition has been seen in a cottage and on the drive way. The house reportedly had other manifestations (the house was investigated around 1900), which are covered later.

DUNANS CASTLE, in Glendaruel on Cowal in Argyll, is an impressive Franco-Scots baronial mansion, originally a property of the Fletchers, whose mausoleum is further downstream on a wooded ridge. The mansion stands in a fantastic remote location, about eight miles south of Strachur. It suffered a fire in recent years.

The house has a Grey Lady.

MONYMUSK CASTLE, some miles south-west of Inverurie, also has a Grey Lady. The apparition seems concerned for unattended children, and emerges from a cupboard in the nursery. Another sighting of a ghost described the phantom as a 'pale' lady, who crossed one of the upper chambers, as well as a bathroom. There are other manifestations here.

95

CARELESS NURSEMAIDS AND HOUSEKEEPERS

T*hese are a small number of these type of stories, although a greater number where a servant, nanny or housekeeper is murdered through no fault of their own.*

A IRTH CASTLE is a substantial mansion, situated about four miles north of Falkirk in central Scotland, and incorporates old work, including the 14th-century Wallace's Tower. About 1470 it was held by the Bruce family, and some 18 years later was burned by the forces of James III. The castle later passed to the Elphinstones, then the Grahams.

Accounts record that in the 17th century two children were killed in a blaze in one of the bed chambers. Their housekeeper had not taken proper care of them, and the story goes that her spirit still searches frantically through the rooms at Airth, looking for the youngsters.

S et in a picturesque and dramatic cliff-top location, DUNSKEY CASTLE is haunted by the spirit of a nursemaid. The woman was holding the baby at a window, when it slipped from her arms and fell to its death on the cliffs below.

Dunskey was a property of the Adairs, who were responsible for the imprisonment and torture of the last abbot of Soulseat Abbey, forcing him to sign the lands over to them. The castle has been abandoned since the end of the 17th century, but is still an impressive ruin. It stands

Dunskey Castle: *haunted by the ghost of a nursemaid, who dropped her charge from a window over the cliffs.*

about half a mile south-east of Portpatrick in the very far south-west of Scotland, and is apparently to be restored.

A similar ghost story, which is associated with DUNTULM CASTLE on Skye, is that of a nursemaid who was cradling a baby at a window overlooking the cliffs. The infant slipped through her arms, fell through the window, and was killed on the rocks below. The nursemaid was stricken, then slain for her carelessness. Her terrified screams have reportedly been heard.

Two male ghosts are also recorded, but these accounts are given later.

There is also a tragic tale at KINGCAUSIE, where a small infant fell through the arms of his nanny and was killed on the stairs of the house. In this case, however, it is the spirit of the boy who haunts the building. A fuller account is given elsewhere.

OLD LADIES

These are stories where the phantom is that of an old woman (and no colour is recorded). In the following accounts, there is no certain reason why the haunting occurs, although in some it can be guessed. As seen in some stories about inns and hotels, the ghost may be 'hanging around' because in life the person had particularly liked or loved the place they haunt. The White Lady of Biel may also fall into this category, covered above, although the apparition at Nivingston House probably does not.

Lying some three miles south-west of Kinross, NIVINGSTON HOUSE dates from 1725 and was a hotel for many years. There have been at least three sightings of an apparition since 1980. The phantom of an old woman in her night clothes was observed, leaving a bedroom and entering another bed chamber, although this was formerly a bathroom. It is believed that this is in connection with the suicide of a former male owner in the early 1900s. Other activity includes the sound of phantom footsteps and doors closing, and these noises always come from the same area of the house.

The stories of ghosts were enough to spook Raith Rovers, a football team from Kirkcaldy, who were staying in the hotel in 1994 before a cup tie against Airdrie. Nothing supernatural happened, but they went on to win the semi-final, then beat Celtic in the final.

SKAILL HOUSE, a complete 17th-century mansion north of Stromness on Orkney, was built for Bishop Graham in the 1620s. It is haunted by the phantom of an old woman, with a shawl over her head, and there have also been reports of ghostly footsteps from unoccupied areas. A dog in one of the rooms got into great distress about 3.00 am and started howling from its refuge under the bed. Another account has a weight, like someone sitting, on the end of a bed, which got up when the occupier of the room himself got out of bed to investigate.

A dozen skeletons were excavated from near the house in 1996, and Skaill was probably built beside an old burial ground. Human remains were also found beneath the stone flagstones of the hall.

Beneath the Cairngorm mountains, and standing in four acres of grounds in a wild and unspoilt spot, GAIRNSHIEL LODGE was used by Queen Victoria, and is now a family-run guest house. The apparition of an old woman has been seen here, believed to be the spirit of a former owner. There are also stories of the sound of feet, horses and carts heard from the old military road, which runs nearby, although nobody is apparently about.

Another story linked to the CARTLAND BRIDGE HOTEL is that the hotel has a Blue Lady, as well as the ghost of a wee girl. The phantom of the old lady was reported in 1978, when it was seen by three members of staff on the same occasion. The apparition was reported coming down the stairs, clad in a pale-blue dress, apparently with a veil. Another sighting was made by guests, several weeks later, in a private lounge. The building had had stories of the ghost old woman before the apparition was seen, and she has been tentatively identified as one of the Scott family.

BALLACHULISH HOUSE, which also has tales of other ghosts, is haunted by the phantom of an old woman. She is believed to be the ghost of Sophia Boulton, who died in 1900. This tale has a twist though: the apparition was reported many years before Sophia died, and a then occupier of the house was able to confirm that it was her when Sophia visited the house for the first time.

There were several tales of ghosts in the old mansion of ROTHIEMAY, which has been demolished despite being a fine building. One was the apparition of an old woman, clad in a plaid shawl, which was observed sitting by the fire, although it soon faded away. It was identified as one of the Duff family from a portrait that hung in the castle. There were also reports of a male apparition, and the weeping of children.

Rothiemay: *there are several tales of ghosts here, including the spirit of an old woman, observed sitting by a fire.*

Standing some miles north of Oban, Barcaldine Castle is a restored L-plan tower house, which was built by, and is occupied again, by the Campbells. It is haunted by a Blue Lady, the spirit of Harriet Campbell, who died around 1900. She was the spinster sister of Sir Duncan Campbell (who restored the old castle), and a lover of music. Her apparition has been seen several times in one of the chambers, and ghostly piano can sometimes be heard on windy nights.

About one mile south of Innerleithen in the Borders, Traquair House is reputed to be the longest continuously occupied houses in Scotland, and dates from as early as the 12th century. It had a succession of owners before coming to the Stewarts in 1478. Mary, Queen of Scots, visited in 1566, along with Lord Darnley, and the fourth laird of Traquair was one of those who helped her escape from Lochleven Castle two years later. Bonnie Prince Charlie visited in 1745, and the house has a collection of items associated both with Mary, and the Bonnie Prince and the Jacobites.

The grounds around Traquair are haunted by an apparition of Lady Louisa Stewart, who was the sister of the eighth and last Earl of Traquair. Louisa died in 1875 at the ripe old age of 100, and her portrait hangs at Traquair. An account in 1900 has her apparition passing through two locked gateways. The walk from the house, by the Quair Water, is called Lady Louisa's Walk.

One story also has Bonnie Prince Charlie haunting here, but this tale has been dismissed.

Earlshall in Fife is haunted by the apparition of an old woman, who is said to have been a servant. The fine building also has stories of a male ghost.

LADIES OF DIFFERENT AND NO COLOUR

T*his is a miscellaneous collection of other stories concerning female apparitions, either where the ghost has no colour or where there is no story behind the manifestations or there is not much recorded about the haunting. More than a third of stories do not record the 'colour' of the apparition.*

D ELGATIE CASTLE, near Turriff in the north-east of Scotland, is haunted by the phantom of a young woman, known as Rohaise. She has been witnessed in a bedroom off the main stair, which now bears her name, and she is reputed to visit sleepers in the chamber (although only men). The story goes that Rohaise was a spirited young woman (with red hair in one account) who defended the castle from attack, but there are no details as to her death. Tales of her ghost, and other mysterious occurrences, were enough to make soldiers billeted here flee from the building on two occasions. The castle was thoroughly searched but no explanation found for the soldier's disquiet – other than Rohaise, of course.

The castle is a fine old building, held by the Hays since the 14th century. The family were created Earls of Errol in 1452, and Mary, Queen of Scots, stayed at Delgatie in 1562.

W INDHOUSE stands in a remote spot of the Shetland island of Yell, and has gained a reputation for being haunted – by at least four different ghosts. The building dates from the beginning of the 18th century, was extended and remodelled in the 1880s, but was abandoned in the 1930s and is now ruinous. The lands were a property of the Swanieson family, but had passed to the Nevens early in the 17th century.

The ghost of a housekeeper and mistress, dressed in silk, has been witnessed here. The swish of her skirt was heard at the top of the stair, a stair down which she had fallen and broken her neck. One account describes that the ghost would walk (unseen) around the landing, and then a sigh would be heard. Foul play could not be ruled out, although it may have been an accident, and a further detail is that the remains of a woman were found under the floor boards at the foot of the stairs. There is, however, another tale of a skeleton, a man's in this case, being recovered from a shallow grave near the house, and a third abut a child's, so the three stories may have become confused.

The house has other tales of restless spirits.

S tanding at Duror, some miles south of Ballachulish on the west coast of Scotland, AUCHINDARROCH was a property of the Stewarts of Appin. It is haunted by a ghost known as the Maid of Glen Duror. The ghost is said to be the spirit of a MacColl, who in life had looked after the family who lived here. A different version is that she was a dairymaid and when out working was swept away by a torrent through the glen, along with her cows.

There may be several different apparitions here. One is that of a small woman, clad in grey, which has been seen in a remote part of the glen around dusk, and in and around the house, sometimes looking in from outside at different windows. The same, or another, ghost has also been witnessed: one describes an old woman who moved across a lawn, while another has a hooded figure in the house at the foot of the stairs.

There are several reports of crashing noises, witnessed by groups of people, but nothing could be found to explain the sounds, despite thorough investigations. These noises would recur two or three times on the same night, prompting even more desperate searches. It would also sound like windows and doors were being slammed shut, but again nothing was discovered. One room is thought to be the centre of the haunting, and items have been found scattered around in the chamber, again without explanation. It is also said to have an especially cold atmosphere at times.

L ying beneath the imposing hill of Bennachie, PITTODRIE HOUSE stands five miles north-west of Inverurie in Aberdeenshire. The house has at its core an old castle, which was later altered and extended into a large mansion. It was a property of the Erskine family from 1558, but is now a fine hotel.

The former nursery of the house is haunted by a ghost, which is believed to be the spirit of a servant. The story goes that her duties included looking after children, and that she died in about 1640 by falling down a turnpike stair during a fire. There have been recent reports of other manifestations, including unexplained footsteps, cries and screams, and the smell of burning, which are centred on an old stair.

G UTHRIE CASTLE is a fine baronial mansion, incorporating an ancient castle, and stands in 150 acres of mature woodland about six miles east of Forfar in Angus. It was long a property of the Guthrie family, who were embroiled in a messy feud with the Gardynes, who had their own stronghold nearby. This apparently started in 1558 with a marriage between the two families, although the Guthrie husband was stabbed to death by his wife's family. This resulted in a cycle of bloodshed, which was not resolved until both families were forfeited by James VI. The Guthries recovered their lands and castle, although the Gardynes were less fortunate.

The castle is believed to have a very benign ghost, the spirit of one of the Guthrie ladies who is concerned for the welfare of guests and likes to ensure they get a good night's rest.

Lying in a lovely situation by the bank of Loch Lomond, two miles south of Luss in Dunbartonshire, is ROSSDHU HOUSE. This is an attractive Adam-style mansion, which was built for the Colquhouns of Luss in 1772. It replaced, and used materials from, an ancient castle, one gable of which survives. The building is now used as the clubhouse for the Loch Lomond Golf Club.

The new house was visited by Johnson and Boswell in 1773. Lady Helen, wife of Sir James Colquhoun, 25th laird of Luss, was none too enamoured of the good doctor when he waded through her new drawing room, water pouring from his boots after returning from a boat trip on the loch. Indeed, Helen is believed to have been very house proud, and her ghost returns to the house she loved. It has been most often reported in the staff quarters.

MELVILLE CASTLE, dating from the 18th century, is a fine symmetrical mansion which was designed by William Playfair. It replaced an old stronghold of the Rosses, which was sold to the Rennie family in 1705, then passed by marriage to Henry Dundas, Viscount Melville, when he was wed to Elizabeth Rennie. Dundas was a very powerful figure in both Scotland and England, and has been called the uncrowned king of Scotland. The building was latterly used as a hotel, was then abandoned, but has been restored and reopened in recent years. The castle is located about a mile and a half west of Dalkeith in Midlothian.

The house is haunted by the apparition of a woman, believed to be the ghost of Elizabeth Rennie, Dundas's wife. Her phantom was observed during the renovation, when it was seen disappearing through a wall. This was later found to be a blocked-up doorway.

Abbout four miles west of Forres in Moray, BRODIE CASTLE, held by
the Brodie family from 1160, is a large Z-plan tower house. It was
remodelled and added to over the years, but is now cared for by The
National Trust for Scotland. A phantom of a woman was reported in
1992 in the nursery room. A possible identity is Lady Margaret Duff,

Brodie Castle: *the sighting of an apparition has been linked
to a tragic fire, but a child's skeleton was also found here.*

who was the wife of James Brodie, 21st laird. In 1786 she fell asleep too
close to the fire, which set her clothes, and the chamber, alight: the
poor woman was burned to death, despite the desperate efforts of her
husband to save her.

It may be, however, that the apparition is linked to the discovery of a
child's skeleton, found when a turnpike stair to one of the corner towers
was being renovated. The skeleton is on display in the Charter Room.

ORD HOUSE HOTEL, lying just west of Muir of Ord, ten miles west
and north of Inverness, dates from the 17th century and was a
property of the Mackenzies. It is a fine old building with 60 acres of
gardens and woodland, and is now used as a hotel.

The building has the apparition of a lady, which has been witnessed
both in corridors and sitting at the end of a bed in one of the rooms.
The ghost has also been blamed for removing pictures, presumably
because of a dislike for them, and propping them neatly and unbroken
against walls.

S tanding some three miles from Thornhill in Dumfries and Galloway, DRUMLANRIG CASTLE, dating mostly from the 17th century, is an impressive towered mansion, although it contains much older work. It was long a property of the Douglases, later Earls and Dukes of Queensberry, before passing to the Scott Dukes of Buccleuch in 1810. The building is open to the public, but it was from here that a painting by Leonardo de Vinci was stolen in 2003.

The castle is haunted by the spirit of Lady Anne Douglas, seen dressed in white, with a fan in one hand and her head in the other. There is apparently, however, no Anne Douglas who is known to have been beheaded. Mary, Queen of Scots, did visit Drumlanrig in 1563 ...

A second phantom, which has not been identified, is a young girl in a flowing dress, who may only appear to people who are ill. One of the corridors, the Bloody Passage, is thought to be the site of a gory murder. Blood which stained the floor could not be removed.

Thomas the Rhymer also made a prophecy about the place, although

Drumlanrig Castle: *there are several eerie stories about the castle, including the headless wraith of a woman.*

this did not apparently come true until the 18th century.

'When the Marr Burn runs where never man saw
The House of the Hassock is near to a fall.'

The House of the Hassock is another name for Drumlanrig Castle. The third Duke of Queensberry, Charles Douglas, diverted the Marr Burn to provide water for a fountain he was constructing south of the castle. Needless to say, when his two sons both died young the burn was returned to its original course.

JOHNSTOUNBURN HOUSE is a fine old mansion, dating from the 18th century, but later extended and altered. It nestles beneath the Lammermuir Hills, some eight miles south-east of Dalkeith, near the village of Humbie. There was an earlier castle or house here, and the lands were held by the Borthwick family, before passing to the Browns then the Ushers, noted whisky blenders. There is an large doocot, which has boxes for 2000 birds.

The hotel is haunted by the ghost of a lady, but she is said to be gentle and not frightening. There are also accounts of a strange presence being felt in some of the bedrooms.

There are also stories of a secret tunnel, which ran from here to the top of Soutra Hill, some two or so miles away.

Standing five miles east of Earlston in the Borders, MELLERSTAIN is a fine castellated mansion, built in the 18th century for the Baillie family by the famous architects William and Robert Adam. There are magnificent interiors, and a fine terraced garden. The house is still owned by the Baillie-Hamiltons, Earls of Haddington.

The house is reported to have several ghosts, and heavy footfalls have repeatedly been heard from empty rooms. One guest woke to find the apparition of a lady, wearing a cap, standing over the bed. The phantom faded away; until then the guest believed it was a member of staff who had come to bring him a cup of tea. The ghosts are said to be friendly rather than frightening.

An impressive mansion in a scenic location, BARBRECK HOUSE is an 18th-century house of the Campbells, located about four miles north of Kilmartin in Argyll. Barbreck's Bone was a talisman believed to be a cure for madness. It was found in a burial ground near Kilmartin, and was reputed to have fallen from heaven. It is about seven inches long and is made of elephant ivory (it is now held in the Museum of Scotland).

Near the house is a rock where the phantom of a young woman has been witnessed. The apparition, dressed in a dark-tartan plaid and a hood, has a pale face with long hair. Should the phantom be closely approached, it fades away and then vanishes.

KELLIE CASTLE, a splendid edifice with a grand garden and 16 acres of grounds, stands four miles north of Elie in Fife. It dates substantially from the 16th century, and was built by the Oliphant family, before passing to the Erskines, who were made Earls of Kellie. The organic walled garden has a fine collection of old roses, fruit trees and herbaceous plants.

The castle is haunted by the spirit of Anne Erskine (possibly the wife of the third or the fourth Earl, who were both called Anne, sometime in the 17th century), who was killed when she fell from an upstairs window after running up a turnpike stair. The reason for her death, presumably suicide, is not given. Although her apparition has rarely been seen, ghostly footfalls, dashing up the steps, have often been heard on the turnpike stair.

BEDLAY CASTLE, which is haunted by a bearded apparition, has other eerie manifestations. At dusk some summer evenings a coach and horses are heard on the old Stirling to Glasgow road. The coach is heard approaching the rear entrance of the old building, and at this point the phantom of a girl appears briefly by the roadside. A distant scream is heard, and then nothing.

In the attractive burgh in West Lothian, LINLITHGOW PALACE is a fabulous although ruinous palace, once the home of kings and queens. Ranges of buildings surround a central courtyard with a finely carved Renaissance fountain as its centrepiece. The palace was associated with many of Scotland's most famous monarchs, and Mary, Queen of Scots, was born here in 1542. The building was accidentally burned out by government troops stationed here in 1746. It stands in a fine location in a park on the banks of a loch, and the interesting parish church of St Michael, with its unique steeple, is located nearby. The ruins of the palace are in the care of Historic Scotland, and the church is also open to the public.

Queen Margaret's Bower, crowning one of the stair-towers, is haunted by a spirit, identified as either Margaret Tudor, wife of James IV, or Mary of Guise, the queen of James V. Mary of Guise is believed to have loved the palace, and it is said that she was waiting for James V to return. Margaret Tudor, however, apparently had no such love for James IV.

An apparition in a blue dress is reputed to have been seen walking from the entrance of the palace to the threshold of the nearby parish church of St Michael. The phantom disappears within a few feet of the wall of the church. The rustle of her dress has also been reported. The ghost is believed to be seen mostly in the month of April, but also sometimes in September, at about nine o'clock in the morning.

D ALKEITH HOUSE is a classical mansion, incorporating an ancient castle, and stands in acres of parkland on the outskirts of the burgh. It was long held by the Douglases, then was sold to the Scotts of Buccleuch in 1642. It was to here that many nobles fled after the nearby Battle of Pinkie in 1547, and were here captured; and Charles I visited in 1633. James IV and James VI were other notable visitors. The building is now used as a school by colleges from Wisconsin State.

The building is haunted by a female ghost. One account has one of the students waking from sleep to find the phantom at the end of their bed, with its head in its hands. A voice told the resident to leave: perhaps a rather unnecessary request in the circumstances. Other reported manifestations include unexplained footsteps, and voices and laughter. Doors also open and close by themselves.

L ocated in a fine location near the shore of Loch Lomond some four miles north of Dumbarton, AUCHENDENNAN is a grand mansion, dating from the middle of the 19th century. It was owned by the Chrystal family, but is now used as the Loch Lomond Youth Hostel.

One of the chambers of the tower is haunted by the apparition of a girl, who has been witnessed crossing the room. There is no story as to her origin, but she is known as Veronica.

M ANDERSTON HOUSE, just over a mile east of Duns in the Borders and lying in 56 acres of formal gardens, is a fine Edwardian mansion, which features the only silver staircase in the world. There was an old castle here, nothing of which survives, a property of the Homes.

Manderston: *the fine mansion is said to be haunted by the apparition of a woman, seen on the main stair.*

The wife of Home of Manderston was accused of witchcraft by Alexander Hamilton (see Penkaet Castle). In 1890 the property passed to Sir James Miller.

An apparition of a woman, identified in one account as Eveline, Sir James's wife, is said to have been seen on the main stair. This story, however, is refuted.

About five miles south-west of Nairn, CAWDOR is a strong and splendid castle, dating from the 14th century, with fine gardens and grounds. The property was held by the Calder family, but then acquired by the Campbells after they abducted the young heiress, Muriel Calder, in 1511. In due course, she was married to Sir John Campbell, son of the Earl of Argyll. The castle is still owned by the same family.

Cawdor is haunted by the phantom of a lady in a blue gown.

Near Laurencekirk in the old county of Kincardineshire, FASQUE is a fine mansion, dating from 1809 but on the site of an older castle. The house passed to the Gladstone family in 1829, one of whom, William Ewart Gladstone, was Prime Minister four times between 1830 and 1851. Fasque is still owned by the Gladstones, and is haunted by the spirit of Helen Gladstone, youngest sister of the Prime Minister. One account has the ghost as Sir Thomas Gladstone, elder brother of the Prime Minister.

INCHDREWER CASTLE has stories of a strange haunting. The apparition of a woman has been seen here, but also the phantom of a white dog, believed to be the woman in another guise. Why she would manifest in such a way is not recorded.

CULZEAN CASTLE, the magnificent mansion of the Kennedys, is haunted by the phantom of a young woman wearing a ball gown. Sightings were made in 1972. Another (or perhaps the same) apparition was seen on the main stair by two visitors in 1976, when it was described as a peculiar misty shape. Culzean also has a phantom piper.

One of the bedchambers at EILEAN DONAN CASTLE is haunted by the ghost of a Lady Mary.

SECTION TWO
Portents, Gruagach & Brownies

CHAPTER ONE
Harbingers & Heralds of Death

These are either the spirits of the dead, or living corporeal creatures. They appear, or are heard, or undertake a particular action, when something of note is going to happen to members of the resident family of a castle or great house. The Banshee from Irish belief is one such example, as is the Bean Nighe, a supernatural being which would be seen washing the shirts of those about to die: if the shirt could be identified, then so could the deceased. This entity features in the story of the Headless Horseman of the MacLaines, but was also reputedly seen before the collapse of the roof of the church of Fearn Abbey in 1742, when 44 people died. The Bean Nighe is described in different disguises, depending on the part of Scotland from where the story comes. One is that she had enormous but drooping breasts (it was possible to control the Bean Nighe by sucking on the nipple), that had to be slung over her shoulder while she was at work; but another that, although small and stoutly built, she was clad in fairy green.

The specific stories of Green Ladies and other female apparitions said to appear before a death in the family are covered in more detail elsewhere. Strongholds with this kind of spirit include Abergeldie Castle, Crathes Castle, Fyvie Castle, Pinkie House, Sanquhar Castle, the Cobbler Hotel, Stirling Castle and the grounds around Birkhall House (the White Lady of Sterin, the former name of Birkhall, is described below). In one account, the Grey Lady of Glamis also appeared before a death in the family.

Gruagach, also covered below, feature Green Ladies at Dunstaffnage, Huntingtower, Skipness, Castle Loch Heylipol and Caisteal Camus.

It should be said that the Victorians recorded, and no doubt embellished, many ghost stories, according to the tastes of the day. Their interest in the paranormal, spiritualism, speaking to the dead and portents

110

of death influenced the themes and detail of stories they collected and recorded.

Usually the portentous appearances will continue, even when the resident family changes. Lillias Drummond, identified as the Green Lady of Fyvie, is said to have appeared to the Gordons in the 19th century as a herald of death. Lillias was the wife of Alexander Seton, who owned the castle in the 17th century. Why did Lillias not continue to appear to the Setons after they had moved elsewhere, rather than to the Gordons? Incidentally, Lillias did not even die at Fyvie. It could be, of course, that this is a confusion of tales.

There portents were not always very specific. In some cases, the appearance or phenomena occurred some time, even many months, before a tragedy. To the cynic, this might seem a little far off. In a large extended Victorian noble family it was likely that someone would be ill or would die within many months. It could be that the facts were fitted to the story, rather than the other way around.

Scotland is also by no means the only country to have such tales: there are example of harbingers of doom in Ireland, England and elsewhere.

Thomas the Rhymer and the Brahan Seer also made prophecies about certain strongholds. These stories are covered under the articles of the castles of Drumlanrig, Fyvie, Hermitage and Fairburn.

Spirits

CORTACHY CASTLE is an impressive and imposing pile, and stands some miles north of Kirriemuir in Angus. It dates from the 15th century, and has a long association with the Ogilvie Earls of Airlie, who still own it. The castle was sacked by Cromwell in 1650, but was restored. The Ogilvies fought for the Jacobites and were forfeited, and they did not recover the title of Earl of Airlie until 1796. This may account for the confused numbering of the Earls in the stories.

Cortachy has a fascinating ghost story, a phantom drummer, who is heard drumming, along with other spectral music, when one of the family is about to die.

There are at least three versions of the tale behind the haunting. One is that the drummer failed to warn the family when their castle was about to be attacked. Another that the man was romantically entangled, or so the Earl thought anyway, with the Earl's wife. Either way, the poor man was forced into his own drum and then cast off the battlements. Just before he died, he cursed the family, warning them he would be

Cortachy Castle: *a ghostly drummer was heard several times in the 19th century as a herald of death.*

heard playing as a herald of bad news. A third version is that he was burnt to death here in 1645 after being taken as a hostage.

It is recorded that several times in the 19th century the music was heard, and that they preceded deaths in the family, including three of the Earls and their wives. The drummer is also said to have been heard at Achnacarry, near Fort William, and even abroad in South Africa.

The manifestation was heard before the death of Clementina Graham of Duntrune, the then Countess of Airlie, in 1835. Her husband, David Ogilvie, Earl of Airlie, himself heard the music while at a house in England. News soon reached him that his wife had died because of a premature birth. The Earl remarried three years later to Margaret Bruce of Cowden.

A guest at Cortachy Castle, Miss Margaret Dalrymple, heard the drummer from below her window in 1845, and then her maid, Ann Day, heard it again the following day (although she reported it along with a piper): this time it grew louder until it seemed to fill the whole building. Margaret was not aware of the story, and asked the Earl about the music. He was obviously somewhat perturbed after the death of his first wife, and Margaret left the castle in consternation when she found out about the herald of death.

The Countess of Airlie, Margaret Bruce, then died in the June of 1845 at Brighton during childbirth (she had twins, one of whom also died), which was some months after the manifestation of the phantom drummer. The Countess apparently believed the drummer had come for her, but the many months in between might seem somewhat far in advance to some (several accounts call this within a short time!). It would not have been unusual for women to die in childbirth, particularly with twins, in Victorian times.

Four years later a guest of David, Lord Ogilvie, the son and heir of the Earl of Airlie, is reported to have heard drumming some distance from the castle in August 1849. The guest returned to Cortachy to find that Lord Ogilvy had been called to London because his father had been taken ill. The Earl apparently died on the day after the drumming was heard.

The next Earl, another David Ogilvie, died in 1881 in New Mexico in the USA, and this time two of his relatives heard drumming, although this time at Achnacarry. It was calculated afterwards this was on the day he died.

The drumming also apparently presaged the death of the Countess of Airlie in 1884; and the death of the next Earl (yet another David) in 1900 during fighting in the Boer War in South Africa.

There are no tales that it has been heard since.

E DINBURGH CASTLE has a spectral drummer, sometimes described as being headless. The drums have been heard on several occasions, and were believed by some to herald an attack on the castle. The first time is believed to have been in 1650, before the siege by Cromwell. An account of the drummer comes from 1960, however, and presumably not as a herald to an attack on the castle: the last time Edinburgh Castle was besieged was in 1745.

M OY CASTLE is a plain old tower in a beautiful location on the shore at Lochbuie on Mull. It was held by the MacLaines, an independent branch of the more famous MacLeans: the MacLeans of Duart had their own spectacular stronghold, Duart Castle, further north, guarding the Sound of Mull. Moy Castle is now a ruin, having been replaced by a nearby mansion, Lochbuie House, in the 18th century. This house is still occupied.

On the road from the ferry at Craignure to Iona, which runs through Glen Mor, is a small loch, Loch Squabain. A small island at the north end is said to have been the home of Ewan MacLaine, son and heir of the fifth chief of the MacLaines. Their residence on the isle may have been somewhat basic: the story goes that Ewan's wife, perhaps a daughter of MacDougall of Lorn, was so dissatisfied with their home that she prompted her husband to rise up against his father and secure his inheritance. Ewan raised a small army and marched on his father. The chief of the MacLaines, aided by the MacLeans of Duart, marched to meet him. The year was 1538.

Before the battle Ewan met an old woman (described in one account as being dressed in green) washing bloody shirts, a Bean Nighe, and unfortunately for him one of the shirts was his, meaning that he was going to perish in the following battle. No doubt somewhat disheartened, Ewan went into battle mounted on his horse. During the fighting, he was struck with an axe, which cleanly severed his head. His horse bolted, galloping along Glen Mor for some two miles before coming to rest, Ewan's headless body still upright in the saddle.

From that day on, the headless horseman was reputedly seen, galloping along Glen Mor (or at Lochbuie) on a black horse, whenever one of the MacLaines was ill or about to die. One version has him sometimes accompanied by a black hunting dog, and it is said that on one occasion in 1909, when Murdoch MacLaine died, only the dog was seen. Indeed, Lochbuie House, which stands near the old castle, was reported as being haunted by a black dog, being both seen and heard, at one time.

One story is that Ewan's ghost has been seen three times in recent times, and has also appeared on the island of Coll.

CULZEAN CASTLE is simply one of the most magnificent buildings in Scotland. It stands some miles west of Maybole in Ayrshire, and was built by the architect Robert Adam for the Kennedy Earls of Cassillis, although it incorporates much of an old stronghold. It has a very fine interior, and a suite of rooms within the building were reserved for President Dwight Eisenhower as thanks for his help during World War II. The building stands in a country park of 563 acres, and there are miles of woodland walks, a walled garden and a visitor centre.

Culzean has a ghostly piper, who is reputed to have been searching caves beneath the castle when he disappeared. The pipes are said to be herald the announcement of a marriage, and also to be heard on stormy nights. His apparition is also said to have been seen in the grounds around the castle, both on Piper's Brae and near the ruinous collegiate church. There are other stories of ghosts here.

FYVIE CASTLE has the famous story of the portentous Green Lady, the ghost of Lillias Drummond. But it also has a phantom trumpeter (or drummer, depending on the version), who is heard playing when trouble is to come. The story comes from around the beginning of the 18th century, when the castle was held by the Gordons.

It is believed this is the spirit of Andrew Lammie, who fell head over heels in love with Agnes Smith, daughter of the local miller. Agnes's parents were not enamoured of their daughter's suitor, and Andrew disappeared, either sent off to Edinburgh, or sold into slavery, a disappearance in which the owners of Fyvie may have been involved. A different version has Agnes as the daughter of the keeper of the castle, and the then laird desired Agnes for himself. Agnes, on learning of her lover's disappearance, wept herself into an early grave, or perhaps she was even murdered by her parents. Andrew eventually returned to Scotland, weak and ill, only to find Agnes was dead. Before expiring himself, he cursed the lairds of Fyvie, declaring that he would return and his trumpet would be heard both within the walls and outside the castle.

The story goes that Lammie's trumpet is heard whenever one of the owners are near death. A foreboding apparition was also seen near the castle, but would disappear if anyone approached. There are many small statues around the walls, and one of them is a trumpeter. It is interesting that the Green Lady also is reputed to appear at times of death, and there are also the Weeping Stones of Fyvie.

When the castle was first built, stones are said to have been removed from a local monastery for the building, and some of these fell into a river. Thomas the Rhymer, the famous 13th-century seer, tried to visit Fyvie, but he was refused shelter at the castle. Thomas foretold that unless three lost stones were recovered the castle and lands would never be held by the same family for more than two generations. Only two of the stones were recovered: one is in the Charter Room, while another is said to be built into in the foundations. The stones are said to weep, to ooze, when tragedy is going to strike. The stones do, or did anyway, 'weep'. This can be explained by climactic conditions as at least one of the stones is made of a porous sandstone, which absorbs and exudes water, depending on humidity.

So, if the Green Lady has appeared on the main stair, there is a trumpet playing somewhere, and the Weeping Stones are weeping, it should be safe to say that trouble is on its way.

Formerly known as Sterin, BIRKHALL is an early 18th-century house, with later modifications and extensions, and stands a couple of miles south of Ballater in Royal Deeside. It was built by the Gordons of Abergeldie, and was bought Prince Albert in 1848. It was used by the Elizabeth Bowes Lyon, the Queen Mother, until her death in 2002.

The grounds around Birkhall are haunted by the White Lady of Sterin. The appearance of the phantom heralds a death in the resident family (or the Gordons, anyway): one sighting was reported in 1901, apparently before Queen Victoria died, but it is recorded that this claim is untrustworthy. The apparition was witnessed in 1926, when it was described going through the grounds of Birkhall, before disappearing with a shriek into the River Muick. There is no story given as to the identity of the apparition.

Nothing remains of JEDBURGH CASTLE, once an important Scottish stronghold in the fighting between England and Scotland, the site occupied by a later jail. Malcolm the Maiden (IV) died at the castle in 1165, while Alexander III was married in the Great Hall to the lovely Yolande de Dreux in 1285: she was to be his second wife. At the wedding celebrations, a strange figure was seen, apparently a portent of trouble to come and Alexander's impending demise.

The figure was clad in death clothes (a hooded shroud) and wore a death's mask like a grinning corpse: at first it was thought it was some sort of show as part of the celebrations. One account has one of the king's men wrestling with the figure, or indeed a whole troop of guards, but the apparition then melted away and only the shroud and ghastly mask were left.

This apparition is said to have been witnessed several times, and was always the portent of death.

Alexander desperately needed an heir as his first wife and son had already died. He was at Edinburgh on 19 March 1286 and decided to visit Yolande at Kinghorn in Fife on a stormy night. Although warned about the dangers of crossing the Forth, he managed to be ferried across at Queensferry safely and without mishap. Thinking his problems were over, he set off along the coast for Kinghorn, but in the dark of the stormy night lost his way and fell over the cliffs to his death: a memorial marks the spot at Kinghorn. This was a disaster for Scotland as the kingdom was left without a direct heir, and the problems culminated in invasion by the English, the Wars of Independence, and hundreds of years of fighting.

There are accounts of Yolande's ghost, a Grey Lady, being seen near Kinghorn, where she is believed to be searching still for her husband.

A warning of the death of a king was also ignored by James IV at St Michael's Parish Church, which stands by LINLITHGOW PALACE. Here a blue-robed but bare-headed phantom, carrying a pike, warned James not to invade England. The king ignored the warning and in 1513 raised a massive army. At first his campaign went well, taking several castles, but his forces were met near Flodden by a English army. Although the Scottish army was larger, it was heavily defeated with the loss of many men, both nobles and soldiers, including the King himself.

Situated a couple of miles west along the coast from South Queensferry, HOPETOUN HOUSE is a large and palatial mansion, first built in 1699-1707, and then remodelled by William Adam and his sons from 1721. It was held by the Hope family, who were made Earls of Hopetoun in 1703. The house has fine interiors, paintings and ceramics, as well as 17th-century tapestries.

The phantom of a black-clad man is reputed to have been seen on one of the paths near the house. The apparition is said to be a harbinger of doom or misadventure in the Hope family.

Lying about five miles west of Aberfeldy in Perthshire, TAYMOUTH CASTLE also has a harbinger of tragedy, but this time predicting events in the lives of the Campbells, its former owners, and perhaps anyone resident here. Ghostly footsteps have also reputedly been heard around the building. During its use as a school in the 1980s, it is said

Taymouth Castle: *a harbinger of doom has been reported here, heralding events in the lives of the Campbells.*

that some students were so scared by unexplained happenings that they refused to stay in the castle.

Taymouth is a large early 19th-century mansion, but incorporates some work from an ancient castle, built by the Campbells in the 16th century. The castle was put up for sale in 1997.

S tanding in a remote spot some miles from Biggar, not much survives of WINDGATE HOUSE except vaulted cellars, and it is known locally as The Vaults. It was built in the 16th century by the Baillies of Lamington. It is said that a couple, garbed in Victorian dress, have been seen here when something of import is going to happen to the Baillie family.

ANIMALS

A IRLIE CASTLE, some miles north and east of Alyth in Angus, is home to the Ogilvie Earls of Airlie, who also own Cortachy Castle (see above). Airlie was an old and strong castle, but it was sacked by the Earl of Argyll in 1640, the events recounted in the old ballad *The Bonnie House o' Airlie* (although it may actually have been at Forter Castle). The lady of the house and her young son were turned out of their home, while the castle was looted and destroyed by Argyll's men: Campbell is said to have taken a hand with the destruction himself using a hammer. The castle was replaced by a mansion in 1793, and is still occupied by the Earls of Airlie.

The castle is reputed to be circled by a ram, known as the Doom of Airlie Castle, when misfortune is about to strike or a death to occur in the family.

S ome miles east of South Queensferry, BARNBOUGLE CASTLE stands by the shore of the Firth of Forth in the grounds of Dalmeny House. The castle was rebuilt in 1880, but incorporates some of the ancient stronghold. Barnbougle was held by the Mowbrays of Barnbougle from the 12th century until 1615, when it was sold to the Hamiltons, and then the Primrose Earls of Rosebery, one of whom was Prime Minister from 1894-5.

The ghost story dates from the time of the Crusades. One of the family, Sir Roger Mowbray, left to fight, but his faithful dog was not to accompany him on the journey. It was in such distress, howling and crying, that Sir Roger finally relented, and the dog was taken with him.

One night, some months after they left, a dog was heard to be howling, a noise so loud that it could not be ignored. It was later discovered that Mowbray had been slain about that time. From that day on, howling would be heard and the apparition of a dog seen as a portent of death of the lairds of Barnbougle. Hound Point, near the castle and now a tanker berth, is said to be named after the ghostly dog.

B RODICK CASTLE, which has other apparitions, also has a harbinger of doom. A white deer is reputed to be seen when one of the family (or particularly the head of the Hamiltons) is near death. Its appearance has apparently been recorded on several occasions.

L ocated some miles south-east of Thornhill in Dumfries and Galloway, CLOSEBURN CASTLE was long associated with the Kirkpatrick family, who owned the property from 1232 until 1783. The buildings consists of an ancient keep to which has been added a 19th-century mansion.

The story dates from when the Kirkpatricks owned Closeburn. Two swans nested on a nearby loch, and would return year after year. One of the laird's sons decided to hunt the birds, and shot and killed one with a bow and arrow. From that time on, a swan with red breast feathers would return to Closeburn as a portent of death in the family. The swan has apparently not been seen since the family moved from Closeburn.

N OLTLAND CASTLE, which has a brownie, is also said to have a ghostly dog, the Boky Hound, which would be heard howling when misfortune or death was about to strike the residents. Good news, such as marriages or births, would be heralded by unexplained spectral lights, observed shining from the walls.

P ITCAPLE CASTLE stands some miles north-west of Inverurie in Aberdeenshire, and is a Z-plan tower house, which dates from the 15th century. It was held by the Leslies until 1757, and the discovery of a robin in the building is said to herald a death in the resident family, the first being found when Sir John Leslie of Pitcaple was killed at the Battle of Worcester in 1651. It is recorded that a robin in Pitcaple was found in 1978, and that a member of the family of the current owners died soon afterwards.

Bells, a Birlinn and a Severed Head

ABERGELDIE CASTLE is haunted by the spirit of Kitty Rankine, and the bell is said to toll as a herald of death.

Abergeldie Castle: *believed to be haunted by the ghost of Kitty Rankie: a bell tolls at times of trouble.*

The bell of St Maddan at the church of Coull is said to have tolled by itself when one of the Durwards of COULL CASTLE was about to die. Not much remains of Coull Castle as it was abandoned in the 14th century after being used during the Wars of Independence. It was held by the Durward family, the 'door wards' of the Kings of Scots. Coull lies about two and a half miles north of Aboyne, in Kincardine and Deeside.

Standing near Loch Fyne in Argyll, INVERARAY CASTLE is the seat of the Campbell Dukes of Argyll, and is a large mansion dating from 1743, although remodelled in the following years. It replaced an older castle which stood nearby and of which nothing remains.

A death in the Campbell family was said to be heralded by the appearance of a spectral birlinn, a boat akin to a small galley, reported to have been seen in 1913 on the death of Archibald Campbell, along with a large gathering of ravens. Inveraray is also believed by some to have other ghosts, including a phantom harper, whose music is said to be heard when one of the Dukes of Argyll dies or during his funeral.

Rosslyn Castle and Chapel lie about two miles south of Loanhead in Midlothian. The castle was once a strong and princely residence, but now much of it is ruinous, although one large block has fine plaster ceilings. It was a property of the Sinclairs, who were Earls of Orkney and then Caithness: Sir William Sinclair was one of those who accompanied the heart of Robert the Bruce to Granada in Spain, and was killed there in 1330. The stronghold was sacked by the English in 1544 and 1650, and it is still owned by descendants of the same family. The are stories that a fabulous treasure is buried somewhere in or beneath the castle, in a hidden chamber protected by an enchanted lady who can only be woken by blowing a trumpet. It is also necessary to be standing on the correct step on one of the staircases.

The nearby 15th-century chapel is very famous and has many legends and stories associated with it, not least tales of Templars and even the

Rosslyn Castle: *ghostly flames are said to be seen when one of the owners of the castle is near death.*

Holy Grail. The building has a fabulously carved interior, with the magnificent Apprentice Pillar, and there are more Green Men here than in any other medieval building. Phantoms of ghostly priests have also been reported as recently as the 1990s, one in a black robe, more commonly clad in grey; and the ghost of the apprentice, believed to have been slain by his master, also haunts the building.

Spectral flames, which flare out brightly from the walls but do no damage, are seen at the chapel when one of the Sinclairs is about to die.

Many of the family are buried in a tomb by the crypt of the church, although they did not use coffins until the end of the 17th century, and were interred only in their armour. When the burial place was opened for a new interment, one of the corpses laid out there seemed to be entire, but when the body was touched it fell into dust. The armour and clothing were almost completely intact, except for some fur around a red cap. The crypt has a cold and foreboding atmosphere.

The castle has tales of the apparition of a dog, the Mauthe Dog, and also has a White Lady. A phantom horseman has been seen several times, riding through Roslin Glen.

Strange spectral lights shone out from NOLTLAND CASTLE when something of note was going to happen to the family: births, marriages and deaths.

Noltland Castle: *there are tales of spectral lights, a phantom hound and a brownie.*

One tale also has a crowd of phantom folk appearing in the great hall of CRAIGIEVAR CASTLE when the resident family, presumably the Forbeses, are in trouble.

Standing by the banks of Loch Lomond, two miles north of Alexandria, CAMERON HOUSE is a castellated mansion, dating from 1830, and altered in later years, although it stands on the site of a castle dating from the 14th century. The property was held by the Lennox family, as well as the Charterises, the Dennistouns and the Colquhouns, but passed to the Smolletts (also see Place of Bonhill) in 1763: Tobias Smollett, the famous author, was from the family. They sold the property in 1986, and the building is now used as a hotel.

The freezing over of Loch Lomond was said to predict a death in the resident family. It would have to be especially cold for this to happen, of course, and during such years many people would be expected to perish in such freezing temperatures. This, however, has been shown not to be true: on years the loch did freeze there were no deaths at Cameron House.

This is perhaps one of the strangest ghost stories of all, and concerns William Boyd, fourth Earl of Kilmarnock, whose seat was DEAN CASTLE, just north of Kilmarnock in Ayrshire.

Some time before the start of the Jacobite Rising of 1745-6, servants in the castle were terrified by an apparition of the severed head of William Boyd, rolling about the floor in one of the chambers. When Boyd joined the Rising, he told the Earl of Galloway about the strange vision, who went on to say that this was a portent of disaster and he predicted that Boyd would lose his head in the Rising.

Boyd was an enthusiastic Jacobite, and became a Privy Councillor to Bonnie Prince Charlie and was a colonel in his guard. Although the rebellion was initially successfully with victories at Prestonpans and Falkirk, the Jacobite army eventually retreated into the Highlands. In 1746, they were defeated at Culloden by Government troops led by the Duke of Cumberland. Boyd was captured following the battle, then taken to London where he was tried and executed for treason: by beheading.

The castle and lands were forfeited but were recovered in 1751, before being sold to the Cunninghams, and then the Scotts. The castle had been damaged by fire in 1735, but was restored in the 19th century. It now houses a museum, and stands in a public park.

CHAPTER TWO
Gruagach & Brownies

GRUAGACH

Gruagach (pronounced groo-uguch) has several meanings in present-day Scottish Gaelic: the first being damsel, or a bride's maid of honour; the others, of interest here, are a household goddess and a brownie.

It is certainly possible that there are so many tales of female apparitions in Scotland's castles because at one time every castle or large house had its own 'household goddess'. Various elements of this have survived in ghost stories throughout Scotland, such as Green Ladies, the idea of a herald of death, and a spirit that looks after children or is searching for its own child: it could be suggested that these gruagach have evolved into the Green, and even White and Grey Ladies, with their own more modern 'genesis' story.

Of course, the character and description of gruagach vary, and have evolved over time and place. Sometimes descriptions are very similar to another supernatural entity from Gaelic areas, the glaistig, particularly when it comes to looking after cattle and taking a libation of milk: it may be that the name was interchangeable depending on location and time. Gruagach seem to have evolved into a hybrid of ghost and fairy woman, some with a bit of brownie mixed in. Beliefs, particularly those handed down by word of mouth, are not always easily standardised.

In this book, as this is about castles and great houses, it is the idea of the guardian spirit, whether fairy woman or ghost or brownie, will be explored.

It should be said that gruagach (and glaistig) bear little resemblance to brownies (covered in the next part), despite what is written in many sources. Gruagach are mostly described as female, normal sized, golden haired, and finely dressed, usually in green; brownies are mostly male, small, hairy and roughly dressed. One reason given for the appearance of gruagach were they were ladies of the house who had died in childbirth or been put under a spell: they were then tied to the site and became the 'guardian spirit', warning the family when trouble was to come by weeping, but also heralding good events by smiling and appearing happy. Brownies, so called because of their brown complexion, had no such powers of prophecy; they appear to have been corporeal creatures rather than spirits, although very long lived; they apparently brought luck; and they could leave a place and move to another.

It is not always possible to tell, then, what is meant by a brownie, whether this is a mistranslation of the Gaelic for gruagach (or glaistig) to the nearest English word or concept. The 'brownie' of Skipness is described as golden haired and dressed in green, and this sounds far more like a gruagach. Because some stories do not elaborate as to their appearance, the 'brownies' of Ardincaple, Castle Lachlan, Lochnell and Invergarry (and others) are listed under brownies. Some of the ghost stories described earlier may also fall into this group: it is interesting, for example, that the Green (or White) Lady of Meldrum, the Pink Lady of Ballindalloch and the Grey Lady of Monymusk describe a ghost looking after or being interested in children, one of the many duties attributed to a gruagach. Indeed, many Green or Grey Ladies are described as being friendly, or even helpful, such as at Inverawe House, Balnagown Castle and Menie House.

D UNSTAFFNAGE CASTLE is a strong courtyard castle on a promontory in the Firth of Lorn, some miles north and east of Oban. This is an ancient site, and is associated with the early Kings of Scots. The castle was built by the MacDougalls, but passed to the Campbells after being besieged and captured by Robert the Bruce in 1309. Flora MacDonald was briefly imprisoned here in 1746. There is a more modern house

Dunstaffnage Castle: *the old stronghold has a gruagach, dressed in green, that foretold events in the resident family.*

built within the walls, and the castle is now in the care of Historic Scotland. A fine ruinous chapel, more eerie than the old stronghold, lies in woodland near the castle.

The fortress is said to be haunted by the Ell (or Elle) Maid of Dunstaffnage, a gruagach, a Green Lady, which was also known as the Scannag. When good events are to come to the family, it would shriek with joy, while bad events would be heralded by weeping and sobbing. It was also said to be able to hand on handicraft skills. Other manifestations reputed to have been witnessed in the more modern house are the sounds of heavy footsteps and banging noises from unoccupied areas, which have also been attributed to the gruagach, as well as the whole house shaking as if hit by an earthquake. It is also said that, when the house was still occupied, children of the Campbells would be teased by the Ell Maid when in their beds, this continuing on over several generations.

J ust a few miles north-west of Perth, HUNTINGTOWER is a well preserved and somewhat stark castle, dating from the 15th century. The castle was originally known as Ruthven Castle, after the family who held it. There are 16th-century mural and ceiling paintings, as well as fine decorative beams in the hall.

The family came to particular prominence, and disaster, in the years before 1600. In 1582 William Ruthven, first Earl of Gowrie, kidnapped James VI and then held him against his will at the castle. James eventually escaped, then had the Earl beheaded. More trouble was to follow. At the Ruthven's house in Perth in 1600, James VI and his followers slew the third Earl (who had gained a reputation as a necromancer) and his brother, and their bodies were hanged, drawn and quartered posthumously after they were found guilty of treason. The King claimed that the Ruthvens had attacked him, but the truth will never be known. The incident became known as the Gowrie Conspiracy. The Ruthvens were forfeited, and their name proscribed: the castle was seized and renamed Huntingtower.

Huntingtower and the lands about the castle are reported to have a Green Lady, My Lady Greensleeves, the appearance of which is said to herald bad events, although her apparition is also said to have been of benefit. Ghostly footsteps and rustle of its gown have been reputedly heard, along with laughter or weeping.

The sighting of the apparition of a 'lady in green' was made in one of the small chambers on the second floor by two visitors in the 1970s.

Huntingtower: the castle has stories of a Green Lady, and the ghost was seen by two visitors in the 1970s.

On one occasion the apparition was witnessed by a traveller staying at the castle as a portent of death: the traveller was killed the next day, drowned in the Tay, although not before telling of his experience. On another, a young girl witnessed the ghost: only to find that her lover had died on his way to meet her.

The Green Lady is said to have appeared in a cottage near Huntingtower, where her touch is reputed to have saved the life of a sick boy. In another cottage, the story goes that she scared off thieves trying to rob an old man.

Located in a lovely spot on the east coast of Sleat on Skye, CAISTEAL CAMUS is a ruinous stronghold, which is also known as Knock Castle. It was first built by the MacLeods, but passed to the MacDonalds who came to control this part of the island. It had been abandoned by 1689.

The castle is said to have had a gruagach, a Green Lady. It would appear when something bad was going to happen, when it would be observed weeping; alternatively, if something good was to happen it would laugh and be happy. It was also believed to take a particular care of children. The stronghold also had a glaistig, which was concerned with looking after livestock.

S KIPNESS CASTLE and House stand in a remote and unspoiled location
on the east side of Kintyre, with fine views over to Arran. A fortress
here was probably first built by the MacSweens, but passed to the
MacDonalds, then later to the Campbells and the Grahams. The castle
is an impressive courtyard building with a later tower house, but was
replaced by the nearby mansion: the castle was used as a farmhouse for
some time but is now a well-preserved ruin. It is in the care of Historic
Scotland and open to the public. The mansion is still occupied, and was
built for the Graham family at the end of the 19th century. There is also
a ruinous chapel, dedicated to St Brendan, overlooking Kilbrannan
Sound. The burial ground has many interesting markers, including some
finely carved grave slabs.

Skipness is said to have had a brownie, but it was described as being
dressed in green with golden hair, although as small as a child. This
sounds more like a gruagach, so it appears the Skipness 'creature' is a
hybrid. Like a brownie, however, it is reported to have helped clean and
tidy, even feeding hens, although one story has it beating up a man it
believed was sleeping in the wrong bed. The poor man was so badly
injured that he died a short time later. The gruagach is said to have been
seen in recent times.

O n a former islet on the Hebridean island of Tiree, the site of CASTLE
LOCH HEYLIPOL, built in the 14th century by the MacDonalds, is
now occupied by Island House, which dates from 1748. The building
was altered down the years, but is still occupied. The island had passed
to the MacLarens, and then the Campbells. The castle, and then the
later house, reportedly had a gruagach, described as being a small woman
clad in green. In the 1970s unexplained sounds of moving furniture
were reported, and strange lights have also been witnessed coming from
the house when it is unoccupied.

The house is also said to be haunted by MacLaren, a former factor.

Brownies

Brownies appear to have been supernatural beings, rather than non-corporeal spirits, although they were very long lived. They were called so because of their brown complexion, and were also known as whippitiestourie. The belief in a household deity or hearth spirit was recorded in Roman times, and no doubt predated this. Brownies are said to be a remnant of this belief. A more prosaic suggestion is that in the 17th century there were many fugitives from the troubles of those times. Someone could be sheltered and not too many questions were asked if the stranger was believed to be a 'brownie'. Brownies were found in castles, large houses, farms, mills and on islands – although it is not always clear whether a brownie, gruagach or glaistig is really meant.

Brownies were usually male, were very hairy or shaggy, small in stature, and were rarely seen by members of the household they had adopted. They would undertake a range of household chores, such as threshing corn, cleaning the kitchen or clearing a slipway of stones – on occasion they are even said to have fetched a midwife for an expectant mother. In return they would want nothing, other than sometimes food. Brownies were extremely touchy, however, and could easily be offended, especially if offered new clothing as a present; or their food or milk was not left out for them; or their work was ever criticised; or there was some change of routine. If this was the case, they would leave their castle or large house (or farm or mill) and not return, taking such luck as they had to offer with them. In some cases, they are said to have sought out a more suitable abode with a neighbour.

On Kintyre, some miles south of Tarbert, LARGIE CASTLE was held by a branch of the MacDonalds, but although once an important seat, little now remains of their old stronghold. The building is said to have had a brownie which also frequented CARA HOUSE on the Isle of Cara, which lies just offshore south of Gigha, and was also a property of the family. The building dates from the 18th century, although it was altered in later years and is now derelict.

This brownie busied himself with keeping the properties tidy, helping to bring in the harvest and move barrels, and washing and keeping things in good order. He would slap careless or lazy servants, and is reputed to have shared the MacDonalds' dislike of the Campbells.

The tale of the origin of this brownie is unusual. He is said to be a ghost, a MacDonald who had been murdered by a Campbell. His apparition was seen in the house, particularly in attic rooms, and he was described in 1909 as 'a neat little man, dressed in brown, with a pointed beard'.

C LAYPOTTS CASTLE, which also has a White Lady, was reputedly home to a brownie, which expected a nightly reward of cream for his services. As in the story above, sloppy servants displeased him, and he is said to have beaten a maid with her carelessly discarded stalks for making a mess when chopping vegetables. He eventually left, giving his former home a 'malison' (a curse or malediction).

C RANSHAWS TOWER stands in a picturesque spot near the Whiteadder River in the Lammermuir Hills in the Borders. It is a fine old tower, and incorporates work from the 15th century. It was long held by the Swinton family, before coming to the Douglases at the beginning of the 18th century, and is still occupied.

Cranshaws also has a story of brownie. One of the tasks he chose to do was to gather and thresh corn, which he undertook over several years. A

Cranshaws Tower: *the castle had a brownie.*

foolish servant made the great mistake of complaining that the brownie was not stacking the corn neatly. The brownie was furious, and immediately left Cranshaws, never to return. He also took the corn and threw it into the Whiteadder River some two miles away, at Raven's Crag, saying:

It's no weel mowed! It's no weel mowed!
Then it's ne'er be mowed by me again!
I'll scatter it ower the Raven Stane,
And they'll hae some wark ere it's mowed again!

D OUNE OF ROTHIEMURCHUS stands about two miles south of Aviemore, and the present mansion dates from the 18th century. It was held by the Grant family, who are said to have had a brownie. The story goes that the brownie had, for a long time, given good service. One night he was tidying up in the kitchen, but was making a terrible din with his clattering of pots and pans, preventing the laird from sleeping. The laird shouted in anger at brownie to be quiet. The brownie fell silent, and promptly departed Rothiemurchus for ever.

N othing remains of DOLPHINSTON TOWER, formerly a strong tower some miles south-east of Jedburgh in the Borders, and the site is occupied by a farm. The property was held by the Ainslie family, but passed to the Kerrs in the 16th century. Again the tower reportedly had a brownie, who, as at Cranshaws, also threshed corn, as well as other chores. This brownie was given a new piece of clothing, made of a very course fabric (harden), and was deeply insulted. It left, with the following lines:

Since ye've given me a harden ramp,
Nae mair o' your corn I will tramp.

N OLTLAND CASTLE is one of the few strong castles in the Northern Isles, and stands near Pierowall at the north end of Westray in the Orkney Islands. The present castle was built by the Balfours in the 16th century: Gilbert Balfour was an incomer from the mainland. He had been implicated in the murder of Lord Darnley, husband of Mary, Queen of Scots, and eventually fled Scotland for Sweden, where he was executed for treason. Noltland had been abandoned by 1760. The building is notable for the profusion of gunloops and a fine staircase.

This is another castle believed to have a brownie. It is said the brownie was an old man, well liked by the resident family. He would help clear roads of stones or help beach boats. The brownie only left when the castle was finally deserted.

South and east of the Border burgh of Moffat, Wamphray Tower, also known as Leithenhall, was once an important stronghold, held from 1476 by the Johnstone family.

The story goes that for some 300 years the building had a brownie, which would only ever appear to the laird on his accession to the property. It would then do what was needed around the castle. A new laird took over Wamphray, but on seeing the brownie thought him famished and in rags. Appalled that a servant of his could be so treated, the laird commanded that the brownie was to be given new clothes and plenty of food. But this present of garments so angered the brownie that he up and left, with the lines:

Ca', cuttee, ca'!
A' the luck o' Leithenha'
Gangs wi' me to Bodsbeck Ha'!

Bodsbeck Ha' or Boadsbeck Tower was a tower house about ten miles away, to the north and east of Moffat.

Another version has the brownie going in the opposite direction, from Boadsbeck to Wamphray. The brownie was usually left only plain food, but when the grateful family one day left out cream for him he departed with:

Ca', brownie, ca'!
A' the luck o' Bodbeck's
Awa' to Leithenha'!

Whatever luck the brownie had to offer did neither castle any good: nothing survives of Boadsbeck and there are only some scant remains of Leithenhall.

The following castles, tower houses and large houses are also said to have had brownies (no doubt there are many others):

Ardincaple Castle, a mansion incorporating parts of an old castle, stood near Helensburgh in Dunbartonshire, but was mostly demolished in 1957. It is said to have had a brownie.

An impressive ruin which dates from the 15th century, Castle Lachlan was a property of the MacLachlans. It was abandoned for the new Castle Lachlan, which stands nearby, after being attacked by a

Hanoverian warship. The old castle also had a brownie, although it is not recorded whether it transferred to the new house.

Dunskey Castle, mentioned earlier, is also reputed to have had a brownie.

Nothing now remains of Gorrenberry Tower, a stronghold of the Elliots, which stood about six miles north of Newcastleton in the Borders. It, too, was reputed to have had a brownie.

Another stronghold with a brownie was Invergarry Castle, the ruins of which overlook Loch Oich, some miles south-west of Fort Augustus. The castle was held by the MacDonnels of Clan Ranald, a

Invergarry Castle: the old stronghold also had a brownie.

branch of the MacDonalds, and was visited by Bonnie Prince Charlie on two occasions, after which it was torched and never restored. It was replaced by a mansion nearby, on the site of which stands the Glengarry Castle Hotel.

Lochnell House, six miles north of Oban in Argyll, was built by the Campbells, and incorporates work from an ancient castle. The building was developed down the centuries into a large mansion incorporating different styles, and it is now held by the Earl of Dundonald. It is also thought to have had a brownie, and ghostly music has also been reported.

133

C ULLACHY HOUSE and INCHNACARDOCH, both near Fort Augustus at the south-east end of Loch Ness, and once held by the Frasers, are both said to have had brownies. There was a castle at Cherry Island (also known as Murdoch's Isle), a crannog (an artificial island) at the east end of Loch Ness.

There are also stories of brownies on Colonsay, Tiree, Berneray, South Uist, and Easdale in the Western Isles, and many more in areas as diverse as Glen Moriston, Orkney, Moray, the Carse of Gowrie, Strathspey, Jedburgh and Dalswinton.

SECTION THREE
Ghostly Men

CHAPTER ONE
Black & Bloody Lairds

M ale apparitions and spirits account for just under one third of the stories covered here. As will be seen, many of the men in the following stories are seen (at least by their contemporaries or by those that compiled the stories) as the perpetrators and aggressors rather than the victims. Some of these dark characters come from the Reforming and Covenanting times of the 16th and 17th centuries, but it is likely they would not recognise this view of themselves, having been demonised by their enemies (who were probably no better or worse than them). Both sides in the troubles of the time committed atrocities. Cardinal David Beaton had heretics burned alive, but his own death at the hands of Protestant Reformers, who hung his naked body from a window, was hardly any less brutal.

In the 17th century Scotland was further consumed by religious turmoil and fighting. Many of the problems stemmed from the role of the monarch in the church and who had the right to elect bishops; while many ordinary people wished to follow a Presbyterian form of worship without any interference. This latter group were known as Covenanters and were outlawed by the authorities. They had to hold their worship out of doors at what were known as Conventicles. These people were outlawed and persecuted, and in the Killing Times, many, such as the Wigtown Martyrs, were summarily executed.

Several opponents of the Covenanters were given the title Bloody (or Bluidy), such as:

'Bloody' Bruce (described below under Earlshall);

'Bloody' Mackenzie of Rosehaugh, who is reputed to haunt his mausoleum in Greyfriars Kirkyard in Edinburgh, as well as the burial ground and several pubs (busy fellow) – indeed, he is blamed even for attacking visitors to the kirkyard, leaving bloody scratches on unexposed areas of skin. The mausoleum was also recently despoiled, a tramp urinated in it, then two youths broke into a coffin and made off with a severed head: they were said to have been playing with it in the burial ground. The two were charged with and found guilty of violating a sepulchre (the first time such as prosecution has been brought in more than 100 years): it would be pleasant to think of his vengeful ghost exacting some suitable revenge;

'Bloody' Clavers or 'Bonnie Dundee', John Graham of Claverhouse who was killed at Killiecrankie in 1689. Claverhouse, it was said, was a demon and could only be killed by a silver bullet;

Sir Tam Dalyell (Bloody Tam) of The Binns was another fellow with a fearsome reputation (musket balls would just bounce off him) and was reputed to have played cards with the Devil.

Sir Robert Grierson of Lagg was said to make water fizz and boil when he put his feet in it, and to have been taken off to hell by a black chariot and horses; a similar story is told about William Douglas, Duke of Queensberry. Grierson's career is discussed in more detail below (under Lagg Tower). In fact, many of the accounts featuring male ghosts originate from the 17th century.

These were violent times, of course, and there were bloody acts by both sides. Although certainly far from a saint himself (he was also reputed to have demonic powers), Archbishop Sharp was still cruelly murdered at Magus Moor in 1679 by the same men who would demonise Dalziel, Bruce, Grierson, Douglas and Claverhouse. Sharp, in the company of his daughter, was dragged from his coach and shot, stabbed and beaten. Prisoners were summarily executed by both sides: camp followers of the Marquis of Montrose, many of them Irish, most of them women and children, were taken out and clubbed to death or shot in cold blood, some at Newark Castle.

And then there are men seen as being too evil to rest, with a list of crimes as long as the road to hell, at least in tales, such as Alexander Stewart, the Wolf of Badenoch, and Earl Beardie, the fourth Earl of Crawford. Perhaps in life they were thought to be possessed by evil spirits, which lived on when their mortal bodies had perished; perhaps it is in human nature to believe someone so strong and wicked cannot be stopped by simple mortality. The evil that men do lives on.

It is interesting to note the large number of male ghost stories which involve the Devil and witchcraft compared to those about women. The vast majority of witchcraft prosecutions, of course, were made against women (something like five to one), but this is not reflected in the tales.

As discussed above, some were certainly men demonised by their opponents, and no doubt they at least believed themselves as good and Godly as their contemporaries. The stories do demonstrate the inequality in power between men and women in medieval and early modern Scotland. Powerful male characters had their perceived wickedness and evil reputation enhanced by being in league with the most powerful evil entity available, the Devil. Women were not in positions of power so there are no corresponding stories.

A further twist can be added. James Pringle, the heir of Buckholm, was involved as a Commissioner in several accusations of witchcraft in 1629-30, while Andrew Kerr of Littledean was a Commissioner for a case in 1662. It would be ironic if these are the two characters who haunt Buckholm and Littledean respectively, one (according to the stories) a sadistic torturer pursued by phantom hounds, the other strangled by the severed arm of his witch lover.

Finally there are tortured souls, driven by insanity or a moment of madness to commit some heinous act with which they then tormented themselves.

Evil Lairds

A selection of ghost stories about some of the more unsavoury or infamous of Scotland's noble men and landowners, who (reputedly) came to a sticky end. It should be said that this labelling of them as evil was often done by their enemies, and embellishment may have exaggerated their wickedness.

HERMITAGE CASTLE is located in a windswept and somewhat desolate position, some miles north of Newcastleton and not far from the English border. It is a strong and imposing ruin, ranged around a small courtyard, and dates from the 13th century. The first castle was built by the De Soulis family, and the fortress was subsequently held by the Douglases, and the Hepburn Earls of Bothwell (one of whom was the husband of Mary, Queen of Scots). It then passed to the Stewarts and the Scotts (the fifth Duke of Buccleuch stabilised and repaired the walls), and is now in the care of Historic Scotland. It has several ghost stories, the blackest certainly about one of the former owners, believed to be William de Soulis, who lived around the beginning of the 14th century (or perhaps his father, Sir Nicholas, King's Butler).

William de Soulis gained an evil reputation, and he was believed to be a warlock who practised all sorts of black magic, having been instructed

Hermitage Castle: *the foreboding ruin has several ghost stories, not least the tale of Evil Lord Soulis.*

by the famous wizard Sir Michael Scott in the Eildon Hills. De Soulis was a huge man, clad in black, who was always seem with his familiar, Robin Redcap, believed to be his link to the Devil. Children began to disappear from the villages and settlements around Hermitage, and rumour had it that they were being kidnapped and killed, and their body parts and blood used in his ever more powerful spells and sorcery. Indeed, Robin Redcap was so called because of the blood which always bedaubed its head.

De Soulis became very powerful, and could not be harmed by hanging or by being smote by iron weapons or bound by manacles (iron was normally seen as some protection against demons, as well as elves and fairies). A mighty champion, the Cout o' Kielder, a giant who had magic armour which protected him from blows by De Soulis, attacked the evil laird. But such was Soulis's cunning that the Cout was slain by being drowned in the Hermitage Water. The Cout's reputed grave is located a short way from the castle, near the ruins of the chapel.

The local people became more and more despairing, and consulted Thomas the Rhymer, the famous seer. He told them that he knew of a way they could get rid of their tormentor. The locals gathered together and surprised the garrison of the castle, seizing De Soulis, and dragging him off to a nearby stone circle, Nine Stane Rig, which survives in woodland about one and a half miles north-east of the castle. The sorcerer had been bound with ropes of sand and was wrapped in lead. He was then boiled in a cauldron filled with the molten metal until he was dead, indeed until his flesh had been dissolved and his bones had been completely melted.

One version has the ghost of De Soulis returning every seven years to a subterranean vault where he used to sacrifice his victims; and where there is a great treasure buried. It is also said that a walled-up room was discovered, and in it was found some human bones, a rusty sword and some chaff. This had been linked to the starving of Sir Alexander Ramsay, although it seems unlikely he would be imprisoned with his sword.

There is, of course, a historic William de Soulis, but he was forfeited for treason in 1320 and imprisoned in Dumbarton Castle. He had been accused of attempting to murder and replace Robert the Bruce as de Soulis, himself, had a claim to the throne of Scots.

The terrifying apparition of De Soulis has been seen at the castle and the area around the old fortress. Ghostly cries and screams of agony have also been heard, thought to be from his many victims. Indeed, the ruins of Hermitage are reputed to have sunk into the ground as they could not support the burden of wickedness that was perpetrated there.

Hermitage is also haunted by a White Lady, possibly the spirit of Mary, Queen of Scots, and the ghost of Sir Alexander Ramsay of Dalhousie.

B ALNAGOWN CASTLE is haunted by a cruel and despicable character, Black Andrew Munro, as well as a Grey Lady. Black Andrew was a man of dark repute in the middle of the 16th century, famed for rapine and murder, and he was particularly unpleasant to women: one tale is that he made his female workers thresh corn completely naked, which would have been excruciatingly painful.

The Rosses (hardly a family noted for their lawful endeavours) eventually tired of the growing list of misdeeds by their neighbour, seized him, brought him to Balnagown, and hanged him from one of the windows. His body was left dangling and kicking by one of the bedrooms off the Red Corridor of the castle.

His ghost then began to haunt the castle, and was most often witnessed in the Red Corridor. Heavy footsteps are said to have been heard coming from the area around midnight; and they have been witnessed on several occasions by different people, including in the 20th century. The ghost also reputedly makes itself known to women who visit the castle, perhaps wishing to torment new victims if only he could.

Three skeletons are supposedly hidden within the walls of the building: the Scottish princess; a man who perished from plague; and a member of the Ross family, walled up in one of the chambers.

INVERQUHARITY CASTLE, north-east of Kirriemuir in Angus, is a restored L-plan tower house of the Ogilvies, dating from the 15th century. One of the family, Alexander, was captured after the Battle of Philiphaugh when fighting for the Marquis of Montrose, and was beheaded in Glasgow. The castle is still occupied, after being rebuilt in the 1960s.

One story is that for many years the castle was haunted by the spirit of a Sir John Ogilvie. The disturbances were so persistent and troubling that Inverquharity was abandoned for a while.

Ogilvie is said to have been a particularly horrible man. The local miller, John White, had an attractive daughter, and Ogilvie desired her above all else. The girl spurned his advances, and her family would have nothing to do with the wicked laird. So Ogilvie had her father hanged, then forced himself on the poor lass, and then also on her unfortunate mother. The local priest was appalled by these terrible acts, and called down vengeance upon Ogilvie, who was then struck down dead. His bogle was not so easily got rid off, however, and returned to cause mayhem in his old home.

GLAMIS CASTLE is often described as one of the most haunted castles in Britain but, as can be seen, it is far from alone in having several ghost stories. It is also not clear how many of the Glamis ghostly tales have any foundation. Two that certainly do are the Grey Lady of Glamis, Lady Janet Douglas; but an equally famous story concerns Alexander Lindsay, fourth Earl of Crawford, known as Earl Beardie and the Tiger Earl.

Crawford was certainly a ruthless and cruel fellow, and his mother no less so: she had suffocated her own brother so that Alexander would inherit the title. Crawford was defeated at the Battle of Brechin in 1452, although later pardoned by James II. Before the fighting, a minstrel had predicted the battle would be lost, and Crawford had the poor fellow impaled on hooks for his trouble: the minstrel would have done better to have kept quiet. Jock Barefoot (who is said to haunt Crawford's now ruinous castle at Finavon) cut a walking staff from the Covin Tree near Finavon, and Crawford had him hanged by the neck as a result.

The story goes that Crawford and the laird of Glamis, one of the Lyon family, probably Patrick, first Lord Glamis, often played cards with their cronies. Their games went on all night, and even into a Sunday: it was bad enough to play cards at any time, but this was, of course, absolutely prohibited on the Sabbath. Alternatively, no Christian gentleman could be found to play on a Sunday. One Saturday night a stranger appeared at the castle and was invited to join the game, which then strayed into the wee hours of Sunday morning.

This dark figure turned out to be the Devil. A curious servant who tried to see what was happening in the chamber, was struck blind when he looked through the keyhole. Crawford was then doomed to play cards until the Day of Judgement.

The chamber in which the game was played then suffered from numerous manifestations. So plagued had it become that it was sealed and no longer used. And so it is said to remain. A count of windows on one side of the building shows that one is unaccounted for, and this is purported to be the haunted chamber.

There have also been sightings of his apparition in the building, described as a large mailed figure in one account; as a huge old man with a long flowing beard in another; and wearing a long dark coat in a third, when the spectre disappeared through a wall. These could, of course, be different ghosts.

An alternative character to Earl Beardie has been suggested: the first Lord Glamis, Patrick Lyon, who was given the title in 1445, a contemporary of Lindsay. He died in 1459. The story itself may be based on an event in 1578 when the eighth Lord Glamis, who was a Chancellor of Scotland and a very rich man, was killed by a follower of the Lindsay family, although the death was an accident. This version records that the two men had been playing cards, and Lyon had been cheating: there is, of course, no historical evidence for this tale.

There are many other stories of bogles. Two more can also be added here: a butler who hanged himself, and a wee black lad, a page to the family in the 18th century.

LORDSCAIRNIE CASTLE is also haunted by Crawford. The ruinous but imposing stronghold stands some miles north of Cupar in Fife, and came to the Lindsay Earls of Crawford about 1350. It was formerly on an island in a loch, but this was drained about 1803.

The ghost of Crawford is said to appear in the castle at Hogmanay, when he is also seen playing cards with the Devil.

The gaunt ruins of RUTHVEN BARRACKS stand near the Highland village of Kingussie in Strathspey. Although the current buildings date from its use as a Hanoverian outpost, this was the site of an ancient castle. The old stronghold was held by the Comyns, then Alexander Stewart, better known as the Wolf of Badenoch. The castle later passed to the

Gordons, but was demolished in 1718 to make way for a barracks. The buildings were torched following the Battle of Culloden in 1746 and never restored.

Alexander Stewart was the fourth son of King Robert II, and was given land in Badenoch in 1371. He added to his possessions by forcing the widowed Countess of Ross, who was heiress in her own right, to marry him, thereby gaining her title and lands (also see Kindrochit Castle). For this and other dastardly deeds, he was excommunicated by the Bishop of Moray. Stewart burned the town of Forres in retaliation, then sacked Elgin and torched the cathedral there, which was the seat of the Bishop (also see Spynie Palace). Stewart gained a pretty impressive reputation as the Wolf of Badenoch, although how much of it was warranted will never be known for sure: one rumour was that he practised witchcraft. What is known is that he died at the relatively ripe age of about 62, and he was buried in Dunkeld Cathedral, where his fine stone effigy and tomb survive.

It is said that around 1406 Stewart was at Ruthven with his men. A dark stranger, dressed from head to toe in black, was admitted, and challenged the Wolf to a game of chess. Stewart was never a man to refuse a challenge, and readily agreed to a deadly wager, one where his soul would be forfeit if he lost. Needless to say, the stranger was the Devil, and in the morning there was nobody left alive in the stronghold.

The phantoms of Stewart and his men are said to still re-enact the fateful match and to haunt the site.

D
UNTULM CASTLE is reputedly one of the most haunted castles in Scotland. Ghosts include the one-eyed Margaret MacLeod of Dunvegan and a nursemaid who dropped her charge from one of the windows. It is also said to have two male ghosts.

One tale is that the eighth Chief, Donald Gorm MacDonald, haunts the remains of the castle. He was a boisterous and wild character, and his feasting with spectral companions is still reputed to be heard at times.

Another ghost story dates from the turn of the 17th century. Hugh MacDonald, who built his own stronghold, Caisteal Uisdean, down the coast, some miles south of Uig on Skye, was reputedly a wicked fellow. He was outlawed for piracy, having been involved in attacks on fisherman from as far away as Fife. For this he was pardoned and, perhaps perversely, made Steward of Trotternish.

Hugh then decided to raise himself to chief by murdering his kin. He planned to lure his relatives to his own castle, and there, during a feast,

Duntulm Castle: *did the many ghosts drive the MacDonalds to build a new house on a different site?*

have them all slain. His plotting was not very efficient, and the plan was discovered when he mixed up letters, and sent the wrong message, the one intended for the assassins, to his family at Duntulm. He fled from Skye across to North Uist, where he sheltered at Dun an Sticar. This is an old Iron Age stronghold, the interesting ruins of which, along with its stone causeways, survive. He was besieged here, and eventually captured and taken back to Duntulm.

Here he was imprisoned in a dark pit. Food was brought to him, along with a jug. Hugh consumed the salted beef hungrily, but then found the jug was empty. When the pit was finally opened, Hugh was dead, mad with thirst: he is said to have destroyed the jug with his teeth.

His skull and thigh bones are said to have been kept on show in the local parish church (little of which now remains) at Kilmuir, until they were finally buried in 1847. The burial ground survives, and Flora MacDonald is also interred there.

Hugh's ghost then troubled Duntulm, and ghostly groans, screams and cries were often heard coming from the prison where he died.

Hugh MacDonald is not the only person said to have died in this horrible manner. John Sinclair, Master of Caithness (heir to the earldom) was imprisoned at Girnigoe Castle in Caithness in 1571. His crime had been to try to reconcile his own family with the Sinclairs' long-term enemies, the Earls of Sutherland. The story goes that he was held for seven years, before also being fed on salted beef, and then denied any water. He also died raving and mad with thirst.

Lying on Orwell Road in Edinburgh, DALRY HOUSE dates from 1661, and was the country home of the Chiesly family. The white-washed building has hexagonal stair turrets, and is now used as an old people's day centre.

The house has a fascinating ghost story. John Chiesly was involved in a messy divorce settlement with his wife, having some 11 children to support. But Sir George Lockhart of Carnwath, Lord President of the Court of Session, found against Chiesly, awarding his wife a large sum of money. Chiesly was furious, swore revenge, and in 1689 shot and killed Lockhart: a crime for which he was captured, tried and sentenced to death. Before he was hanged, he was tortured and his arm was hacked off, then Chiesly died swinging from the gallows. The arm was stuck on a spike at the West Port, one of the gates into the city.

Strangely, his corpse was cut down and taken from the gallows, although nobody knows by whom – or why. His phantom then appeared, screaming and weeping. It is said to have been witnessed often, and became known as Johnny One Arm.

When Dalry House was being renovated in 1965, the skeleton of a one-armed man was reportedly found, under a hearth stone in one of the chambers of the house. When the remains were buried, the hauntings are believed to have ceased.

Standing in a picturesque location above the River Tyne, some two miles east of the Midlothian town of Gorebridge, CRICHTON CASTLE is a magnificent ruin, and dates from the 14th century. The castle is arranged around an internal courtyard, and was extensively remodelled at the end of the 16th century. One block has a fine Renaissance arcaded and diamond-faced facade.

The castle was built by the Crichtons, but when they were forfeited for treason in 1448, passed to the Hepburns. One of them was James Hepburn, fourth Earl of Bothwell, and the third husband of Mary, Queen of Scots; Mary was present at a wedding here in 1562. Crichton then passed to Francis Stewart, who added the Renaissance block, but he eventually had to flee abroad when he fell out of favour with James VI. The castle is now in the care of Historic Scotland.

There are also the ruins of a two-storey stable block outside the castle. This building is haunted by the spirit of Sir William Crichton, Chancellor of Scotland. On the anniversary of his death, his phantom is seen leaving the stables and entering the castle tower.

Crichton was a very important man during the reign of James II in the

Crichton Castle: *the stables are haunted by the ghost of Sir William Crichton; there is also a ghostly horseman.*

15th century. The Black Douglas family had become very powerful, and Crichton wanted to reduce their standing, taking somewhat direct means. In 1440, he invited the young sixth Earl of Douglas and his brother to Crichton, where they were lavishly entertained, and they proceeded to Edinburgh Castle. At a dinner with James II (who was friends with the young Earl), and on the production of a black boar's head, the two young Douglases were set upon and stabbed to death. The event is known as the Black Dinner. Whether Crichton felt any guilt for this treacherous act is not recorded, but he did found the nearby collegiate church, a fine sturdy building near the castle, so that prayers might be said for his soul in perpetuity. Crichton and Edinburgh Castles were sacked by the Douglases after the murders.

The power of the Black Douglases was not broken, however, until 1455 and the Battle of Arkinholm. Three years earlier James II had murdered the eighth Earl of Douglas at Stirling Castle: he then had the corpse carelessly thrown out of a window. James had promised the Earl safe conduct. It is not difficult to see from whom he learned his diplomatic skills.

The DREADNOUGHT HOTEL in Callander is said to be haunted by the ghost of Francis MacNab, 16th Chief, who had a building constructed here in 1802. He was the chief of the MacNabs, and there are stories which cast him as an unpleasant character. He died in 1818, and most of the family property had to be sold two years later. There are other ghost stories here, possibly as a result of deeds by MacNab.

145

ENEMIES OF GOD

This selection of tales covers the Covenanting period of the second half of
the 17th century. This was a time of major instability and upheaval,
both social and religious, and there were periods of warfare, invasion, famine
and even plague. This century was also noted for its witchcraft prosecutions
and panics, and has been characterised as a century of fear. Two of the
stories (Littledean and Penkaet) mention threads being used in spells: this
was a common belief, both in charming (white magic) and maleficium
(black magic). Science in its early manifestations (in forms such as natural
magic, alchemy and astrology) was also feared, which perhaps explains the
last two tales (Skene and Kinnaird).

BUCKHOLM TOWER has a tale of a wicked laird. The old tower is now
a ruin, and stands on the west side of Buckholm Hill, near Galashiels
in the Borders. It was long a property of the Pringles, who were convicted
of treason in 1547 and the tower torched. It was restored, but the roof
has now fallen in. The vaulted basement is said to have rusty old meat
hooks hanging from the stone ceiling, which ooze a kind of red fluid
like blood.

One of the Pringle lairds was feared as a rabid persecutor of Covenanters,
and he would spend his time and energy trying to locate Conventicles
and capture or kill those attending them. He also wished to learn of the
location of the preachers organising the meetings. When he was not out
hunting the locals, which he often did with huge dogs, he spent his time
drinking, abusing his servants and tenants, and so tormenting his wife
and son that they fled and went into hiding.

Andrew Bruce of Earlshall (see Earlshall) arrived one day at Buckholm
with the news that Alexander Peden, a preacher and one of the leaders
of the Covenanters, was in the area. Bruce and Pringle, with a force of
dragoons, attempted to surprise a Conventicle on Ladhope Moor. The
Covenanters had sentries and all of them escaped except for an old man
and his son, who Pringle found using his fearsome dogs. The old man
was badly wounded, but Pringle had the two prisoners carried off to
Buckholm, where he imprisoned them in one of the vaults. Here he
interrogated them for information, or just tortured them for fun, but
when they refused to talk he had them impaled on the meat hooks by
their jaws. They both died in great agony. Pringle declared that swine
should be treated like swine, having hung them there like a side of pork.

The wife of one of his victims, discovering that her husband had been
tortured to death, was distraught and brought down a terrible curse on

Pringle, predicting that he would be hunted by hell hounds for all of eternity. For the rest of his life he is then said to have been in great fear, awaiting that awful doom. He became more and more terrified until eventually he died, a dreadful expression etched into his face.

From then on, or so the story goes, on the anniversary of his death, and at other times as well, his spirit is seen near the tower, being hunted down by a pack of ravening dogs. Screams and cries of pain are also heard, coming from the basement chamber.

S ome six miles west of Kelso and by the banks of the River Tweed, LITTLEDEAN TOWER is a ruinous Border stronghold, consisting of a rectangular block and a D-shaped tower. It was built by the Kerrs, and was burnt in 1544 by the English, although it was later restored.

It is said to have been the home of a notorious Kerr laird, known as the Deil of Littledean, another man who hunted and persecuted Covenanters. The story goes that he spent his time, when not pursuing those attending Conventicles, drinking and brawling with others of wicked disposition until Margaret, his wife and a gentle and pious creature, despaired: for some reason her name is recorded, while his has been lost.

Following a bitter argument with his wife, his last retort being: 'I would rather be wedded to a fiend from hell than you', he rode out into a black night. It began to pour with rain and he found a hovel in a clearing where he hoped he could shelter. Here he met a rather fetching young woman at a spinning wheel. The girl snapped a thread in his face, no doubt casting a spell over him. The laird fled at that time, but could not forget the beautiful stranger. He searched high and low for her. One day he came upon her and they started a passionate affair, which lasted many weeks. Kerr even gave the girl a ring his wife Margaret had formerly worn.

The frolicking couple were not very discreet, and soon rumours spread about the laird's new mistress, even reaching the ears of his wife. But Margaret could not find out who the woman was.

Then one night the laird returned home in a terrible state, saying that he had been pursued by devils disguised as a party of hares. Drool coming from their mouths, the hares had darted around him and started launching themselves at the terrified laird. Drawing his sword, he had slashed at them, and severed one of their paws, at which point they had abandoned the chase.

The paw had become trapped in his pistol holder, but when he got back to the tower, he found the hare's paw had turned into a woman's arm, and on one of the fingers was Margaret's ring. Even more horrifying, the hand still twitched.

Kerr tried to get rid of the arm, stabbing it with his sword. He rushed from the tower and rode off, and when far enough away threw the arm into a local burn. On the way home, and near where he had first met his lover, he came across an evil old crone, doubled up in pain, with a stump for one of her arms, no doubt gushing blood. With utter dread, the laird realised this was his lover in her real guise. In great pain and near death, the old woman cursed him, telling him that he would never be free of her severed limb. Kerr struggled back to Littledean, to find that his wife had done the sensible thing and deserted him.

Then to his horror, he found something wriggling in his pocket, and again found the severed arm. He ran to a window and threw it out, shutting and barring the windows and doors. Eventually he retired to bed, first making sure everything was secure. But he found the arm beneath his pillow. This time threw it onto the fire, and watched it burn. But he was determined not to sleep, and managed to stay awake until the dawn.

It the late morning the Deil of Littledean had still not appeared for breakfast. On investigation, his servants found him dead, sprawled across his bed. The furniture was smashed as if a terrible fight had happened. There were marks around Kerr's neck as if he had been strangled.

On some nights, especially when it is stormy, a phantom horseman is seen galloping madly through the fields and woods near the tower, pursued by some unseen foe.

The story does not make it clear which Kerr of Littledean features, but it is interesting to note that Andrew Kerr of Littledean is recorded as being a Commissioner involved in a witchcraft investigations against a Bessie Morrison and a Grizel Murray in 1662.

Penkaet Castle stands about one mile from Pencaitland in East Lothian, and was held by the Lauder family from 1685 until 1922. The building dates from the 16th century, although it has been altered down the years.

One of the stories associated with Penkaet Castle is that it is haunted by the spirit of Alexander Hamilton. The tale goes that Hamilton was a beggar, but he was refused any charity at the castle and roughly ejected from the grounds. As he was leaving, he became very angry and cursed the family by binding the bars of the castle gate with a blue thread, a spell with murderous intent. Soon afterwards, the lady of the house and her eldest daughter both died from a sudden illness. Hamilton was eventually imprisoned in Edinburgh, where he was tried for witchcraft and found guilty, then executed. He had apparently bragged about causing their deaths.

This appears to be Alexander Hamilton (or Hammiltoun), who was executed in 1630. His was a notorious case, involving an accusation by him against the wife of Sir George Home of Manderston and many others. Hamilton eventually retracted his statement against Home's wife, although others were loss fortunate. Hamilton confessed to meeting the Devil in many guises, including a man dressed in black or grey and several types of animals: a cat, dog, rook and a foal. He also tried to kill Home and his household by leaving a dead bird in his barn, which only killed several horses. Hamilton was also a healer, although he said that he got his power from the Devil. It does seem that at the trial in Edinburgh, the authorities were concerned that he had been pressurised into making the confessions. Hamilton, however, was found guilty, and was strangled and then burned at Castle Hill in Edinburgh.

Hamilton's spectre has been seen near Penkaet Castle.

The castle has several other eerie tales, including an investigation into the different hauntings.

L ying just east of Leuchars in Fife, EARLSHALL is an impressive courtyard castle, which dates from the middle of the 16th century. The hall is a fine panelled chamber, and the second-floor gallery retains a tempera-painted ceiling of 1602. The castle was a property of the Bruces, and is still occupied although it has passed from the family.

The castle is haunted by the ghost of Sir Andrew Bruce, known as the 'Bloody' Bruce. Bruce hunted down Richard Cameron, who was the leader of a group of radical Covenanters famed for their repudiation of the King, known as the Cameronians. Bruce caught up with Cameron at Airds Moss in Ayrshire in 1680, and slew him and his followers. Cameron's head was chopped off, as were his hands, and Bruce took these back to Edinburgh, where his body parts were tried for treason.

Bruce's apparition has been seen several times at Earlshall, and heavy footsteps heard on one of the turnpike stairs when nobody is – apparently – about. Other manifestations in the castle include objects being moved around, and a bed appearing as if it had been slept in even when it had not been used.

THE BINNS, some miles from Linlithgow in West Lothian, is a fine mansion dating from the 17th century, but stands on the site of an old castle. It was originally a property of the Livingstone family, but was sold to the Dalyells in 1612. The house in now in the care of The National Trust for Scotland, is open to the public, and lies in grounds with a fine woodland walk.

The most famous member of the family was Sir Tam Dalyell, who was born at the turn of the 18th century. He was a staunch royalist, and he fought and was captured at the Battle of Worcester in 1651. Tam was imprisoned in the Tower of London, but managed to escape and, when the Royalist cause looked doomed, joined the Tsar's Cossacks in Russia. He gained a notorious reputation when he is said to have roasted prisoners in Russia, and he is also said to have introduced thumbscrews to Scotland. After the Restoration of Charles II, he became commander of forces in Scotland from 1666 to 1685. Tam led the forces that defeated the Covenanters at the Battle of Rullion Green: musket balls aimed at Tam are reputed to have bounced off him without harming him.

Whatever the truth behind his reputation, he, like many of his contemporary 'bloody' men, lived to a good age, dying in 1685 at the age of about 85.

An apparition of Tam has been witnessed at The Binns, both in the house and the grounds. The phantom is sometimes described as riding a white horse up to the entrance to the house. A famous story is that Tam played cards with the Devil, but Tam being Tam he actually won. The Devil was furious that he had been beaten by a mere mortal, and threw the heavy marble table, on which they had been playing, at Tam's head. Tam ducked and the table sailed through a window of the house into the Sergeant's Pond. When the water was low in the Pond, following a period of drought, the marble table was found (in about 1885, some 200 years after Dalyell's death). The cards, goblet, spoon and table, reported to have been used in the game, are preserved in the house. His boots, too, can be seen here, although they are said to vanish when his ghost is riding around the grounds.

There is also another story about a tunnel, this time running from The Binns to Blackness Castle, some miles along the coast.

LAGG TOWER is about seven miles south-east of Moniaive, and consists of a ruinous 16th-century tower house. It was a property of the Griersons of Lagg from 1408.

This was the home of Sir Robert Grierson, who became notorious for persecuting Covenanters. In 1685 he surprised a Conventicle, slew some of the worshippers (reputedly he put his victims in a spiked barrel and rolled them down a hill), and then denied them a Christian burial: a memorial marks the place where this happened. Grierson went on to be a Jacobite, for which he was fined and imprisoned. He died in 1733, at Dumfries, well into his 70s, and was buried in the cemetery of the old parish church at Lagg. By then he was extremely fat, and it was said that part of the wall in the house in Dumfries had to be demolished to remove his corpse from the building.

One account records that on the night he died, a ship in the Solway Firth is said to have seen a chariot, drawn by six horses and surrounded by black clouds shot through with lightning and booming thunder, accompanying Grierson's soul to hell. It was also said that when he placed his feet into cold water (he had gout), the water would boil and fume with 'hellish' heat. His spit could burn holes where it landed, and wine would turn to congealed blood when given to him.

Grierson had a pet monkey, which was killed by his servants on his death, and the animal haunts Rockhall.

A similar tale of a phantom black carriage seen by a ship at sea concerns William Douglas, Duke of Queensberry, who was responsible for the building of DRUMLANRIG CASTLE. Douglas was also notorious for his treatment of Covenanters. A former tenant claimed that, while in Sicily, he had seen a black coach bearing Douglas towards the top of a volcano. Just to confirm the identity, an evil voice was heard to say: 'Open to the Duke of Queensberry'. The tenant then claimed that he had seen the coach and its occupant just shortly after Douglas died.

This is probably not one of the most believable of tales.

E DINBURGH CASTLE, mentioned elsewhere, has another strange story. Colin Lindsay, Lord Balcarres, was in charge of Jacobite prisoners held at the fortress, and was disturbed to find John Graham of Claverhouse, Bonnie Dundee, lying in his bed. The apparition slowly faded and then disappeared. Balcarres was probably perturbed, although somewhat more so when news came the next day that, although the Jacobites had been victorious at the Battle of Killiecrankie, Claverhouse had been killed. Presumably this would have been by a silver musket ball (his enemies had dubbed him a demon). One account states that Claverhouse's spectral corpse is still sometimes seen at the castle.

According to some accounts, Claverhouse, himself, was visited three times the night before the battle by the phantom of John Brown of Priesthill, its head gushing blood, who is said to have cried: 'Remember Brown of Priesthill!' Hard to believe Claverhouse would have forgotten him after such a manifestation.

Some four years earlier, Brown had been executed by Claverhouse because he was a Covenanter (and had arms stored in his house). As stated above, Claverhouse was mortally wounded with a musket ball at the battle; and, according to one account, was finished off by a looter of the dead.

KINNAIRD CASTLE is a large and impressive mansion, mostly dating from the 19th century, but incorporating work from the 15th century or earlier. It was long a property of the Carnegies, and is still occupied by the Earls of Southesk. The old castle was torched by the Lindsays following the Battle of Brechin in 1452, as the Carnegies had been on the opposing side.

James Carnegie, the second Earl of Southesk, was a learned man, and is believed to have spent much time in Padua. He died in 1669, and the tale went that while on the Continent he had learned much black magic (the Devil was said to be one of the lecturers at Padua), even losing his shadow to Satan. Carnegie is said to have always walked in the shade so that nobody would notice.

It is not clear what Carnegie actually did to merit this reputation, but on his death a black coach, with black horses, is reported to have taken his corpse from the house and straight to hell.

Kinnaird Castle: *the story goes that James Carnegie was summoned to hell by a black coach and horses.*

S KENE HOUSE, near Westhill in Aberdeenshire, has a very similar story. The house includes an old castle in the large castellated mansion. As the name suggests, it was a property of the Skene family, who held it from 1318 until 1827. The house is still lived in.

Alexander Skene of Skene also studied on the Continent, and was reputedly a warlock, getting up to all sorts of black mischief, including the defiling of graves and also losing his shadow. He was said to have had four familiars, a crow, magpie, jackdaw and hawk, and he would procure them the unbaptised corpses of new-born babies on which to feast.

When he died in 1724, a black carriage, carrying him and the Devil, is said to have whisked him away. It is reputed to be seen every midnight on New Year's Eve, speeding across the Loch of Skene, only to sink as it approaches the bank.

REFORMATION DEVILS

*A*s was to happen to those men who opposed the Covenanters, enemies of the Reformation were also vilified. Cardinal David Beaton was certainly a controversial figure, and was as much (if not more so) a politician as a churchman. Whether he deserved a brutal death at the hands of other men of God is debatable. He certainly remains one of the most controversial characters from this period, which is perhaps why – along with Mary, Queen of Scots – there are stories that he haunts so many places.*

S ome miles north and west of Brechin, MELGUND CASTLE is a strong L-plan tower house, and was built by David Beaton, who was Bishop of Arbroath, then Archbishop of St Andrews, also Chancellor of Scotland, and, not least, also a Cardinal of the Catholic church. Beaton was very unpopular with the religious reformers of the times, not least when he had George Wishart burnt alive for heresy at St Andrews in 1546. St Andrews Castle, where Beaton was staying at the time, was seized by his opponents. Beaton was murdered, and his fleshy naked body hung from one of the castle windows. The stronghold was then held by the Reformers, joined by John Knox, until overwhelmed by a large French force after a long siege.

Beaton built Melgund for his wife and mistress (he was married, but as a Cardinal had to be a single man so the marriage was annulled) Marion Ogilvie, with whom he had several children, and he haunts the building.

Melgund passed to the Gordons in the 17th century, and then to several other families. It fell ruinous, but restoration has been undertaken.

E THIE CASTLE, some miles north-east of Arbroath, also in Angus, also has associations with Beaton. It incorporates an ancient castle of the Beatons, which passed to the Carnegies in 1549: they were made Earls of Ethie in 1647. The castle has changed hands since, but is still occupied.

Ethie was one of the residences favoured by Beaton when he was abbot of Arbroath in the 1530s, and then Archbishop, until his death in 1546. He spent much time here with his mistress. His apparition has been seen in the castle, described in one account as small and fat, with a ruddy face, wearing a red cloak; although it has also been described as a stately figure. The sound of ghostly footfalls, climbing a turnpike stair, have been reported. The footsteps are recorded as being halting, described as being thump-step, thump-step (Beaton is believed to have had gout). Noises of something heavy being dragged across the floor

Ethie Castle: *haunted by the spirit of Cardinal David Beaton, as well as a Green Lady.*

have also been heard, but it is not clear if these are connected with the Cardinal. Ethie is also said to have a Green Lady, and the ghost of a child haunted a chamber for some time.

Nothing survives of BALFOUR HOUSE, some miles east of Glenrothes in Fife, except a mound of rubble, but this was once a strong L-plan tower house, later remodelled into a large castellated mansion. The lands were held by the Balfour family, but later passed to the Beatons, who held them until the end of the 19th century. The building was deliberately blown up in the 1960s in an attempt to clear the site.

This is another of the sites once haunted by Beaton.

Beaton's ghost has also been seen riding in a spectral carriage through the streets of St Andrews, and one account has him haunting ST ANDREWS CASTLE (see below).

Claypotts Castle is haunted by a White Lady, said to be an apparition of Marion Ogilvie, Beaton's wife and mistress. The figure is reported to be seen at one of the windows on the anniversary of the Cardinal's death: one description had it waving a white handkerchief. It does not appear, however and as already mentioned, that there was a castle at Claypotts in 1546. If Marion was to haunt a stronghold, Ethie or Melgund seem better candidates; Claypotts has no apparent historical connection with Beaton or Marion.

S T ANDREWS CASTLE is a shattered ruin standing by the sea in the attractive and historic city. The castle was used by the Bishops and Archbishops of St Andrews as their residence, and is close to the cathedral. The cathedral is largely destroyed, but enough remains to show that this was once one of the most magnificent buildings in Scotland, and one of the longest churches in Britain. The castle saw action in the Wars of Independence, and was rebuilt by Bishop Trail at the end of the 14th century.

It might have been thought that being a man of the church was a safe profession, but this was far from the case. Patrick Graham was the first Archbishop, but he was imprisoned in his own castle in 1478. Archbishop Alexander Stewart, the illegitimate son of James IV, was slain with his father at Flodden in 1513. As described above, Cardinal David Beaton was murdered here in 1546, and hung naked from one of the windows by Protestant Reformers. The resultant siege to oust the Reformers led to siege mines being dug: the mines can still be entered although they

St Andrews Castle: *haunted by an apparition of Archbishop Hamilton.*

are not for the claustrophobic. The Reformers were eventually defeated by a large French force, and many were used as galley slaves, including John Knox. Archbishop James Sharp, as mentioned already and one of the Protestant bishops, was brutally murdered at Magus Moor in 1679.

John Hamilton was elevated to the position of Archbishop in 1546, on the death of Beaton, after being Bishop of Dunkeld. He was involved in helping his own family and their ambitions to the throne. It was Hamilton who agreed to annul the marriage of James Hepburn, fourth Earl of Bothwell, to his first wife Jane Gordon, so Bothwell could wed Mary, Queen of Scots. Jane, of course, was not a happy bunny and got her revenge by having Bothwell imprisoned in Denmark after he had fled Scotland. When Mary abdicated and was imprisoned in England, Archbishop Hamilton continued to support her: his family's interests lay in that direction. But when the Earl of Lennox, the Hamiltons' mortal foe, was made Regent for the young James VI, Archbishop Hamilton was captured at Dumbarton Castle and accused of being involved in the murder of Lord Darnley and the assassination of the Regent Moray. Hamilton was hanged at Stirling in 1571.

His ghost has been seen in the ruins of St Andrews Castle.

L INLITHGOW PALACE is mentioned in connection with a Blue Lady, but there is also a very curious incident involving James V in 1539. One night James was asleep in his bed when he was suddenly awoken. Before him was an apparition of Thomas Scott of Balwearie, a Lord of Session and James's Justice Clerk, accompanied by a party of devils. James was told by the apparition that Scott was damned to everlasting hell for serving him. Scott is said to have died the same night at Balwearie Castle, an event which James could not have known of beforehand.

What Thomas Scott of Balwearie might have done to merit such punishment is not clear.

S cott's apparition, although hopefully without the devils, has also been witnessed on occasion at BALWEARIE CASTLE, which lies two or so miles south and west of Kirkcaldy in Fife. The old stronghold is now a ruin, half the tower having fallen, but was long a property of the Scotts, before passing to the Melville family.

Tortured Souls and Evil Bogles

T*his small section consist of just four stories. The first two are about men who should be pitied rather than condemned.*

The last two are interesting in that they feature a particularly violent and nasty spirit. There are very few stories about ghosts in Scotland's castles actually physically harming the living. Two other tales can be mentioned here; one regards the house of Gilbert Campbell. He lived in Glenluce in the south-west of Scotland, and numerous disturbances plagued his home in 1655. Campbell had apparently been cursed by a peddler, Alexander Agnew. Agnew was hanged, and the activity then ceased. The house of Andrew Mackie in Auchencairn had similar poltergeist activity in 1695. His home was believed to have been built on the site of a murder. Most usually, accounts do not involve physical harm, and these are the exceptions.

It appears even the ghosts were more violent in the second half of the 17th century.

C ULLEN HOUSE, standing near Cullen in the north-east of Scotland, has been divided into several different residences, but the building incorporates a 16th-century L-plan tower house. Extensions were made by Robert Adam, and in the 19th century the house had 386 rooms. The estate was originally held by the Sinclairs, but was long a property of the Ogilvie Earls of Findlater, after passing to them by marriage.

The house is haunted. The story goes that James Ogilvie, the sixth Earl of Findlater (who was also the third Earl of Seafield), although in good mental health most of the time, would suffer from uncontrollable and violent rages. In November 1770, during one of these attacks, he murdered his own factor in a frenzied assault. When he came to, he was in despair, climbed the stairs to the top of the building, and killed himself in one of the attic rooms by slitting his own throat.

An apparition of the Earl has been reported in the building, both on the stairs and in the corridors, including in 1943 when a servant reported she had seen a ghostly re-enactment of the murder. Footfalls were often reported from areas of the house which were unoccupied, and were heard often on the stairs. Disturbances are said to come mostly from the library, where the murder took place, and in the Pulpit and Church Rooms at the top of the stairs. On one occasion a couple staying beneath the Church Room described hearing loud unexplained noises from the chamber above.

Newspaper journalists, who were staying at Cullen House in 1964, heard unexplained footsteps and experienced an extremely unpleasant atmosphere. They were staying in nearby rooms, the Pulpit and Church Rooms, and heard footsteps ascending the steps. The noises stopped outside one of the men's doors, the handle seemed to rattle, but then the footsteps receded again.

D OUNE OF ROTHIEMURCHUS is said to be haunted by the spirit of a son of one of the lairds. The poor man suffered from bouts of madness, during one of which he strangled an unfortunate serving girl. This was on the main stairs of the house, and he then fell from the top and was killed. His spirit is said to haunt the house, and is mostly witnessed in one of the bed chambers.

T he scant remains of DUCHAL CASTLE are located a few miles west of Kilmacolm in Ayrshire. The castle was built in the 13th century, and held by the Lyle family, who became Lord High Justiciars of Scotland. The property passed to the Montgomerys, then the Porterfield family, and the castle was replaced by Duchal House, and allowed to fall into ruin.

The castle has a ghost story from the 13th century. Duchal was haunted by the ghost of an excommunicated monk, a very malevolent and powerful spirit. It would stand on the walls and roof of Duchal, and swear and shout at the occupants and passers-by. The Lyles did everything they could to rid themselves of the spectre. They shot at it with arrows, but the arrows melted away when they hit the ghost.

The son of the house decided to take a hand, being a particularly pious, strong and virtuous young man. He confronted the ghost in the great hall of the castle. The fight lasted many hours, and in the morning it was found that the hall had been devastated – and the lad was bloodied and dead. But the ghost never troubled Duchal again.

G ALDENOCH CASTLE is a ruinous 16th-century L-plan tower house, which stands some miles north and west of Stranraer in Galloway. It was built by the Agnews of Lochnaw.

At one time Galdenoch was haunted by a particularly unpleasant spirit. It would hurl things at people, and even picked up an old woman bodily and dumped her in a nearby river. Disturbances continued to plague the building, until finally one last minister was called. His mighty singing so daunted the spirit, that it departed and Galdenoch was left in peace.

CHAPTER TWO
Men Too Wronged to Rest

T hese are a selection of stories where the man was the victim, and his ghost returned because of the wrongs done to him. Of course, some of the people in the previous chapter may also fall into this category, such as Alexander Hamilton, said to haunt the grounds of Penkaet.

S PEDLINS TOWER, near Lochmaben in Dumfries and Galloway, has a famous story, dating from the end of the 17th century, and for years was haunted by the spirit of a local miller, Dunty Porteous. The building dates from the 15th century, and was owned by the Jardine family. It was replaced by Jardine Hall and became ruinous, but Spedlins was restored in the 1970s and is now occupied again.

For reasons which are not clear, Dunty Porteous attempted to burn down his own mill. He was imprisoned in the dungeon of Spedlins Tower while it was decided what to do with him – imprisonment was not usually a form of punishment for crimes in early modern times. Unfortunately, the laird of Spedlins, Sir Alexander Jardine, was called away to Edinburgh on business, and he took the key for the dungeon with him, forgetting about the miller.

Porteous could not be given any food, and became more and more desperate as hunger consumed him. His woeful cries could be heard, becoming weaker and weaker, but there was nothing the servants could do, or at least there was nothing they chose to do. When Jardine finally returned (or according to one version: had the key returned as soon as he discovered he had taken it) it was too late. The dungeon was finally opened, and it was found that Porteous had gnawed at his own hands and feet, before dying from starvation or dehydration. Some have suggested that Jardine's wife, Margaret Douglas, allowed Porteous to starve as she was renowned for her miserliness and could not bear the expense of feeding him. Another account has Jardine finding the rotting corpse of Dunty manacled to the wall months later. The miller had ripped off his own hands in an attempt to escape from the chains.

Whether by accident or design then, Dunty died, although he was not to rest in peace.

Almost as soon as he died, the tower was plagued with his shrieking apparition, rushing through the building, crying 'Let me out! Let me out! I am dying'. The family and servants were terrified, and hardly got a moment's peace. Jardine called in ministers to perform an exorcism, but to no avail. The disturbances went on and became even more fearful.

Porteous's spirit was eventually confined to the dungeon by using a large bible (described as dating from 1634 and being bound in calf skin) at the entrance, although the restless ghost could not be silenced. His anguished cries could still be heard coming from the prison. Sticks pushed through the lock would come back stripped and mangled as if the bogle was still desperate for food. The bible had to be left in a stone wall cupboard by the door to the dungeon.

In 1710 the bible was removed and sent away to be rebound. Dunty immediately escaped the confines of the dungeon and went wailing around the castle. Finding the place abandoned, he travelled to Jardine Hall and terrified the household there. The ghost is even said to have thrown Jardine and his wife out of their beds. The bible was quickly returned to its niche and the ghost contained.

The old tower eventually was abandoned and the roof fell in. Stories still continued, however, of unexplained moaning being heard from the ruins. Several people also reported seeing the apparition of a tall white-haired man in the vicinity of the tower, described as being in great distress – and having no hands.

Whether the spirit of the miller then departed is not known, but there have apparently been no manifestations since the castle was restored and reoccupied.

H ERMITAGE CASTLE is haunted by several ghosts, including the evil William de Soulis and an apparition of Mary, Queen of Scots. It also has a third ghost.

Alexander Ramsay of Dalhousie was a prominent nobleman in Scotland. He was well thought of by most people, having retaken Roxburgh Castle from the English and having resisted Edward Balliol in the 1330s. Ramsay was at worship in St Mary's Church in Hawick when he was seized by William Douglas, the Knight of Liddlesdale. Douglas carried the poor man off to Hermitage Castle, where he had him incarcerated in one of the vaults. It seems that Douglas was peeved that Ramsay, rather than he himself, had been made Sheriff of Teviotdale by David II: after all, Douglas had retrieved Hermitage Castle from the English in 1338.

Ramsay was not given any food. His life was prolonged by grain coming from a storeroom above his prison, but eventually he died a lingering and excruciating death from starvation. It is said that he gnawed his own fingers. Years later it is said that his place of imprisonment was discovered, and in it were found bones, a rusty sword and some chaff, the remains of the corn. Perversely, Douglas was then made Sheriff of Teviotdale.

Anguished cries and groans have been heard within the castle walls, and an apparition of Ramsay seen here.

Douglas himself was to come to a sticky end. He was captured by the English in 1346, and only secured his release by making a treaty with his captors. He tried to block his godson, another William Douglas, from obtaining the lordship of Douglas and the castle of Hermitage. The younger man was to prove as ruthless as his godfather: in 1353 he ambushed the older man and summarily slew him.

There are other vague reports of other apparitions, some in blood-stained armour, seen during thunder storms, as well as headless phantoms.

D UNTRUNE CASTLE lies on the north side of Loch Crinan, some miles north and west of Lochgilphead in Argyll. The building dates from the 13th century with a later L-plan house in one corner. It was long held by the Campbells, was besieged in 1644, and then burned in 1685, Duntrune was sold to the Malcolms of Poltalloch in 1792, and they still own the castle. There are fine stone effigies for members of the family who were buried in Kilmartin cemetery.

Duntrune is haunted by the ghost of a MacDonald, the Phantom Piper of Duntrune, and the tale dates from 1615. Coll Ciotach MacDonald was active in the area, raiding and fighting the MacDonalds' enemies, the Campbells. A MacDonald, Coll's piper, was sent to the castle to spy on the Campbells. He was seized and imprisoned in an upstairs chamber, a turret in some accounts, although the present building does not have any. (Or he was the last member of a garrison of MacDonalds who had seized the castle before he had been retaken by the Campbells: the rest of his comrades were slaughtered.) The Campbells were laying in wait to ambush the MacDonalds, who planned to besiege Duntrune. The piper could think of nothing to do but play his pipes, and his kinsmen were warned and withdrew. He paid for his bravery: the story goes that the Campbells chopped off his fingers. The piper bled to death.

From then on the sound of ghostly bagpipes would often be heard, with no explanation as to from where the music came. This along, with other manifestations, so troubled one occupier, a minister, he had the

162

Duntrune Castle: *the old stronghold has tales of a phantom piper and a fingerless skeleton.*

basement exorcised, for it was here that most of the disturbances were thought to occur. There are reports, however, that the spirit was still active in the 1970s: unexplained knockings and footsteps, and things being thrown about rooms were described.

In 1870 a fingerless skeleton was found, sealed beneath the stone flags of the floor in the kitchen of the basement. It was given a proper burial, but this does not seem to have affected the disturbances.

About one and a half miles east of Inverkeithing in Fife, DONIBRISTLE HOUSE was a large mansion, of which only two service wings survive, but it stood on the site of a castle. It was to suffer at least two fires, the second in 1858, which left the building a ruin. The lands were sold off in the 1960s, and the many housing estates, which comprise Dalgety Bay, were built.

James Stewart was the second of that name to hold the title of the Earl of Moray. The first, another James, was the illegitimate brother of Mary, Queen of Scots, and she gave him the title in 1563. This was much to the chagrin of the (Catholic) Gordon Earls of Huntly, who had previously had the title.

When the first Earl of Moray was murdered in 1570 at Linlithgow by Hamilton of Bothwellhaugh (see Old Woodhouselee), he left a daughter. She was married to another James Stewart, this time of Doune, and their son, yet another James, was made Earl of Moray in 1592. This James was close to the militant Protestant faction in Scotland at the time, only making the feud with the Gordons worse. There is also a suggestion, at least in the ballad, that the Bonnie Earl was taking an undue interest in Anne of Denmark, James VI's wife. Indeed, Moray was suspected of being involved in a plot against the king, and the Earl of Huntly was given a commission to hunt him down and capture him: it seems unlikely that James VI would not have realised the likely outcome – Moray's murder.

The Gordons besieged Moray at Donibristle and, when he refused to surrender, torched the building and slew anyone they found. Moray managed to evade capture, and fled to caves on the shore; but here he was discovered, pursued and then cornered on the beach. Gordon of Gight slashed him across the face, prompting the remark from the dying Earl 'you have spoilt a better face than your own'. Moray's mother had a painting made of her son's corpse, showing the various wounds, so that this could be used as evidence. The famous picture is kept at Darnaway Castle, which is still the home of the Earls. The events are also commemorated in the ballad *The Bonnie Earl o' Moray*. The Earl of Huntly was never prosecuted for the slaying as he had been given the commission by the king.

The story goes that an apparition of Moray, his hair blazing with flames, has been seen near the spot where he died.

INVERARAY CASTLE has accounts of several ghosts, although the stories are refuted by those at the castle. The old castle, which has long been demolished but stood near the present building, had a phantom harper,

Inveraray Castle: *there are several ghost stories associated with the building, including a ghostly harper.*

believed to have been one of the victims resulting from Montrose's attack in 1644: the poor man was hanged. An apparition, dressed in Campbell tartan, has been reported, usually seen by women rather than men, and the soft sounds of a harp heard. This is believed to occur mostly when one of the Dukes is near death or at the time of a funeral.

The apparition of a young servant, who was murdered by Jacobites in the 1745-6 Rising, has been seen in the MacArthur Room. The are also other manifestations in the library, where unexplained crashing noises have been heard.

S et in a fine location four or miles south-west of Alford in Aberdeenshire, CRAIGIEVAR CASTLE is one of the best preserved and interesting of towers houses in Scotland, and is now in the care of The National Trust for Scotland. It was completed in 1626 and, while the lower storeys are relatively plain (and were plainer when first built), the upper storeys are brought to life with an extravagant profusion of turrets, gables, chimney stacks and corbelling. The building is washed in a fetching tone of pink. The interior is particularly fine, and the hall has magnificent plaster work and a carved fireplace. Many other chambers have fine panelling and plaster ceilings.

The castle was begun by the Mortimer family, but they ran out of funds and it was sold to the Forbeses, who held it until 1953.

Craigievar is haunted by the spirit of a member of the Gordon family: the Gordon and Forbes families were bitter enemies. The Gordon was murdered by being forced from one of the windows of the Blue Room at the end of a sword by the 'Red' Sir John Forbes, third Laird: John was called 'Red' because of his ruddy complexion, not for any bloody deeds. The problem with this tale is that the windows are small and formerly had bars, which casts some doubt on the account. Whatever the truth of it, ghostly footsteps, described as firm and fairly heavy, have also been heard ascending the stair.

The castle is also haunted by a fiddler, who was drowned in the well beneath the floor in the kitchen, and only appears to members of the Forbes family. One tale also has a crowd of phantom folk appearing in the great hall when the family are in trouble.

W INDHOUSE, a small ruined mansion on Yell in Shetland, has several ghost stories. One is that it was plagued by the apparition of a large man, clad in a black cloak and a top hat. The phantom would appear out of the ground at the same spot near the building, and then would walk to the side of the house and there disappear through the wall.

The skeleton of a man was uncovered near the house in 1878, and the ghost is thought to be the spirit of a peddler who was murdered and then buried at the spot where the ghost appeared.

Other ghost stories include a lady, a child and a dog.

The grounds of ASHINTULLY CASTLE, which also has a Green Lady, is haunted by two male spectres.

One is the apparition of a tinker, called Robertson, who was caught trespassing on the lands. He was summarily hanged by one of the Spalding lairds, but cursed the family before he died. The Spaldings are said to then have lost the property within a generation. The phantom of the tinker has been witnessed in an avenue of trees, the site of his execution.

The second phantom is known as Crooked Davie, who is believed to have been killed for not delivering a message. He had been sent off to Edinburgh with important correspondence, and managed to return that same evening (which would have been some feat) with a response. One version has him romantically entangled with a servant of the castle, and hence his speed so he could visit her that night. Davie was exhausted after riding all day and, while waiting for the laird, fell asleep in the hall. The laird thought he had not yet set out, and was so angry that he slew the poor man while he slept.

FINAVON CASTLE is now very ruinous, but was once a magnificent castle and residence. It stands some four miles north-east of Forfar, and was for hundreds of years the seat of the Lindsay Earls of Crawford. As mentioned in relation to Glamis Castle, Alexander Lindsay, the fourth Earl, was a cruel and ruthless fellow. Among his many dark deeds was the hanging of Jock Barefoot from the Covin Tree for cutting a branch for using as a walking stick. Jock's spirit returned to haunt the castle.

Finavon was sold in 1629, and passed to the Carnegies, and then the Gardynes. It was replaced by a mansion, although an old doocot, with roosting places for some 2000 birds, survives and is in the care of The National Trust for Scotland.

SANQUHAR CASTLE is haunted by a White Lady, but has a second ghost, believed to be the spirit of John Wilson. In 1597 Wilson had been sent to Sanquhar to deliver a message on behalf of Sir Thomas Kirkpatrick of Closeburn, and was one of his tenants. But Robert Crichton of

Sanquhar Castle: *home to both a White Lady and the spirit of a man who was wrongly executed.*

Sanquhar had the poor man imprisoned. Douglas of Drumlanrig, Crichton's friend and ally, had a dispute with Kirkpatrick, and Wilson became the unwitting pawn in their debacle.

The Privy Council ordered that Wilson should be freed, but Crichton had him hanged instead. Crichton was himself executed in 1612 for murder, but he escaped justice for the slaying of Wilson.

Strange noises were reported in the castle, the sounds of chains and the groaning of a man's voice. This has been linked to the cruel and unjust death of Wilson.

These manifestations, however, may be connected to the discovery of a skull-less skeleton, which was found in a coffin in the ruins of the castle about 1840.

Located more than a mile north-east of Crail, BALCOMIE CASTLE dates from the 16th century and was built by the Learmonth family. It later passed to the Hopes, then the Scotts and the Erskines. The building is still occupied, but is now used as a farmhouse.

The house is plagued by the sound of ghostly whistling. Some time in the past, a young lad worked at Balcomie, presumably a jolly sort. It was his habit to whistle as he went about his business, and would not desist no matter how often he was asked. Eventually, his habit became so irritating that he was imprisoned without food to teach him a lesson. Unfortunately, he died, although this did not, apparently, stop the poor fellow whistling.

E DINAMPLE CASTLE is a restored 16th-century Z-plan tower house, and lies about one mile from Lochearnhead in the heart of Scotland. It was built for Sir Duncan Campbell of Glenorchy, also known as Black Duncan, around 1584. The ghost story comes from this time. The tower was supposed to have had a parapet walk, but the builder either forgot to add this feature or it was left out of the original plans. He decided to prove to Campbell, however, that it was possible to walk around the roof of the building, as he did not want his fee reduced. Black Duncan solved the dispute quite suddenly by pushing the builder from the top of the castle. He was dashed on the ground below, so saving Campbell the whole fee.

At certain times a spectre of the builder can still be seen scrambling around the roof of Edinample.

Indeed, St Blane, a 6th-century holy man, cursed the place, saying that the owners would be neither rich nor lasting. Grave slabs from a local cemetery were used in the construction of the castle. A local wise woman (or witch) advised that 'You'll put the estate through your backside yet with the gill stoup!', meaning that the laird would drink his way through his money and the estate. This apparently is what at least one laird did.

B EDLAY CASTLE lies some miles east and south of Kirkintilloch in central Scotland, and is haunted by a large bearded apparition, recorded as being seen in the 1970s, dressed in clerical robes. The wife of the then owner reported being repeatedly touched by invisible hands. Manifestations also include the often-heard sounds of heavy footsteps from unoccupied areas, either walking down corridors, or pacing to and fro. There was a period of increased activity in the 1880s, and the then owners had the castle exorcised. It does not appear that this was successful.

The castle was built by the Boyds in the 16th century, but the ghost is thought to be that of Bishop Cameron, who was found face down in a nearby loch: foul play was suspected. The date is given as around 1350 in two versions of the tale. There was, however, no Bishop of Glasgow called Cameron at this time: presumably, this story refers to John Cameron, who was bishop of Glasgow from 1426-1446. An alternative identity for the spectre has been given as James Campbell, one of the lairds, who died in the 1700s.

The lands were originally held by the Bishops of Glasgow, but passed to the Boyds at the Reformation, then later to the Robertsons, the

Campbells and the Christies. The castle is still occupied.

There are other manifestations at the castle.

Lying three miles from Granthouse in the Borders, HOUNDWOOD HOUSE is a castellated mansion of the 19th and 20th centuries, but has an old tower house at its core. The lands were held by Coldingham Priory, but were acquired by the Homes at the Reformation, and then passed through several families. The house is still used as a residence.

Houndwood has several eerie tales, not least that is visited by a ghost known as Chappie. Manifestations reported in the 19th century included unexplained deep breathing and moans, heavy footfalls, and banging and rapping. The apparition of the lower half of a man was witnessed in the grounds outside the house. The legs and lower torso were dressed in riding breeches. Chappie is believed to have been slain in the 16th century, and his body cut in two.

The sounds of ghostly horses have also been reported, linked to a visit by Mary, Queen of Scots in 1565.

HAILES CASTLE is a picturesque ruin in a lovely spot by the River Tyne, some one and a half miles south of East Linton in East Lothian. It dates from the 13th century, but was developed down the years into a large stronghold, some of which is now fragmentary. It was held by the Hepburns for much of its history, but was burned in 1532 and captured by English forces 15 years later. Mary, Queen of Scots, was brought here after she had been 'abducted' by James Hepburn, fourth Earl of Bothwell, in 1567. The castle was sold in 1700 to the Dalrymples, who moved to Newhailes near Musselburgh. Hailes is now in the care of Historic Scotland, and is open to the public.

The castle has two deep and claustrophobic pit prisons, and one of these is haunted. The ghost is believed to be that of a man who was having an affair with the wife of one of the lairds. The man was thrown into the prison and left to starve.

There are also tales of a secret tunnel from the castle, which runs all the way to Traprain Law.

ARBIGLAND HOUSE is haunted by the daughter of one of the Craik lairds, known as the Ghost of the Three Crossroads. Her lover, Dunn, is believed to have been murdered, and his ghost, on a phantom horse, has been reported near the main gates of the house.

The area around PITREAVIE CASTLE is haunted by the phantom of a headless Highlander, one of those slain at the Battle of Pitreavie in 1651. The story goes that a party of MacLeans had sought refuge in the castle following the battle, but this was refused and they were fired on.

KNIPOCH HOTEL is a large building, now used as a hotel, and stands in a lovely position on the banks of Loch Feochan, some six miles south of Oban in Argyll. The hotel is on the site of an older house, a property of the Campbells, which was the scene of the murder of John Campbell of Cawdor in 1752. The murderers were later captured and tried.

Campbell's ghost is believed to haunt Knipoch.

Some stories have BARCALDINE CASTLE (or House) haunted by the spirit of Colin Campbell of Glenure, the Red Fox, who was shot in 1752 (the Appin Murder), his slaying featuring in *Kidnapped* by Robert Louis Stevenson. Campbell is buried at Ardchattan Priory. One account records that his apparition has been seen in the castle, as well as by people walking in Lettermore Wood.

One report describes a kilted apparition, large and well built, armed with a dirk, by the Glendhu Burn. The witness saw the phantom walking for about half a mile through the woods before fading away. The witness thought that this ghost might be Campbell of Glenure, but this seems unlikely: Campbell would never have worn a kilt or even plaid. The Campbells supported the Hanoverian government, and wearing Highland dress was proscribed following the Battle of Culloden in 1746.

The owner of the castle, however, was not aware of its second ghost, but Barcaldine does have a Blue Lady.

CHAPTER THREE
Some Other Male Bogles

These are a selection of stories where the reason for the appearance of a ghost is not certain or, in the later sections, where the identity has not been confirmed with any confidence. These characters may or may not have been any less good or wicked than those men mentioned in the first chapter of this section, the Black Colonel of Inverey or the Duke of Lauderdale being good examples. There are also several famous characters among these tales, not least William Wallace, Bonnie Prince Charlie and Sir Walter Scott. Ghosts are often said to return to places they loved, rather than because they were evil or wronged. As before, the fragmentary or brief tales are covered at the end.

FAMOUS GHOSTS

Stories where the identity of the spirit is known, and the person was reasonably famous (or infamous). No male ghost, however, can claim to haunt as many places as Mary, Queen of Scots.

INVEREY CASTLE stood some miles west of Braemar, but was completely demolished following the Battle of Killiecrankie in 1689 and nothing survives. It was a property of the Farquharsons, one of whom was John Farquharson of Inverey, also known as the Black Colonel. His exploits became famous: he murdered John Gordon of Brackley in 1666, the events recorded in an old ballad; and defeated a government force at Braemar, then burnt that tower. Farquharson summoned his servants by firing a pistol, and his adventures avoiding capture by the government became legendary (although his castle was destroyed in 1689).

Farquharson left clear instructions behind that when he died he was to be buried at Inverey alongside his mistress, who had predeceased him. When he died, his wife and family decided to inter him in the family vault at St Andrew's churchyard at Braemar. This was obviously against his wishes, but he was buried as his wife wanted. Then his coffin appeared above ground. Thinking there was some mistake by the sextant, he was buried again, but twice again his coffin appeared above ground.

If this was not enough to change his wife's mind, his apparition then began to terrorise her and his family. Finally they relented, and

Farquharson was buried at Inverey by the side of his mistress.

There is also a postscript to the tale. Years later, two diggers accidentally broke into his coffin when excavating a new grave. They each took one of the Black Colonel's teeth as a souvenir. That night his vengeful ghost appeared to both of them: and his teeth were soon reunited with the rest of his remains.

Perhaps the youths who broke in and took a skull from Mackenzie of Rosehaugh's mausoleum in Greyfriars Kirkyard in Edinburgh should take heed.

B RAEMAR CASTLE, which has stories of a female ghost, is also believed to be haunted by Farquharson. His ghost leaves behind a lighted candle, perhaps as a reminder of his torching of the tower house.

T HIRLESTANE CASTLE, which stands just north-east of Lauder in the Borders, is a magnificent mansion which includes an ancient castle. Among its many treasures are several fine 17th-century plaster ceilings. It was built by the Maitlands, who for several generations were very important in the history of Scotland.

One of the family was John Maitland, who was elevated to Duke of Lauderdale, and who had much of Thirlestane built as it appears today. He was the Secretary of State for Scotland from 1661 until 1680, although he was replaced following the uprising of Covenanters the previous year. He was a pragmatic politician, but his regime was noted for its corruption and deceit. He died in 1682 and was buried at a magnificent (and expensive) funeral in St Mary's Church in Haddington, where there is a fine marble tomb to his family. His intestines and brain were apparently kept separate in a large lead urn near his coffin. His coffin reportedly moved around in the vault, and for a while it was thought there could only be a supernatural explanation. It was later discovered, however, that it was probably because of flood water from the River Tyne, which flows beside the church.

Maitland haunts both Thirlestane and St Mary's, and an apparition has been witnessed on occasion in both buildings. His phantom has been described as an important-looking figure with long curly hair, which might not distinguish too many 17th-century nobleman, but there is a full-length portrait in the house. Maitland has been seen in several rooms, but mostly in a chamber on the third floor, which is currently not accessible to the public.

CULLODEN HOUSE, which dates from the second half of the 18th century, has cellars from a 17th-century tower house built into the basement. The house, which stands in 40 acres of grounds, was a property of Alexander Stewart, Wolf of Badenoch. Later it passed to the Mackintoshes, Strachans and Forbes family, and is now used as a hotel. It stands some miles east of Inverness, near the famous battle site, where in 1746 the Jacobites were defeated and slaughtered by the Hanoverian army led by the Duke of Cumberland: Bonnie Prince Charlie used the house as his base before the fighting. Wounded Jacobites were brought to the house, and there received a form of severe medical treatment: they were all shot or had their heads staved in with musket butts.

There are accounts of the apparition of a tartan-clad man, with a plaid of grey, seen in many parts of the building, including the lounge, passages and bedrooms – identified by some as the spirit of Bonnie Prince Charlie.

TRAQUAIR HOUSE also has stories of a male apparition, identified by some as Bonnie Prince Charlie, seen on the avenue of trees from the house to the Bear Gate. The story has been dismissed, however.

THUNDERTON HOUSE in Elgin, may include work from the 14th century, and was held by the Sutherland family, then the Dunbars of Thunderton. The house was altered down the centuries, and is now a public house. One story is that the building is haunted by the ghost of Bonnie Prince Charlie, who stayed here for 11 days before going on to defeat at the Battle of Culloden; an alternative identity for the ghost is Lady Arradoul, who was his hostess for the visit. Other manifestations include the faint sounds of bagpipes and voices coming from the second floor when it is not occupied, and items being mysteriously moved about.

The Bonnie Prince is also said to have haunted the Country Hotel in Dumfries, but that building has been demolished.

THE ghost of Henry Stewart, Lord Darnley, who was the second husband of Mary, Queen of Scots, is believed to haunt the site of KIRK O' FIELD, which is at Old College in Edinburgh. Nothing of the house in which they were staying has survived. Darnley may have been murdered at the instigation of James Hepburn, fourth Earl of Bothwell, who went on to became Mary's third husband. Kirk o' Field was blown up with gunpowder, but Darnley and his servant were found dead in their nightclothes some distance from the building. They had been strangled.

L ying in the outskirts of Edinburgh, CRAIGCROOK CASTLE is a fine extended tower house, which dates from the 16th century. It was probably built by the Adamsons, but then had a succession of owners, including Archibald Constable, who published many of the works of Sir Walter Scott. It passed to Lord Francis Jeffrey, Lord Advocate and a Lord of Session; and editor of the *Edinburgh Review*. Jeffrey had the castle remodelled, and died in 1850. The building is still occupied.

Craigcrook: *the house has been plagued by many ghostly manifestations, attributed to the spirit of Lord Jeffrey.*

The ghost of Jeffrey has been witnessed here. Manifestations, many reported in recent times, include ghostly footsteps and noises, and objects being moved around and thrown about rooms. The library is often exceptionally cold and can have a disturbingly chill atmosphere. The doorbell has also been rung many times, only to find that there is nobody at the door: a phantom chapper.

A RDROSSAN CASTLE stands on a headland by the sea in the town in Ayrshire, and is a shattered ruin on a neglected site. It was held by the Barclay family, and later passed to the Montgomerys, who had to take refuge here in 1528 when their main seat at Eglinton was burned during a feud with the Cunninghams.

The castle was the scene of a famous incident from the Wars of Independence. William Wallace captured Ardrossan from the English garrison, taking many prisoners. The garrison, however, was then put to the sword, and their corpses piled into the basement. The castle was slighted and torched. The episode became known as Wallace's Larder (see Douglas Castle for Douglas's Larder).

Wallace's ghost is sometimes seen in the vicinity of the building on stormy nights.

A BBOTSFORD, which stands in a pretty spot by the Tweed near Melrose in the Borders, has stories of two apparitions.

The house was built by the famous Scottish historian, poet and novelist Sir Walter Scott, who bought the property in 1812, when it was known as Cartley Hole. The old house was demolished and a new mansion built, which Scott called Abbotsford. Scott was behind the rediscovery of the Scottish Crown Jewels at Edinburgh Castle; wrote such famous works as *Ivanhoe* and the *Waverley* novels; recorded Border ballads; and was Sheriff Depute of Selkirkshire. He collected many historic artefacts, including Rob Roy MacGregor's musket, purse, sword and sgian dubh, the Marquis of Montrose's sword, and the marriage contract of Flora MacDonald. The library and study have some 9000 books, many of them very rare. Scott worked himself into an early grave trying to repay huge debts after Constable, his publisher, and Ballantyne, his printer, both ran into trouble.

After suffering several strokes, Scott died on 21 September 1832 in the dining room at Abbotsford, and his apparition has been reported here, including in recent times by visitors to the house.

A second ghost is the spirit of George Bullock. He was in charge of supervising the rebuilding of the house, and died in 1818. One manifestation is a sound like heavy furniture being dragged over the floor.

B ALGONIE CASTLE, also haunted by a Green Lady, has several other eerie stories.

A phantom seen here has been identified as Alexander Leslie, Earl of Leven, who died at Balgonie in 1661. After serving in Swedish forces as a Field Marshall, Leslie was a general in the Scottish army which was defeated by Cromwell at the Battle of Dunbar in 1650. Leslie was imprisoned in the Tower of London and sentenced to death, and it was only the intervention of the Queen of Sweden – Leslie had given good service – that earned him a reprieve. He was released four years later.

Another apparition which has been reported here is that of a soldier, dressed in 17th-century garb. He is witnessed with an arm out, as if opening a door: an outhouse formerly stood at the spot where it appears.

It has also been seen walking through the gateway of the Balgonie. Other ghosts are a hooded figure and a further apparition, dressed in medieval clothes, as well as a spectral hound.

CESSNOCK CASTLE is haunted by one of the ladies of Mary, Queen of Scots, along with the spirit of John Knox, which has been witnessed quoting scriptures.

Cessnock Castle: *haunted both by an apparition of John Knox and one of the ladies of Mary, Queen of Scots.*

KELLIE CASTLE, mentioned previously in relation to the ghost of Anne Erskine, is also haunted by the spirit of James Lorimer, the father of the famous Scottish architect Sir Robert Lorimer. James's apparition has been seen, seated on a chair in one of the corridors.

OTHER NAMED GHOSTS

As well as having a Green Lady or gruagach, CASTLE LOCH HEYLIPOL is also troubled by the spirit of one of the factors, a MacLaren. The old castle was replaced by Island House, which had been built on the orders of MacLaren, and was completed in 1748. He died on the threshold, however, before he could take possession of his new dwelling. Unexplained noises were reported here in the 1970s, and strange lights have been seen burning out from the house.

The story goes that the factor had forced many of the locals to help build a causeway to the house. He made one old man work late into the night, and was told by that individual that he would not live to enjoy his new house. Whether this was a curse or a prediction is not clear, but MacLaren took ill and died before he could enter his swanky new dwelling.

BALLECHIN HOUSE, the remains of which stand some four miles east of Aberfeldy in Perthshire, dated from 1806, but was extended in later years. It was partly demolished because of dry rot in 1963, although a wing of 1884 survives. The property was held by the Stewarts until it was sold to the Honeyman family in 1932.

The house was haunted, reputedly by the spirit of Major Robert Stewart, who died in 1876. Manifestations included unexplained footsteps, banging and rapping, groans and shrieks, disembodied voices, and other noises (these noises were dismissed by some as being caused by the plumbing). The disturbances went on for many years, and one family renting the building in 1896 left because of the haunting, as had a governess three years earlier (although she seem to have been more worried by other people's reports than her own experiences). Apparitions were reported, one a Grey Lady, who moved along a corridor, another a hunchback, who noiselessly climbed the stairs.

The house was investigated by psychic researchers in 1897, when noises and apparitions were recorded, although it is not clear how reliable this investigation was. One investigator reported that his bedclothes had been interfered with, and his bed moved, although the account seems somewhat far-fetched. The then owner had not been informed that his house was to be probed for ghosts (he was told it was being used for sporting activities), and was extremely angry when the results were published.

Reports of disturbances continued into the 20th century.

B ALMUTO TOWER, which lies about two and a half miles north of Burntisland in Fife, dates from the 15th century with later additions and modifications. It was long held by the Boswell family, one of whom was killed at the Battle of Flodden in 1513, while another was a favourite of James VI. The tower had become ruinous, but has been restored and is occupied.

One story is that the building is haunted by the ghost of Sir Alexander Boswell. He was slain at Balmuto on 26 March 1822, having engaged in a duel with a descendant of the Earl of Moray.

B ALLINDALLOCH CASTLE has both a Green and a Pink Lady, as well as the ghost of James Grant, who died in 1806. This is a proud bogle, as in life Grant had made improvements to the estate, and the story goes that he rides around the grounds on a phantom horse to admire his handiwork. After taking a tour of the policies, the ghost retires to the wine cellar, for some spirits, no doubt.

C ASTLEMILK, near Glasgow, has been mostly demolished, but has several ghosts stories, with both a White and a Green Lady. Another spectre is known as the Mad Major, witnessed galloping up to the former door on a phantom horse. The spirit has been identified by some as Captain William Stirling Stuart, and the mad ride his return from the Battle of Waterloo in 1815. Another apparition is described as an ancient Scottish soldier. It is supposed to have fired an arrow into the back of the head of one of the locals, who then needed stitches.

D ornoch is a fine old burgh located on the north side of the Dornoch Firth in north-east Scotland. Dornoch Cathedral, the seat of the Bishops of Caithness whose diocese also covered Sutherland, is a fine restored church in the heart of the attractive town. It was not always so pleasant, however. In 1761 the local minister complained that pigs, which were roaming freely in the burial ground, were digging up and eating corpses. Dornoch is also said to be the last place in Scotland to witness the burning of a witch, Janet Horne, in 1722 or 1727. She was dragged through the streets before being burned in a barrel of tar.

Near to the cathedral is DORNOCH PALACE or Castle. This was originally the residence of the bishop, but passed to the Earls of Sutherland after the Reformation. There are stories of a secret passage linking the cathedral and the castle, in which the church's treasure was hidden and sealed. Should the tunnel and treasure be found, this is said to herald the end of the Earls (now Dukes) of Sutherland.

The castle was involved in the feud with the Sinclair Earls of Caithness, and was besieged in 1570. It was eventually surrendered, although hostages given by the garrison were subsequently murdered. The castle was then torched. In the 19th century the building was used as a court and jail, and it is now a hotel.

Dornoch Castle is believed to be haunted by the ghost of Andrew McCornish, who was imprisoned here accused of sheep stealing. There are reports of sightings of his phantom at the end of the 19th century.

INVERAWE HOUSE has a Green Lady, as well as the apparition of Duncan Campbell, who died fighting at Ticonderoga in Canada in 1758.

There is an eerie tale about Campbell. Duncan came across a bloodied man, called MacNiven (or a Stewart of Appin), one day while out on the hills, who begged Campbell to shelter him. This Duncan swore to do, and found him a refuge in a cave (or at Inverawe). When he returned to Inverawe, Campbell discovered that MacNiven had slain Donald, his foster brother.

Campbell was stricken, but he had given his word and felt he had to honour it: so he continued to shelter his brother's murderer. But that night the spectre of Donald appeared to Duncan, demanding vengeance, but Duncan could not agree, despite his own feelings. The ghost appeared again, but all Duncan could do, following his oath, was to help MacNiven flee the area. Donald's phantom appeared for the last time that night, saying: 'We shall meet again at Ticonderoga'. Duncan had no idea to what this might refer.

Duncan Campbell joined the army and went to fight in Canada. His regiment was besieging a French position, but his fellow officers, to whom he had told the tale of his foster brother, did not inform him the name of the fort in the tongue of the Native Americans. Duncan was mortally wounded, his last words were reportedly: 'You deceived me. This is Ticonderoga ... for I have seen him.' It may be, however, that Duncan Campbell did not die until 1760 in Glasgow, although from wounds received at the battle.

Duncan's apparition has been seen here, a tall phantom in a uniform of the 18th century.

Standing in a fine position with splendid views, RAMMERSCALES HOUSE is an Adam-style mansion dating from the 18th century. It stands some miles south of Lockerbie in Dumfries and Galloway, and is still occupied, having a fine collection of contemporary art and library with many rare volumes.

The house is haunted by the ghost of Dr James Mounsey, who died in 1773, and had the house built. He was physician to Tsar Peter of Russia, and when he returned to Scotland, after the Tsar had been assassinated, remained in great fear of his life. Manifestations are centred on the library, which Mounsey had particularly liked. Evacuees from Glasgow, who were sent here during the World War II, were so scared by the ghost that they decided to sleep in the stables.

Lying near the Border town of the same name, DUNS CASTLE is a large mansion, which includes work from the 14th century, and it stands in an extensive park. It may have been built by Sir Thomas Randolph, Earl of Moray, but later passed to the Home family, then the Cockburns and the Hays. The castle was damaged by an English army in 1547.

The Yellow Turret Room is haunted by an apparition of Alexander Hay, who was slain at the Battle of Waterloo in 1815.

Duns Castle: *believed to be haunted by the ghost of Alexander Hay, who was killed at Waterloo in 1815.*

Located three or so miles north-east of Rhynie in Aberdeenshire, LEITH HALL is a picturesque building, arranged around an internal courtyard with small drum towers and turrets. It was held by the Leith family (hence the name) from 1650 until 1945 when it was taken over by The National Trust for Scotland. There is a six-acre garden, woodland walks, and a small collection of Pictish stones.

Several sightings of an apparition have been made at Leith Hall, one report describing the phantom as a Highlander with a bandaged head. The ghost has been tentatively identified as John Leith, who was killed in a brawl in 1763. One sighting was reported in 1968, when the phantom appeared at the end of a bed. Other activity includes heavy footsteps as if coming from 'nailed boots', and the sounds of a party, the latter heard one night, along with a woman's laugh and the swish of a skirt.

HADDO HOUSE, ten miles north-east of Ellon in the north-east of the country, is a large mansion, which was built in 1731-6 for the Gordon Earls of Aberdeen by William Adam. It replaced an old castle, which had been slighted in 1644. John Gordon of Haddo was a supporter of the Marquis of Montrose, and was captured and taken to Edinburgh after being besieged in the castle for three days. He was imprisoned in St Giles Cathedral in a dark recess which became known as Haddo's Hole, and was then executed by beheading. Gordon's son, however, became Lord Chancellor of Scotland; and the fourth Earl of Aberdeen was Prime Minister of Great Britain, although he resigned in 1854. The house is now in the care of The National Trust for Scotland, stands in a country park with walks and monuments, and there is a fine terraced garden.

The Premier's Bedroom is haunted by the spirit of Lord Archibald Gordon, whose apparition has been seen here. He was the son of the first Marquis of Aberdeen (the title was not bestowed until 1915), and was one of the first people in Britain to be killed in a car accident. He died in 1909. His ghost was seen in the 1950s, when it was described as a young fellow with red hair and wearing a Norfolk jacket. The apparition smiled at the occupant of the chamber before leaving. A visitor to the castle also reported seeing a phantom, and was able to determine its identity from a portrait which hangs in the house.

Lying some five miles or so north of Huntly in Aberdeenshire, ROTHIEMAY CASTLE was a fine-looking baronial pile, dating from the 15th century, but extended into a large and imposing mansion down the centuries. It was long held by the Gordons, one of whom was burned to death at Frendraught Castle. Rothiemay was sacked by the Marquis of Montrose in 1644, and held by Cromwell's forces in 1650. It later passed to the Duff family, and then the Forbeses, but was demolished in 1956.

There were several tales of ghosts in the old mansion. The phantom of Lieutenant Colonel J. Foster Forbes was seen several times, including by his grandchildren. He died in 1914, and was identified using photographs. Other manifestations included the sounds of arguing coming from an unoccupied room, and a lady of the house hearing sounds like she was being followed down an unlit corridor.

Rothiemay also had the story of the ghost of an old lady, and the crying of children.

Perched on cliffs above the sea, SLAINS CASTLE is a magnificent atmospheric ruin, the remains of a once grand and imposing mansion, which had extensive grounds and gardens. It stands on the site of an ancient castle, a mile east of Cruden Bay in the north-east of Scotland, and was built by the Hay Earls of Errol. Bram Stoker found inspiration for Dracula's castle from Slains when writing the novel,

Slains Castle: *the ruins are said to be haunted by one of the last owners.*

although at that time it was not a ruin. The Hays sold the place in 1916, and it was stripped and roofless within ten years. There are reports that it is to be rebuilt as a holiday complex.

One story has the ruins being haunted by the ghost of Victor Hay, 21st Earl of Errol, who died in the first quarter of the 20th century.

F ASQUE is haunted by the ghost of a butler called MacBean, as well as the spirit of Helen Gladstone.

C ASTLE CARY has a White Lady, but it also has the spirit of General William Baillie, the Covenanter leader who was defeated by the Marquis of Montrose at Kilsyth in 1645. The ghost is believed to be regretful as a visit by Baillie to Castle Cary resulted in it being torched.

C AWDOR CASTLE, as well as having a Blue Lady, is haunted by the spectre of John Campbell, first Lord Cawdor.

N ORWOOD HALL, which also has a female ghost, is haunted by a spectre of Colonel James Ogston, although no reason is given as to why he should do so. His phantom has been seen in the dining room of the hotel.

A nother ghost at PROVAN HALL is the spirit of Reston Mathers, who was an occupant of the house.

PIPERS

*I*t is perhaps not surprising that there are several stories which feature the bagpipes. There are also several other tales with musical ghosts, such as a harper at Culcreuch, a trumpeter at Fyvie, and drummers, including the famous Ghostly Drummer of Cortachy and the headless spectre at Edinburgh.

The first stories in this group also involve another common belief about castles: that they had underground tunnels which connected them to other places. Tulloch to Dingwall, Castle Huntly to Glamis, Johnstounburn to Soutra Hill, Fetteresso to Dunnottar, Dornoch Cathedral to Dornoch Castle, The Binns to Blackness, and Hailes Castle to Traprain Law are some, more are covered below.

EDINBURGH CASTLE was one of the strongest castles in Scotland, dominating the capital, and making the city one of the most beautiful in Britain or even Europe.

There were tales that the castle was joined to Holyroodhouse (which has a White Lady), about a mile down the Royal Mile. One day the opening to a tunnel was found at the castle, and a piper was despatched to search the passageway and see where it emerged. The skirl of his pipes were followed from the ground, and proceeded down Castle Hill. But the sounds became fainter and fainter, and it could no longer be identified from where they came. Those above ground were forced to give up the investigation, and the piper never returned from his search. The faint sound of the bagpipes can still sometimes be heard, coming from a great distance, issuing from some tunnel beneath the Royal Mile.

There are many other vaults and passageways beneath the old town of Edinburgh, several with their own ghost stories.

Kirkwall, the capital of Orkney, is a fine old town, and has many buildings of interest, most notably the medieval cathedral of St Magnus and the Earl's and BISHOP'S PALACES. The cathedral survived the Reformation, and is a magnificent building which stands in an interesting burial ground. Over the road is the ruin of the Bishop's Palace and the adjacent Earl's Palace. This latter building is an impressive Renaissance residence with large oriel windows, built by the Stewart Earls of Orkney in 1607. The Stewarts were incomers to Orkney, and oppressed the islanders, and both Patrick, the Earl, and Robert, his son, were executed.

The Bishop's Palace has a large round tower, and it was here that

Haakon, King of Norway, died after being defeated by the Scots at the Battle of Largs in 1263.

There is a story of a secret passage connecting the Bishop's Palace and the cathedral. This tunnel also has a phantom piper.

G IGHT (pronounced Gecht) CASTLE lies about four miles east of Fyvie in Aberdeenshire, and is a ruinous fortress, which was a property of the Gordons. In the 18th century the estate was held by Catherine Gordon in her own right. She married John Byron, but he was a terrible philanderer (or a very good one!) and Gight had to be sold to pay off his gambling debts. They had a son, the famous poet Lord Byron.

The story goes that a subterranean passageway was found beneath the castle. A piper was sent into the tunnel to discover where it went. He played his pipes so that his progress could be monitored, but gradually the music became more and more distant. The piper never found his way out of the passageway, but sometimes ghostly pipe music can still be faintly heard.

The Gordons of Gight were apparently a wicked lot, and there are tales of witchcraft and diabolic occurrences. One account still has phantoms of the family occasionally seen cavorting with the Devil at a nearby pool.

P LACE OF BONHILL stood just south of Alexandria in Dunbartonshire, but was demolished in the 1950s and the site is occupied by a school. The house incorporated an old castle, and was held by the Lennox family and then the Smolletts.

The house also had a phantom piper, and the story behind the haunting is similar to Edinburgh and Gight. A hidden passageway was found behind the fireplace in the drawing room. A piper was sent to explore where the tunnel went: it apparently led towards the bank of the River Leven. His pipes could be heard for a long time, but from further and further away. Faint pipe music could then sometimes be heard in and around Place of Bonhill.

T he pretty village of CULROSS lying on the shore of the Firth of Forth in Fife also has an account of a piper, along with his dog, searching a tunnel under the houses which led off from a vault at Newgate. It was hoped that treasure would be found. Again his piping could be heard, and was followed from above ground. The music got softer and softer, until eventually it could no longer be heard. The piper was never seen again, but pipe music is still heard from time to time, wafting its way to the surface, coming from the subterranean passageway. It is said that the faithful hound managed to escape, but it had lost all its hair, and died soon afterwards.

Culross has many points of interest, including the remains of the abbey, the choir of which is used as the parish church; Culross Palace, which was built between 1597 and 1611 and has original interiors; and the Town House and Study.

MUCHALLS CASTLE, which has a Green Lady, was thought to have a tunnel to a sea cave about a mile away. The story of a phantom piper is associated with the cavern, however. An opening was discovered at the back of the large cave, and a piper was despatched to find where it went. The man was never seen again, but at times the faint sound of the bagpipes can still be heard.

DUNOLLIE CASTLE occupies a prominent but now overgrown site, about one mile north of Oban in Argyll, and defends the sheltered bay. This is an ancient stronghold, and there was a fortress here of the Kings of Dalriada, which was captured in 689. The MacDougalls of Lorn had a castle on the site, but this was sacked by Robert the Bruce in 1309. It was attacked in 1644, and besieged in 1647 and again in 1715. The castle was replaced by nearby Dunollie House, part of which may date from the 17th century and which is still owned by the MacDougalls.

Dunollie Castle: *the ruinous stronghold has tales of an apparition of a piper.*

One story is that in 1971 a party of scouts were visiting the old castle when several of them saw the apparition of a piper in Highland dress. The phantom was apparently transparent, and trees could be seen through it. The ghost has been observed on other occasions.

S PYNIE PALACE, which lies in a fine location north of Elgin in Moray, is actually more of a fortress than a palace, and was held by the Bishops of Moray. This shows what a precarious position several found themselves in, not least Bishop Innes, who built the castle after the cathedral and city of Elgin had been torched by Alexander Stewart, the Wolf of Badenoch, who is mentioned elsewhere. Further work was needed when Bishop David Stewart excommunicated the powerful Gordon, Earl of Huntly. Stewart built a great keep, which is known as Davy's Tower. This was further fortified with gunloops by the last bishop.

Following the Reformation, the lands passed to the Lindsays, but the castle was used by the Protestant bishops in the 17th century. One tale is that the last bishop, Bishop Hepburn, was in league with the Devil, and that at Halloween witches could be seen flying to the castle. Unexplained lights and strange unearthly music would be heard coming from the bishop's chambers. The building has tales of a piper, as well as (perhaps) the ghost of a lion.

The palace became ruinous, and was put into the care of Historic Scotland in 1973.

C OLQUHONNIE CASTLE, some miles north of Ballater in the north-east of Scotland, is a very ruinous 16th-century tower house, built by the Forbeses. Three of the lairds are thought to have died supervising construction work, and the tower house may have never been completed. Indeed, one of the Forbeses, a piper, fell from the upper part of the building and was killed. A ghostly skirl of the pipes can sometimes be heard from the vicinity of the castle and the nearby hotel.

F ORT GEORGE, some ten miles north-east of Inverness, stands near Ardersier, and is an impressive Georgian artillery fort, built just after the Jacobite Rising of 1745-6. By the time it was finished in 1769, it was no longer needed, although it covers 16 acres and could billet 2000 men. The fort is open to the public, although it is still a working army barracks. The fort also has a spectral piper.

CULZEAN CASTLE also has a ghostly piper as does DUNTRUNE CASTLE.

UNKNOWN GHOSTS

S tories where the ghost has not been identified. Many of the later stories are fragmentary.

E DINBURGH CASTLE sits on a rock in the middle of the capital, and is a magnificent collection of buildings. The oldest part is the small chapel of St Margaret, dating from the 11th or 12th century. The stronghold was developed down the centuries, until it was, along with Stirling, one of the two most important fortresses in the country.

The castle was in English hands from 1296 until 1313, when a force, led by Thomas Randolph, climbed the rock and surprised the garrison. It had another English garrison in 1341, but was retaken by Scots disguised as merchants. It was besieged in 1440 for nine months after the treacherous murder of the Earl of Douglas at the Black Dinner. In 1566, Mary, Queen of Scots, gave birth to the future James VI here, and it was held by men loyal to her until 1573 when it finally fell. The fortress was captured by Covenanters in 1640, and then by Cromwell in 1650. It was besieged by Jacobites in 1745.

Among many things of interest, the castle houses the Scottish Regalia and the Stone of Destiny, as well as the famous cannon, Mons Meg, and the Scottish War Memorial.

Edinburgh has a spectral drummer, sometimes described as being headless. The drums have been heard on many occasions and, less often, an apparition has been seen. The first time is believed to have been in 1650, when sentries on several different nights heard and saw the

Edinburgh Castle: *the stronghold above Scotland's capital has several ghost stories, including a headless drummer.*

drummer, and even fired on him. This preceded the attack by Cromwell, although presumably the garrison knew the English were on their way. Manifestations were recorded in 1960, though not to herald an attack on the castle.

There are also tales of a piper and a phantom dog.

Eilean Donan Castle has become the archetypal Scottish stronghold, having been much photographed and used in several movies, including *Highlander* and *James Bond*. It stands in a wonderful location near Dornie in Lochaber, by the road to Skye. It was, however, quite ruinous at the turn of the 20th century, and was rebuilt and restored between 1912 and 1932.

The castle was long held by the Mackenzies, with the MacRaes as keepers, and in 1331 Thomas Randolph executed 50 men here and had their heads spiked on the walls.

Eilean Donan saw action in the small Jacobite Rising of 1719, and it is from then that the ghost story originates. William Mackenzie, fifth Earl of Seaforth, had the castle garrisoned, and a force of 300 Spaniards landed here. They were joined by local Jacobites, but the small army remained low in numbers and unimpressive. A government force marched to meet it, and the armies engaged at Glenshiel. The Spaniards and Jacobites were defeated, and many Spaniards were captured after the battle, although they were eventually released and returned to their home country. Eilean Donan was battered into surrender by three government frigates, and the castle was seized and blown up using 343 barrels of gunpowder.

An apparition of one of the Spaniards has been witnessed in the castle, with his head under his arm. It is thought that he was killed at the battle or during the bombardment of the castle.

Monymusk Castle, which stands about six or so miles south-west of Inverurie, dates from the 16th century. The lands were a property of the priory here, but passed to the Forbes family, and then the Grants, who still occupy the castle. Monymusk has associations with the famous Monymusk Reliquary, a casket which carried the relics of St Columba, now on display in the Museum of Scotland. A carved Pictish stone, which formerly stood at the castle, is now on display in the parish church.

The castle is haunted by at least three ghosts, one a Grey Lady. Another has been called the Party Ghost, and is described as being dressed in a kilt and sporran, a laced shirt, and a jacket with silver buttons. The spirit is believed to barge through guests when there is a function here. Other manifestations include laughing and joking, and footsteps running on the stairs, heard by guests sleeping in the upper chambers.

Another phantom has been witnessed in the library, sitting in one of the chairs, apparently reading a book. The ghost fades away should it be approached.

A nother ghost at Brodick Castle, along with stories of a Grey Lady, is the spectre of a man dressed in a green velvet coat and light-coloured breeches, which is said to have been witnessed in the 17th-century library.

R osslyn Castle has other stories, but there are also at least three accounts of a phantom horseman, dressed in black armour and with a visor, which has been observed in and around Roslin Glen.

A s well as the ghost of William Crichton in the stables, Crichton Castle has a ghostly horseman, who rides up to the old stronghold through the original entrance: which has long since been blocked up and is now a solid wall. This has been tentatively identified by some as William Crichton.

R oxburgh Castle, about a mile west of Kelso in the Borders, was formerly one of the most important strongholds in Scotland, and there was a royal burgh here, although little now remains. It was a royal castle, but was repeatedly captured and held by the English. During a siege by the Scots in 1460, a cannon exploded, killing James II: a holly tree between Roxburgh and Floors is believed to mark the spot. Roxburgh was subsequently stormed and demolished.

Accounts have a phantom horseman riding up to the site of the castle.

B allachulish House, which is located some miles south of Fort William, dates from the 18th century, but there was an earlier building here. It was held by the Stewarts of Appin, and it was from here that the order was given to begin the Massacre of Glencoe in 1692. It was also near the house that the gun which shot the Red Fox, the Appin Murder, was found: it is now in the West Highland Museum (also see Barcaldine Castle). Ballachulish House is now used as a hotel.

The house has stories of several ghosts. An apparition has been seen, riding up to the house on a phantom horse, when it then dismounts and fades away before the door of the house. It is believed to be one of the Stewarts of Appin. The unexplained sounds of horses' hooves have also been reported.

Another spectre is believed to be that of a tinker, which has been seen at the gates of the house, reported on autumn nights.

L ittle survives except some walling with a gunloop of CASTLEHILL, a 17th-century tower house, which stood a mile south of Wishaw in central Scotland. The lands were held by the Bairds, then the Stewarts, the Somervilles and the Lockharts. The tower was gutted by fire in 1810, and was replaced by nearby Cambusnethan House. The apparition of a headless horseman has been reported in the grounds around the castle.

B LEBO HOUSE, dating from the early part of the 19th century, stands in fine wooded grounds four miles east of Cupar in Fife. The lands were a property of the Beatons.

A phantom coach, with a headless coachman, has been reported, being driven furiously along the back drive of Blebo House.

C LONCAIRD CASTLE is located four miles east of Maybole in Ayrshire; and the Gothic mansion, dating from 1841, has an old castle of the Mure family at its core. The castle is still occupied.

The apparition of man has often been seen on the stairs, including in recent times, but there is no clue as to his identity.

A RDVRECK CASTLE has a tale of a daughter of the house who jumped to her death. Another apparition seen here is a tall man, clad in grey. The ghost is described as being friendly, but can only speak in Gaelic.

B ALVENIE CASTLE has a White Lady, but there is also a report from 1994 of an apparition of a red-haired groom with two horses, which were being led across the courtyard. The noises of the horses continued for some time after the apparition had disappeared. Other activity includes the mysterious sounds of a flute playing, and a disembodied voice.

D UNNOTTAR CASTLE is a wonderful ruin on a cliff-top location, and has a phantom of a girl. Another apparition, this time of a

Scandinavian man, was seen going into the guardroom at the main entrance, and there vanished. There are also stories of a deer hound, and noises of a meeting coming from Benholm's Lodging when the building was unoccupied.

F AIRBURN TOWER is an impressive building and lies about four miles west of the Muir of Ord in the Highlands. It dates from the 16th century and was held by the Mackenzies. It was replaced by nearby Fairburn House, itself now a nursing home, and fell derelict. It has undergone restoration.

One the Brahan Seer's predictions features the tower: that the family line of the Mackenzies of Kintail and Seaforth would fail when a cow had calved in one of the watch-chambers at the top of the castle. The tower was not occupied at the time, and crowds came from far around to see the spectacle. The family died out in 1850 as predicted.

One story is that an unfortunate ferryman took an apparition of one of the lairds across the Conon River. Unfortunate because the laird had died some hours earlier.

F LOORS CASTLE is a massive mansion, the largest inhabited house in Scotland, and is the seat of the Duke of Roxburghe. It is located just north-west of Kelso, and was designed by William Adam and then remodelled by William Playfair.

The main entrance to the castle is haunted by the spirit of a gardener, although a presence is witnessed far more often than an apparition.

G ARLETON lies in a picturesque spot in the Garleton Hills, a mile or so north of Haddington in East Lothian. Much of the castle is ruinous, while one block has been remodelled as cottages. It was a property of the Lindsays, and one of the family was David Lindsay, who wrote *The Satire of the Three Estates,* but later passed to the Tower family, then the Setons.

The apparition of a man was seen in the castle at one time, along with the sound of heavy footfalls coming from unoccupied areas.

G RANGE HOUSE was a impressive castle and mansion in the Grange area of Edinburgh, but it has been completely demolished and nothing remains. It was held by the Wardlaw family, before passing to the Cants, the Dicks and the Lauders. Bonnie Prince Charlie visited in 1745.

The house had many bogles, one being that of a miser. The story goes that his spirit would often be heard rolling a large barrel filled with gold around the building.

H ALLGREEN CASTLE has several ghosts, including the apparition of a woman and two serving girls. It also has the phantom of a man shrouded in a cloak, which has been seen in one of the vaulted passageways.

L IBERTON HOUSE, on the south-east side of Edinburgh, dates from about 1605 and is a fine old L-plan tower house. It was built by William Little, Provost of Edinburgh, and is still occupied.

The house is haunted. A photograph taken at the beginning of the 20th century apparently shows the image of the apparition of a man, although there was nobody visible when the photo was taken. Other manifestations include electrical equipment switching itself off and on, including a fan heater and burglar alarms.

L ocated eight miles north of Campbeltown in Argyll, SADDELL CASTLE is an impressive stronghold, dating from the 16th century, and stands by the sea. The castle was built with materials from the nearby abbey, little of the monastery now survives except some splendid stone effigies, formerly burial markers, and a 15th-century cross. The abbey was founded in the 12th century, but was never a rich or large establishment, and it was dissolved some years before the start of the Reformation. The lands were held by the Campbells, and the castle was itself replaced by nearby Saddell House, a mansion dating from 1774. The castle became ruinous, but was restored by the Landmark Trust in the 1970s, and it can be rented as holiday accommodation.

The castle has a White Lady, but another story is that there is also an apparition of a monk. It is thought that the ghost may have translated from the abbey to the castle along with the building materials.

A nother ghost at CASTLE OF PARK is believed to be of a monk, who was walled-up in one of the ground-floor chambers. There are other manifestations here, including a Green Lady.

S TIRLING CASTLE, along with accounts of a Green and Pink Lady and phantom footsteps, has accounts of a kilted apparition. One sighting took place in 1952, when the castle was still occupied by the army. Two soldiers of the garrison observed the phantom walk from the Douglas Gardens, move along the wall of the King's Old Building, and then vanish at a spot at the angle created by a tower.

A photograph, taken in 1935 by an architect working on the castle, also apparently shows a kilted figure walking through the arched entrance to the upper square.

Another ghost at the ROXBURGHE HOUSE HOTEL is reputedly that of a soldier: there are also accounts of a Green Lady. The soldier may be one of those imprisoned here during the World War II; or one of the family who formerly lived at the house, as many of them were in the military. The ghost has been witnessed on the top floor of the house, which is currently only used for storage space. The apparition is dressed in brown, military-style clothing.

A third manifestation is felt rather than seen, and one of the rooms has had a strange aura from time to time. A guest in 1990 reported that she awoke suddenly at night with a strange sensation as if something cool was brushing down her entire body.

The administration offices, housed in the old laundry in the oldest part of the building, are also said to be haunted.

The grounds of THE BINNS are supposedly also haunted by the spectre of an old man, gathering firewood. He is described in one account as being a Pict, clad in a brown cloak; although what criteria was used to distinguish a Pict from a Scot, Angle or Briton is not recorded.

SECTION FOUR
Other Eerie Tales

MASSACRES

There were, sadly, several incidents of massacres in Scottish history, and, perhaps not surprisingly, there are ghost stories associated with some of the most notorious.

The most famous massacre in Scotland is that at Glencoe in 1692, and there are stories of ghosts from the site where most of the MacDonalds were slain. They, of course, did not have a castle, and this is one of the reasons they were singled out.

NEWARK CASTLE is an impressive ruin, consisting of a large tower and its courtyard. It lies in the grounds of the magnificent mansion of Bowhill, home to the Duke of Buccleuch, a few miles west of Selkirk in the Borders. Newark was held by the Douglases, but passed to the Crown after the fall of that family in 1455. The castle passed to the Scotts, and was burned by the English in 1548.

It was near here that the Battle of Philiphaugh was fought in 1645. The Marquis of Montrose had led a skilful campaign round Scotland, defeating all the forces sent to stop him in a series of crushing victories. But his force was surprised in its camp, and slain or scattered by the Covenanter general David Leslie. Montrose escaped the battle, but was executed in 1650 after being defeated at Carbisdale in the far north of Scotland.

Many prisoners were taken to Newark after the battle and imprisoned in the courtyard, mostly such camp followers as had associated themselves with the Marquis's army. Most of these prisoners were Irish women, many of them pregnant, and their children. But they were shown no mercy by men who thought of themselves as servants of God.

In an orgy of killing, the camp followers were shot, stabbed or bludgeoned to death in the courtyard of the castle. Patrick Gordon of Ruthven (who was a Royalist but also criticised his own side for their excesses), describes what happened thus 'there were 300 women, that being natives of Ireland, were the married wives of the Irish; there were many big with child, yet none of them were spared with such savage and inhumane cruelty ... for they ripped up the bellies of the women with

Newark Castle: *ghostly manifestations have been witnessed, attributed to a massacre of women and children in 1645.*

their swords, till the fruit of their womb, some in the embryo, some perfectly formed, some crying for life, and some ready for birth, fell down upon the ground ... in the gory blood of their mangled mothers.' Others were taken to the Mercat Cross at Selkirk and there butchered.

The courtyard and area around Newark Castle are haunted by the spirits of those slain here. Both apparitions and desperate ghostly cries and anguished screams have been reported.

Located in a picturesque spot in a mountainous area some ten miles north-west of Ballater, Corgarff Castle is a fine restored tower house with star-shaped emplacements. The property was held by the Earls of Mar, but passed to the Forbeses. The tower was torched by the Jacobites in 1689, then again in 1716, this time by Hanoverian forces. The government acquired Corgarff in 1748 and turned it into a barracks, although latterly it was used as a base in the fight against illegal whisky distilling.

The darkest moment in its history was in 1571. The Forbes and Gordon families were both powerful players in the north east, and inevitably they ended up bitter enemies. Adam Gordon of Auchindoun raided and ravaged through the Forbes family's lands. Gordon demanded that Corgarff be surrendered to him. Most of the men were away, and the castle was held by Margaret Campbell, wife of Forbes of Towie. She refused point blank, and matters came to a head when she shot one of Gordon's men in the knee with a pistol.

Gordon had wood piled up around the building, and set it ablaze. The smoke and flames killed all those in the building, including Margaret, her young son and the rest of the household: womenfolk, children and servants, some 27 people in total. The tale is told in the old ballad *Edom o' Gordon.*

Ghostly screams and cries are reported to have been heard from the castle. The restored barrack room is believed to be the most haunted part of the building.

It is possible that these events actually took place at Towie Castle, another Forbes' property, the site of which is some three miles or so south of Kildrummy in Aberdeenshire. Towie was certainly rebuilt in 1618, but the last remains of this castle were cleared away in the 1980s.

D UNPHAIL CASTLE is a very ruinous stronghold, some miles south of Forres in Moray, but was once a strong castle of the mighty Comyn family. The Comyns were ruined following the Wars of Independence as they were enemies of the victorious Robert the Bruce. After Bruce died, David, his young son became king, but Scotland was controlled by a Regent, Andrew Moray.

Alasdair Comyn of Dunphail decided to try to ambush and kill Moray (or Thomas Randolph), but the plan backfired and he and his men were surprised themselves, and fled back to Dunphail. Moray had them besieged in the castle, but the Comyns had made scant provision for such a chance. They were starving, and Comyn of Dunphail and four companions slipped out of the stronghold on occasions to find food, throwing bags of oatmeal over the castle walls to the garrison.

Moray became aware that they were eluding capture, and had a constant watch put on the walls. Comyn left the castle on a further foray, and was captured along with his men. The five were summarily executed by beheading, and their severed heads were flung over the walls into the castle, with the cry to the starving men within, 'Here's beef for your bannocks' (or 'meat for your oatcakes' as we might say now).

The Comyns were appalled by this turn of events, and fled in despair from the castle. But every one was hunted down by the Regent's men and slaughtered. One story is that their heads were spiked on the battlements of the castle. From that day, the eerie sounds of fighting and ghostly groans have been heard from around Dunphail from time to time. Some stories are that apparitions of headless men have been seen here. During work near the castle in the 18th century, five skeletons missing their heads were found.

C ASTLE SPIORADAIN, which means 'castle of the ghosts', stood near Bona Ferry, some miles south-west of Inverness, but the last vestiges were removed when the Caledonian Canal was constructed. During that excavation, human remains were found at the castle site.

The lands were a property of the MacLeans, and in the 15th century they had a prolonged feud with the Camerons of Lochiel. The feud led to repeated bouts of fighting, and on one occasion a party of Camerons were seized, slaughtered, and their corpses hung from the walls of the castle. When the Camerons found out, they sent out a large force and many of the MacLeans were slain in revenge.

Following the deaths, the castle and surrounding area were plagued by the restless spirits of those from both sides who were killed. The manifestations became increasingly terrifying, local people were tormented by the ghosts, and the castle gained an evil reputation, resulting in its name.

L ying close to a large car park in Braemar, KINDROCHIT CASTLE is a shattered ruin, but was formerly a large and important fortress. In 1390 the castle was granted, along with the Earldom of Mar, to Sir Malcolm Drummond, who strengthened Kindrochit. He was, however, kidnapped while overseeing building work and he died in captivity in about 1402. This may have been at the hands of Alexander Stewart, the Wolf of Badenoch, who could have seen Drummond as a dangerous rival. Stewart certainly turned the situation to his advantage. He forced Isabella, Countess of Mar in her own right and Drummond's widow, into marrying him at Kildrummy Castle two years later. Stewart then acquired both the Earldom of Mar and the Lordship of Garioch, although he was soon separated from his wife, who (it would be fair to say) bore him no love. Further details on Stewart's life are covered in the ghost story concerning Ruthven Barracks, where Stewart is supposed to haunt.

Kindrochit Castle was ruined by 1618, and the Erskine Earls of Mar built a new tower house, Braemar Castle, some distance away (it also has its own ghost stories).

Some time around 1618 an outbreak of plague was reported at Kindrochit, and many of the victims were in the castle. Plague was, of course, greatly feared, and the sick were barricaded inside the old stronghold. Cannon were used to destroy the walls and anyone left alive inside.

In 1746 a way through its roof into one of the vaults was discovered by some Hanoverian troops. As far as they could tell, it had survived the destruction of the castle intact and was a vast chamber; and they hoped that they might find treasure there. One fellow was lowered by a rope into the castle to investigate, but soon returned with a harrowing tale: the vault was not empty, there was a great treasure there. But down its centre ran a long table, with chairs at each side. The table was piled with skulls, and a ghostly company were arranged around the table. The vault was hastily resealed.

When the castle was excavated in the 1920s, no such chamber was unearthed, but the Kindrochit Brooch was found. There was some treasure to be discovered, after all.

One of the stories about GLAMIS CASTLE is that a party of Ogilvies was being pursued by the Lindsays, and sought refuge in the stronghold. They were shown to a chamber, but there barricaded within and the died of starvation. This was in a room in the Western Tower, from which sounds of ghostly groans and cries were held.

As time went on, the deaths of the Ogilvies were forgotten, but the noises still often came from the chamber. When the room was finally opened, the grisly contents were discovered. The men had apparently gnawed at their own arms in desperation. The chamber was immediately sealed again. There is an account of the groans and sounds being heard in the 20th century, but this is one of the stories given no credence by the staff at the Glamis.

The story of a secret room with ghostly manifestations is, of course, similar to the haunted chamber when Earl Beardie played cards: the two may have become confused.

BLOOD STAINS

There are a stories where blood stained the floor following a murder, and then the gore could not be washed off, whatever was tried. There are such tales at Holyroodhouse (David Rizzio), Fyvie Castle, Castle Fraser (a girl killed in the Green Room), Wellwood House (a girl murdered on the stairs) and Drumlanrig (where blood could not be washed from the Bloody Passage). These stories are all described above.

Glamis Castle also has a story of a blood stain, in King Malcolm's Room, where Malcolm II was reputedly murdered in 1034. This last tale is one to be taken with a huge pinch of salt: no such room existed at the time.

GRANDTULLY CASTLE is a hugely impressive and well-preserved fortress, dating from the 16th century and long was, and still is, a seat of the Stewarts. It stands about two and a half miles north-east of Aberfeldy in Perthshire, and its strategic position meant it was used by many commanders, including the Marquis of Montrose and Bonnie Prince Charlie.

The Battle of Killiecrankie was fought nearby, at which a government army was defeated by a Jacobite force led by Bonnie Dundee, John Graham of Claverhouse, although he was killed during the fighting. Following the defeat, government troops took shelter in Grandtully. In one of the corner turrets, an argument flared up between an officer and one of his men. The soldier killed the officer, and the man's blood stained the floor. No matter how the floor of the turret was cleaned, the stain could not be washed off.

LINTHILL HOUSE, which lies more than a mile south-west of Eyemouth in Berwickshire, is a fine old mansion which was developed out of a 17th-century tower house. It was a property of the Home family, and is still occupied.

It was here that in 1752 the widow of Patrick Home of Linthill was viciously murdered by her servant, Norman Ross. Ross was captured, tried and executed, and he has the dubious distinction of being the last man in Scotland to be mutilated before being hung in a gibbet. It is said that his bloody hand prints from the murder cannot be washed away.

Another manifestation is a bang on the floor, heard coming from one of the upper chambers. Sometimes this has been preceded by the sound of an unseen carriage coming up to the house. It is not known if this phenomenon is related to the murder.

CHILDREN
Some tragic tales of children.

KINGCAUSIE (pronounced 'Kincowsie') is a modern mansion but it includes much work from a 17th-century building. There was an earlier castle here, although there are no remains. Kingcausie has long been held by the Irvine family, and is still occupied.

The house has a tragic ghost story. James Turner Christie was just two years old when he slipped through his nanny's arms and fell down the main stairs of the house. The wee lad was killed, but the pattering of small feet have been heard several times when there is apparently nobody about or there are no children in the house. One instance was in 1962, at about 3.00 am, when small footfalls were heard rushing along a corridor.

ETHIE CASTLE has stories of a Green Lady and the ghost of Cardinal Beaton.

At one time, it also had the spirit of a child, activity being centred in one particular bed chamber. A new governess started at the castle. From her room, she could hear the soft patter of small feet, and sounds as if toys were being played with on the floor above – and forlorn weeping, apparently coming from the chamber on the upper floor.

It was found that this room had been sealed many years before, although nobody knew why. When it was broken into, the small skeleton of a child was subsequently found, along with the remains of some toys. When the remains were buried, the haunting is believed to have ceased.

DALHOUSIE CASTLE is said to have another ghost as well as the Grey Lady: a student, from when the building was used as a school. The lad is believed to have jumped from the battlements, and his apparition has been seen here.

WINDHOUSE, on Yell in Shetland, has several ghosts. One account has the persistent crying of a child, which was heard in the kitchen, as well as a witness being touched as if by a small cold hand. During renovation, the skeleton of an infant was found beneath the floor. This was the third skeleton said to have been discovered here. On other occasions that of a man was found outside the house, and that of a woman, believed to have been a housekeeper, below the floor beneath the stairs. There are ghost stories associated with each set of skeletal remains, but it is possible the stories have become confused. Another explanation might be that the house is built on a burial ground or cairn.

D UNNOTTAR, two miles south of Stonehaven, is one of the most spectacularly sited of all Scotland's castles, and is a fantastic complex of mostly ruined buildings on a cliff-top promontory. External shots of the castle were used in Mel Gibson's version of *Hamlet*. The stronghold was the seat of the Keith Earls Marischal. William Wallace is said to have captured the castle during the Wars of Independence, and slaughtered 4000 Englishmen here.

Several ghosts have been witnessed in different parts of the castle. One is the phantom of a young girl, about 13 years of age in appearance, and dressed in a 'dull-coloured' dress. She has been seen in the brewery, where she leaves by a door and then vanishes.

C ASTLE OF PARK has several strange stories, including the unexplained sounds of a child's voice and a music box, heard in the upper quarters. Sudden drops of temperature have also been experienced, and objects disappear, only then to reappear. Vague shapes have also reputedly been seen moving across rooms. The manifestations are not said to be frightening.

The building also has tales of a Green Lady and the apparition of a monk.

A lthough now demolished, ROTHIEMAY CASTLE also had accounts of the unexplained sounds of children's crying, coming from the corner of one chamber, which was known as Queen Mary's Room (Mary visited here in 1562). A chaplain, who was staying in the room, heard the weeping on several nights. When he exorcised the room, the sounds apparently ceased.

O ne of the bedrooms of the DREADNOUGHT HOTEL in Callander is believed to be haunted by a child, as the unexplained weeping of a youngster have repeatedly been heard. One story is that the infant was drowned in an old well in the basement of the hotel, the illegitimate child of Francis MacNab. MacNab is also said to haunt the building, along with the phantom of a girl.

Originally known as Baronald House and once the private home of Captain James Farie of Farme, the CARTLAND BRIDGE HOTEL stands one mile from Lanark, and has been a hotel since 1962. The building is haunted by a ghost of Annie, the seven-year-old daughter of the then family. The wee girl was killed in a riding accident in the policies of Baronald, and buried in a private burial ground overlooking the River Mouse. There is a large portrait of her in what is now known as the Portrait Room Restaurant. Annie's ghost mostly frequents the chamber which was formerly her Dolls' Room.

Another story is that the hotel also has a Blue Lady, the apparition of an old woman, which has been seen in the building.

AUCHEN CASTLE, about two miles south-west of Moffat in the Borders, is a ruinous castle of enclosure, dating from the 13th century. There are said to be many underground passages and chambers. It was held by several families, including the Dunbars, then the Douglases, then the Maitlands. A large new mansion, also called Auchen Castle, was built about half a mile to the north by General Johnstone in 1849, and the property passed by marriage to the Youngers. This later mansion is now a hotel.

The mansion is haunted by the apparition of a child. Reports include sightings in the corridors and on the main stair in the small hours of the night. The phantom has also been described playing in the formal gardens, both at twilight and in the early morning.

DOGS, HOUNDS, MONKEYS AND A LION

*T*ales *of phantom dogs and other beasts. There are also eerie stories of portentous canines at Barnbougle, Moy Castle (Lochbuie House) and Noltland (all covered above). Other creatures, although not apparently ghosts, are also covered in the section on Harbingers &Heralds of Death.*

R OSSLYN CASTLE is mentioned in connection to ghostly flames seen at the nearby chapel, but is also haunted by the apparition of a dog. The tale comes from the Wars of Independence: an English army was ambushed by a Scottish force in Roslin Glen in 1302, and many of them killed. One man, accompanied by his dog, made it almost to the castle, but here they were both slain. The ghost of the canine, known as the Mauthe Dog, has been heard howling on many occasions.

D OUGLAS CASTLE, just north of the village of Douglas in Lanarkshire, was formerly a large castle, which was rebuilt in the 18th century by the Adams as a magnificent mansion. Subsidence due to mining activity resulted in the building being demolished between 1938 and 1948.

The castle was built by the Douglases, who established themselves as one of the most important families in Scotland. Sir James Douglas was

Douglas Castle: *a black dog is said to haunt the area.*

a companion and captain of Robert the Bruce. Douglas Castle was captured by the English in 1307, but Douglas retook the stronghold, capturing the garrison when they were at church. The garrison was slaughtered to a man, their corpses dumped in the vaulted basement, and then the whole castle was torched. This incident became known as

Douglas's Larder: there is a similar story concerning William Wallace at Ardrossan.

The grounds around the castle are haunted by the phantom of a large black dog.

A round the ruins of LOUDOUN CASTLE an apparition of a fearsome hunting dog, with glowing eyes, has been seen on many occasions. The castle also has a Grey Lady.

I NCHDREWER CASTLE has the phantom of a white dog, which is believed to be the spirit of a woman in another guise (the 'why' is not explained).

E DINBURGH CASTLE is haunted by the spirit of a dog, which has been seen around the buildings and is buried in the pets' cemetery. The magnificent stronghold also has a phantom drummer.

T he apparition of a black canine has been reported from WINDHOUSE, which has several other stories. A black dog was claimed to have prowled around a bed chamber, terrifying the occupant.

T he apparition of a young deer hound has also been witnessed at DUNNOTTAR CASTLE. The phantom faded away near the tunnel above the entrance.

B ALGONIE CASTLE has a Green Lady, the ghost of Alexander Leslie, and the apparition of a 17th-century soldier, as well as other stories, including the phantom of a hound.

D ALHOUSIE CASTLE, home to a Grey Lady, also has accounts of the apparition of a dog, called Petra, which has been seen several times. The dog fell from the upper part of the building in the 1980s.

R OCKHALL, located six miles east of Dumfries, is an altered tower house, which dates from the 16th century. This was home to Sir Robert Grierson of Lagg, a notorious persecutor of Covenanters.

Grierson had a pet monkey, which would often blow a whistle. The servants tired of the creature after Grierson died, and killed the monkey. They were not so easily rid of the sound of it. The noise of whistling was still heard repeatedly, believed to be from the ghost of the pet.

D RUMLANRIG CASTLE is also haunted by the ghost of a monkey, seen in the Yellow Monkey Room of the mansion. The beast has been witnessed on more than one occasion in the 19th century. In one account, two girls saw a furry beast running down a corridor towards them; in another a woman saw the apparition of a large monkey sitting in a chair in the room. One explanation is that the monkey was kept as a pet or curiosity, and died in the building. The chamber has apparently been called the Yellow Monkey Room since 1700, and also had a reputation for being haunted. There are other tales of ghosts at Drumlanrig, including an apparition of Lady Anne Douglas.

A long with a phantom piper, the ruins of SPYNIE PALACE, a fortress of the Bishops of Moray based at Elgin Cathedral, also has the ghost of a beast, perhaps a lion, which is believed to have been kept as a pet by one of the bishops. The apparition of the beast has been witnessed both in Davy's Tower, where a large paw print was seen by a visitor, and possibly in the ruinous kitchen range, when some beast jumped out at another visitor.

INSUBSTANTIAL PHANTOMS

*T*here are many stories where a building has accounts of strange activity, but these cannot be attributed to any particular spirit or bogle. Mostly this activity includes knocking and banging on walls and doors, unexplained footsteps, unpleasant atmospheres, movement of objects such as doors opening by themselves, people being pushed aside or feeling a large weight is on their chest when waking, and a range of other phenomena. Such manifestations often occur in conjunction with apparitions in stories, but the appearance of apparitions is actually relatively rare in comparison to this type of activity, at least in modern accounts.

O n a rocky promontory by the sea, the ruins of DUNURE CASTLE lie five miles north-west of Maybole. This was a seat of the Kennedys, a branch of the powerful Ayrshire family, of whom the Earl of Cassillis was chief.

Crossraguel Abbey had been endowed with much land by the Kennedys, but when it was dissolved in 1570 it was the Commendator (administrator) of the abbey, Allan Stewart, who was in control of its property. The Kennedys, under Cassillis, seized him and brought him to Dunure. In one of the vaults, they had him placed in a cauldron and heated in sop, slowly raising the temperature until the man was in excruciating pain. When he could not longer stand the torture, Stewart signed over the lands to the Kennedys. Another branch of the family, the Bargany Kennedys stormed the stronghold and released Stewart but, although the Kennedys were required to pay Stewart (who was badly injured) a pension, they kept the lands. The Kennedys had, of course, been one of the main donators of land and money to the abbey, and reckoned that they had some right to the abbey's property.

Ghostly screams and cries of agony are still sometimes heard from the ruins of Dunure, and these have been associated with the roasting of poor Stewart.

The Adairs of Dunskey have a similar tale: they tortured the abbot of Soulseat Abbey into turning over the abbey lands to them.

C ROMARTY CASTLE, which stood just to the south-east of the burgh in the far north of Scotland, has been removed, but was once a strong castle, believed to have dated from the 12th century. It was long a property of the Urquhart family, but passed to the Murrays, then in 1771 to the Ross family. They had the building demolished, and built a new residence, Cromarty House.

When the old castle was being dismantled, human remains were discovered, including some headless skeletons. Indeed, Cromarty Castle had a range of ghostly activity, such as the sightings of apparitions, and numerous instances of unexplained groans and cries being heard there.

B LACKNESS CASTLE is a fantastic, brooding fortress, located on the sea about four miles east of Bo'ness. It was often used as a State prison, and famous prisoners in the 16th century included Cardinal David Beaton and the Douglas Earl of Angus. The castle was captured by Cromwell's forces in 1650, but by the end of 19th century was being used as the central ammunition depot for Scotland. Blackness is now in the care of Historic Scotland, and is open to the public.

One story is that unexplained banging is often heard from different parts of the building, although no work is being done. One account also has a visitor being chased from the castle by the apparition of an irate 'knight'.

T HREAVE CASTLE, built on an island in the River Dee, was a very strong castle, and is an impressive ruin. It stands west of Castle Douglas in Dumfries and Galloway, and was built by Archibald Douglas (known as Archibald the Grim from his fearsome visage during battle), third Earl of Douglas. The Black Douglases became one of the most important and powerful families in Scotland, leading to conflict with

Threave Castle: *the unexplained sounds of breathing, coming from unoccupied areas, has been heard here.*

the king or his advisors. The sixth Earl was murdered at Edinburgh Castle, while the eighth was summarily slain at Stirling Castle by James II. James II then went on to destroy this branch of the family, and Threave was besieged and captured in 1455. The castle was kept by the Crown, and the Maxwells became hereditary keepers. Threave was attacked in 1640 by Covenanters, and after 13 weeks was seized and dismantled. It is now in the care of Historic Scotland (although owned by the NTS), and is open to the public.

There have been several reports of the sounds of voices from areas of the building which are unoccupied.

Located in a remote spot on the island of Unst in Shetland (and the northernmost fortress in the UK), MUNESS CASTLE is a ruinous 16th-century Z-plan tower house, which has many gunloops. It was built by the Bruce family, who were incomers to Shetland. The castle was torched in 1627, abandoned in 1750, and is in the care of Historic Scotland.

An Australian visitor to Muness took an interesting photograph here, which is claimed to show an apparition, perhaps of a man in 17th-century dress (although it looks more like a goblin and could be a shadow ...).

CASTLE STUART is a fine pile, and stands some miles north-east of Inverness. It dates mostly from the 17th century, although incorporates much older work. As the name suggests, the stronghold

Castle Stuart: *one of the chambers on the top floor is believed to be haunted by a terrifying bogle.*

was built by the Stewarts, although on lands formerly held by the Mackenzies: the castle was seized during a dispute over ownership.

One of the turret rooms gained a reputation for being haunted by a terrifying bogle. The owner offered a princely reward should anyone spend a night in the chamber. A burly fellow, Big Angus, agreed. A terrible commotion was heard during the night, but in the morning the corpse of Angus was found on the ground beneath the turret. He had been tossed out of the window, and a terrible expression was frozen on his dead face.

C AROLINE PARK has a Green Lady, but also another eerie story, and possibly one of the strangest. At least twice in its history, both recorded in the 19th century, a cannon ball was witnessed crashing through a window of the Aurora Room. On one occasion it bounced three times before coming to rest against a fire screen. In 1879 the same phenomenon was witnessed, but this time by a different person

On further investigation, however, nothing could be found: there was no damage and no evidence of the cannon ball – despite several people hearing and seeing the event. On other occasions, only the noise of the cannon ball was heard. The occurrence was apparently so common at one time that the servants ignored it.

S TIRLING CASTLE has several ghosts, including a Pink and a Green Lady. There have also been many reports of ghostly footsteps in more than one area of the buildings. They have been witnessed coming from an upstairs chamber of the Governor's Block when unoccupied. This may be linked to the death of a sentry in the 1820s (the man was found dead with an expression of terror on his face), and the sounds were heard both in 1946 and 1956 when the castle was still occupied by the army. When the great hall was being renovated, there were also accounts of unexplained footsteps coming from the roof of the chamber, greatly frightening workmen: indeed, one man was so spooked that he would not return to work on the roof.

There are also reports of unexplained footfalls in the King's Old Building, climbing stairs which no longer exist, and moving down the whole length of a corridor which has been divided.

A CHINDOWN, mentioned above in relation to the apparition of a girl, also has a strange tale of an unpleasant manifestation. One night an owner experienced a mist forming by the fireplace in the drawing room, accompanied by a sudden drop in temperature. The mist seemed to substantiate into a face, which told the man to 'get out': a wise person might have vacated sooner. The owner described the presence as feeling evil, and did as it requested. On another occasion a woman described a further manifestation, when, again with a chill atmosphere, two dogs began to behave very oddly, backing away from some unseen threat. She also described an evil presence, and fled the chamber.

B EDLAY CASTLE is believed to be haunted by the spirit of Bishop Cameron but there is also a tale concerning the mausoleum built in the garden by the Campbells. Many apparitions were seen around the burial place, and when the mausoleum was relocated to Lambhill, the ghosts are believed to have followed, no doubt to the relief of the occupants of the castle.

N ear GIGHT CASTLE is a pool where phantoms of the Gordons, who owned the stronghold, are sometimes seen dallying with the Devil. The family were apparently a wicked lot, and there tales of witchcraft and diabolic occurrences.
 The castle also has a ghostly piper.

V ery little remains of BLANTYRE PRIORY, which stood on a steep bank of the Clyde, and was founded in the 13th century. The establishment was dissolved following the Reformation, and became a property of Walter Stewart of Minto, who became Lord Blantyre in 1606. When the priory fell into their hands, the Stewarts lived in the old buildings. Lady Blantyre became so troubled by the ghostly activity and unexplained noises, which plagued the priory at night, that she refused to stay here and fled the building, taking her daughters. Lord Blantyre was left at the priory. It could be, of course, Lady Blantyre simply wanted a more comfortable and modern dwelling.

C ASTLE VENLAW stands in four acres of wooded grounds just to the north of Peebles in the Borders. The house dates from 1782, but was much enlarged in 1854, and is built on the site of Smithfield Castle. This was a property of the Dicksons, but by the 19th century was held by the Elphinstones. Since 1949, the building has been used as a hotel.
 One story is that repeated sighing has been heard, coming from one of the rooms. It is said that a guest had tried to commit suicide here by jumping out of the window.

Near Drymen in Stirlingshire, Buchanan Castle is a large castellated mansion, now ruined, which has much old work. It was held by the Buchanan family, but in 1682 passed to the Grahams. A golf course is now laid out near the castle.

Buchanan Castle: *unexplained gasping sounds have often been reported from the vicinity of the ruin.*

Many accounts from the vicinity of the ruin describe unexplained gasps or moans, most often heard during summer nights, which begin about an hour before midnight and continue until dawn. The sounds are said to be too loud and regular to come from animals.

There may, of course, be some natural explanation for the phenomenon, but none has been discovered so far.

One of the chambers of Cameron House has been the scene of several unexplained incidents. Items and objects have been observed here, although they do not apparently exist. A portent of death is also associated with the freezing over of Loch Lomond.

Braco Castle, standing six miles north of Dunblane in Stirlingshire, dates from the 16th century and was held for many years by the Grahams. The castle has some strange occurrences, such as doors opening by themselves, and dogs are said to be especially fearful in the old part of the building.

Lying about two miles from Inchbervie, Benholm Castle is reported to be haunted, but there is no detailed story about what form the manifestations take. The ruinous tower stands by a deep ravine, and dates from the 15th century. It was held by the Lundies, Ogilvies, Keith Earls Marischal, and the Scotts.

Standing a couple of miles north-east of New Deer in the north-east of Scotland, Fedderate Castle is a very ruinous stronghold of the Crawford family, and then the Gordons. It was the last castle to hold out for the Jacobites in 1690, and its scant remains are as a result of blowing up the building so that the site could be cleared. The castle was said to be haunted.

Strange noises and crashes, which cannot be explained, have been heard coming from the library at Inveraray Castle. On once occasion the noises are said to have lasted for an hour, but on inspection the library was found to be undisturbed. The castle also has a story of a spectral birlinn and a phantom harper.

The Chinese Room of Kingcausie also has unexplained disturbances, not least the bed clothes being thrown off an occupant of the chamber on two separate occasions. The mansion also has the story of a haunting by a young infant.

Houston House, in Uphall in West Lothian, is a large mansion developed down the centuries, but it incorporates a 17th-century L-plan tower house. It was a property of the Houston family, but passed to the Sharp family, one of whom was Archbishop James Sharp, murdered at Magus Muir, near St Andrews, in 1679. The family sold the property in 1945, and the building is now used as a hotel.

According to accounts from guests, the old part of the house is haunted. On one occasion someone staying in one of the rooms reported being pushed down in her bed by an unseen force, which prevented her from moving or even talking.

Standing on a rocky outcrop a mile north of Cove in Dunbartonshire, Knockderry Castle is a mansion which dates from 1855, but is believed to have been built on the remains of a small castle. The dungeons of this building have stories of ghosts.

LAUDALE HOUSE, which lies on a remote spot on the south side of Loch Sunart in the north-west Highlands, is a three-storey mansion. There are accounts of unexplained noises, as if something heavy was being dragged across the floor. One explanation for the haunting is that this disturbance was caused by the armoured body of Angus Mor. Angus was slain in fighting at Glen Dubh, near Kinlochaline, by a force of Camerons and MacLeans, after he himself had murdered the young chief of the MacIans. Angus's body was brought back to Laudale and apparently kept in the building for several days. Why that would mean the house was haunted by him is not clear.

LAURISTON CASTLE is located in Davidson's Mains on the west side of Edinburgh, near the picturesque village of Cramond. It stands in fine gardens and parkland, and is an attractive tower house and mansion, with impressive carved chimneys and a good Edwardian-period interior. The old tower was built by the Napiers in the 16th century, then was held by several families before being given to the City of Edinburgh in 1926. There are several accounts of phantom footsteps being heard from areas which are unoccupied.

LYING east of the attractive village of Aberlady in East Lothian, LUFFNESS HOUSE is a fine old mansion, which incorporates a tower house, and parts date from the 13th century. The lands were held by the church, but passed at the Reformation to the Hepburn Earls of Bothwell, then in 1739 to the Hope family, whose descendants still own it.

An eerie tale concerns one of the angle towers, which has only one entrance and gunloops for windows. The massive door into the tower, indeed the only way into the chamber, locked itself. The room could be examined from outside through the gunloops, and the key could be seen on a table in the middle of the room.

LOCATED in fine grounds to the north of Perth, SCONE PALACE is a large castellated mansion, which dates from 1802, but incorporates some earlier work. There was an abbey here, and this was where the Kings of Scots were inaugurated on the Moot Hill. The Stone of Destiny (or Scone) was used in the ceremonies, but it was stolen by Edward I in 1296, and was only returned to Scotland in 1996, and is now held at Edinburgh Castle. The abbey was dissolved at the Reformation, and the Ruthvens acquired the property. They were forfeited (see Huntingtower), and the lands were given to the Murrays, descendants of whom, the Earls of Mansfield, still own the palace.

Ghostly footsteps have been heard on several occasions in the south passage. Although the corridor has a wooden floor, the steps sound as if they were walking on a stone floor.

Activity at CASTLE FRASER has been reported, including the sound of a piano coming from the hall, and voices coming from unoccupied areas.

An old military way passes close to GAIRNSHIEL LODGE by a tall arched bridge. There are stories of the sound of feet, horses and carts heard from the old road although nobody is apparently about.

A strange occurrence happened at BRODIE CASTLE in 1889. The butler became concerned when he heard strange noises, such as moaning and rustling, coming from an empty chamber. He could not discover the cause as the room was locked and they did not have the key. Some time later, the news reached Brodie that Hugh Brodie, 23rd laird, had died, and the unexplained sounds have been linked to his death.

Around five miles south of Kelso in the Borders, MARLFIELD HOUSE is a mansion, but it incorporates some of an old castle. It was remodelled in the 18th century and later. It was a hotel for a while, but is now in private hands again.

The house has tales, some of them from when it was being used as a hotel, of a ghost which, although nothing can be seen, forces its way past people in one of the passageways.

MEGGINCH CASTLE, some miles east of Perth, is a Z-plan tower house, dating from the 15th century, but later altered and extended. It was held by the Hays, then the Drummonds, who still live here. The castle has fine gardens, which were first laid out in the 16th century, including an astrological garden, and the 19th-century parterre is surrounded by 1,000-year-old yews.

There are many reports of the whispering of two gossiping women coming from one of the rooms, a former nursery, in the old part of the castle. The sounds are mostly heard after guests have been visiting the building. The whispers stop as soon as anyone approaches closely or the door to the room is opened.

Located one mile south-west of Dalkeith in Midlothian, NEWBATTLE ABBEY was established in 1140 as a Cistercian house by David I, but, following the Reformation, passed to the Kerr family, who were made Lords Newbattle in 1591. They remodelled one range of the abbey buildings, which has a fabulous vaulted undercroft, into a fortified house. This was altered and extended in following centuries into a large mansion, and the building is now used as an adult education college.

Newbattle has a reputation for being haunted, although there are no specific details of what by, but few people, it is said, like to spend time in the old part of the building after dark.

PENKAET CASTLE is described above in connection with the spirit of Alexander Hamilton, but there are reports of many other manifestations here, which do not appear to be connected to him.

There are accounts of activity such as banging on doors and the sounds of furniture being moved, as well as ghostly footsteps and a strange noise, as if something heavy is being dragged across the floor. These have been connected to the murder of, or a murder by, John Cockburn.

Other strange occurrences related to a four-poster bed, which was slept in by Charles I. The bed often appears to have been lain in, although no one has used it. And sometimes breathing and other noises, which might be made by someone sleeping, have also been heard when the bed is not being used.

These manifestations were reported often in the first decades of the 20th century, and the house was investigated for paranormal activity in the 1920s. Many unexplained noises and happenings were recorded, but the reliability of the investigation could be questioned.

VAYNE CASTLE is a ruinous Z-plan tower house, built by the Lindsay Earls of Crawford, and is located seven miles west of Brechin in Angus. The lands passed to the Carnegies at the end of the 16th century, then the Mills. They built a new mansion, and Vayne was abandoned to fall ruinous. The castle ruins are believed to be haunted, but there are few details about what form the manifestations take.

SELECTED FURTHER READING

Adams, Norman *Haunted Neuk*, Banchory, 1994

Adams, Norman *Haunted Scotland*, Edinburgh, 1998

Adams, Norman *Haunted Valley*, Banchory, 1994

Alexander, Marc *Haunted Castles*, London, 1974

Campbell, Margaret *Ghosts, Massacres and Horror Stories of Scotland's Castles*, Glasgow (no date of publication)

Connachan-Holmes, J. R. A. *Country Houses of Scotland*, Frome, 1995

Coventry, Martin *The Castles of Scotland* (3rd edition), Musselburgh, 2001

Coventry, Martin *Haunted Places of Scotland*, Musselburgh, 1999

Coventry, Martin *Wee Guide to Scottish Ghosts and Bogles*, Musselburgh, 2000

Fleming, Maurice *Not of This World*, Edinburgh, 2002

Groome, Francis *Ordinance Gazetteer of Scotland* (5 volumes), Glasgow, c1890 (?)

Halliday, Ron *Paranormal Scotland*, Edinburgh, 2000

Lindsay, Maurice *The Castles of Scotland*, London, 1986

Love, Dane *Auld Inns of Scotland*, London, 1997

Love, Dane *Scottish Ghosts*, London, 1995

Love, Dane *Scottish Spectres*, London, 2001

MacGibbon, D & Ross, T *The Castellated and Domestic Architecture of Scotland*, 1887-92

Mason, Gordon *The Castles of Glasgow and the Clyde*, Musselburgh, 2000

McKean, Charles (series editor) *The Illustrated Architectural Guides to Scotland* (27 volumes by area), Edinburgh, from 1985

Mitchell, Robin *Adam Lyal's Witchery Tours*, Edinburgh, 1988

Robertson, James *Scottish Ghost Stories*, London, 1996

Salter, Mike *The Castles of South West Scotland*, Worcester, 1993

Salter, Mike *The Castles of the Heartland of Scotland*, Worcester, 1994

Salter, Mike *The Castles of Lothian and the Borders*, Worcester, 1994

Salter, Mike *The Castles of Western and Northern Scotland*, Worcester, 1995

Salter, Mike *The Castles of Grampian and Angus*, Worcester, 1993

Tabraham, Chris *Scotland's Castles*, London, 1997

Tales from Scottish Lairds, Norwich, 1985

Thompson, Francis *The Supernatural Highlands*, Edinburgh, 1997

Tranter, Nigel *The Fortified House in Scotland*, (5 volumes), Edinburgh, 1986

Tranter, Nigel *Tales and Traditions of Scottish Castles*, Glasgow, 1993

Underwood, Peter *Gazetteer of Scottish Ghosts*, Glasgow, 1973

Underwood, Peter *Guide to Ghosts and Haunted Places*, London, 1996

Underwood, Peter *This Haunted Isle*, London, 1984

Whitaker, Terence *Scotland's Ghosts and Apparitions*, London, 1991

Wilson, Alan J; Brogan, Des & McGrail, Frank *Ghostly Tales & Sinister Stories of Old Edinburgh*, Edinburgh, 1991

Guidebooks are also available for (virtually) all the castles and mansions which are open to the public.

Thanks to Dr Joyce Miller for the information from the Survey of Scottish Witchcraft, available at www.arts.ed.ac.uk/witches.

The ghost stories in this book were collected over 15 years, from many books, pamphlets, guide books, websites, personal recollections, (as well as from memory), and thanks for the many stories and details from custodians, managers and owners of the castles and mansions. Much of this information came from research originally undertaken for The Castles of Scotland, *a fourth edition of which is now in preparation.*

INDEX OF HAUNTINGS

Page numbers refer to entry for the type of haunting – complete page numbers for each castle is given at the beginning of the book.

OTHER LADIES

PORTENTS AND HERALDS OF DEATH

BROWNIES & GRUAGACH

MALE GHOSTS

ANIMALS & HORSEMEN

CHILD GHOSTS

MAIN INDEX